WHAT KIND OF BIRD CAN'T FLY

WHAT KIND OF BIRD CAN'T FLY

A MEMOIR OF RESILIENCE AND RESURRECTION

DORSEY NUNN

WITH LEE ROMNEY

HEYDAY
50
Berkeley, California

Library of Congress Cataloging-in-Publication Data

Names: Nunn, Dorsey, 1951- author. | Romney, Leora, author.
Title: What kind of bird can't fly : a memoir of resilience and
   resurrection / Dorsey Nunn with Leora Romney.
Other titles: What kind of bird cannot fly
Description: Berkeley, California : Heyday, [2024] | Includes
   bibliographical references.
Identifiers: LCCN 2023039487 (print) | LCCN 2023039488 (ebook) | ISBN
   9781597146326 (paperback) | ISBN 9781597146333 (epub)
Subjects: LCSH: Ex-convicts—California—Biography. | Prisoners—Civil
   rights—California.
Classification: LCC HV9475.C2 N866 2024 (print) | DDC 365/.9794—dc23/
   eng/20231114
LC record available at https://lccn.loc.gov/2023039487
LC ebook record available at https://lccn.loc.gov/2023039488

Cover Art: Khristopher "Squint" Sandifer
Cover Design: Archie Ferguson
Interior Design/Typesetting: Diahann Sturge-Campbell

Published by Heyday
P.O. Box 9145, Berkeley, California 94709
(510) 549-3564
heydaybooks.com

Printed in East Peoria, Illinois, by Versa Press, Inc.

10 9 8 7 6 5 4 3 2 1

CONTENTS

Contents

FOREWORD

Michelle Alexander

Toni Morrison once said, "Just remember that your real job is that if you are free, you need to free somebody else. If you have some power, then your job is to empower somebody else."

As far as I know, Toni Morrison never met Dorsey Nunn. But I can say without hesitation that Dorsey has been living for decades according to the ethical code that she described. It's a code that values what you do more than what you say, and that insists on leaving no one behind. It's a code rooted in a very simple truth: All of us deserve freedom, dignity, and power. All of us or none.

I've known Dorsey for two decades. I've watched him grow and evolve into an extraordinary thinker and leader, someone who has helped to birth and shape movements that are changing the course of history. Today, thanks to movements that Dorsey and many others have built, more than 230 million people in the U.S. now live in jurisdictions that have "banned the box" on employment applications—that dreaded box asking, "Have you ever been convicted of a felony"? In this era of mass incarceration, that box has made survival difficult and sometimes impossible for tens of millions of formerly incarcerated or convicted people, and that box has helped to lock them into a permanent second-class status. But because of the heroic work of Dorsey and all those in the organizations that he led or cofounded, and the powerful movements that he has helped to build, barriers to employment, housing, education, and more have begun to fall away for millions of people—overwhelmingly poor people and people of color—who've been ensnared by our nation's criminal punishment system. The vital grassroots, movement-building work to which Dorsey has dedicated his life has touched and changed countless lives, shifted public consciousness, and demonstrated the brilliance, creativity, and resilience of the very people our nation has treated as disposable.

So much of what I've come to know and understand over the years about the second-class status imposed upon people labeled "criminals" or "felons" I've learned from Dorsey and the people who comprise All of Us or None, an organization he cofounded. Although I have fancy degrees and Dorsey does not, there's never been a time in our friendship in which he hasn't been schooling me—not so much in theory, but in practice. As he notes in the pages that follow, in academic circles people sometimes ask, "What's your theory of change?" Dorsey has much to say about theory, having deepened his political education both in and outside of prison, but what he values most is what people do in practice. As he sees it, theories of change are nice, but "the real question should be, what is your motherfucking practice?"

As long as I've known him, Dorsey's practice has been to show up for those who are locked up and locked out with love, honesty, courage, and a fierce determination to gain power and freedom for all those left behind. He's the first to admit that he's made mistakes, big and small, during his journey from incarceration and addiction to movement leadership, but he's never claimed perfection—only commitment to his practice. In my experience, Dorsey always aims to practice what he preaches.

And oh, can he preach. Dorsey and I first met back in the late 1990s, in the midst of the "get tough" era, when incarceration rates were soaring as Democrats and Republicans were competing with each other to escalate the "war on drugs" and to pass laws imposing ever-harsher sentences on the crimes committed by the least advantaged. We were both living in the San Francisco Bay Area at the time, and we were both working at social justice organizations that were trying to resist the assault on our communities. Dorsey was a staff member at Legal Services for Prisoners with Children—which he would later lead—and I was director of the Racial Justice Project of the ACLU of Northern California, focused mainly on litigation and organizing work challenging racial profiling and police misconduct. I was also teaching a class on race and criminal justice at Stanford Law School. I thought it would be a good idea to invite Dorsey to speak to my students. Little did I know what was to come.

Dorsey blew them away. Throughout the semester, my students had heard from (in person or on paper) legal scholars, criminal justice experts, organizers, public defenders, and prosecutors—including one guest speaker, a local prosecutor, who went on to become attorney general of California and vice president of the United States, Kamala Harris. None of the guests or authors did more to inform, inspire, and challenge my students than Dorsey Nunn. Not even close.

The first thing Dorsey said when he stepped in front of my class was, "Oh shit, I've never been invited to speak at a law school before! I'm a little nervous." He immediately caught himself, clapped his hand over his mouth, and said, "Uh, sorry, can I curse up in here? You know, that's just how I talk."

I laughed and said, "Sure, Dorsey, you can say whatever you want."

And then he let it rip. He told us in his own words, in his authentic voice, about his childhood—all the fear, grief, intermittent joy, and struggle—and he explained exactly how and why he was imprisoned for first-degree murder. He was unflinchingly honest about everything—about the violence and harm that he had experienced throughout his life, as well as the violence and harm that he had inflicted on others. My students were riveted.

Then, without pausing to take a breath, Dorsey told us exactly why he believed that our so-called justice system was "completely fucked up." His scathing critique was full of stories about himself and others that made us want to scream, cry, and revolt. Truth rained down on my class for nearly two hours. Some of his truths hit hard, like hail causing us to flinch and want to run for cover; other stories had us nearly weeping. And sometimes, miraculously, Dorsey had us laughing—not at the tragedies but at the moments of absurdity that could be found amid it all.

His talk was only supposed to last for forty-five minutes, but my students wouldn't let him go. They kept asking questions, hungry for the kind of unfiltered truth-telling that Dorsey was offering straight from the heart. After he left, one of my students said, "I'll never, ever forget that guy." The entire class murmured agreement. Years later, I ran into one of those students on the street. She was working as a public defender and involved in multiple grassroots organizations aiming to dismantle mass incarceration and to support those cycling in and out of prison. "Dorsey Nunn changed my life," she told me. "After he came to class that day and told his story, I knew nothing would ever be the same for me."

I've been hoping that Dorsey would publish a memoir ever since. Many years ago, I told him that. He laughed and said, "Nah, I don't have time for shit like that. Besides, I don't know how to write a book."

Fortunately, my words stuck with him, and all these years later, he's partnered with Lee Romney—an outstanding writer and journalist—to support the writing of this wonderful memoir, one that is even more moving and illuminating than the speech he delivered to my Stanford Law class. Why? Because this book contains the stories of another two decades of organizing, movement building, and personal—as well as political— struggle. The documenting of this history serves our movements, and Dorsey's honesty and vulnerability regarding the deeply personal dimensions of his journey allow us, as readers, to experience transformation and not merely get an education.

Thank you, Dorsey, for this wonderful gift. You've long been an inspiration to me, and this remarkable book reveals exactly why.

PREFACE

I was well into my seventh decade of life when I realized I needed to tell my story. It was a time of urgent work accompanied by deep reflection, and in the rearview mirror I could see my personal and professional journeys intertwined with history like a braid. Like just about everyone I grew up with, I graduated from street thug to prisoner just in time to experience one of the most violent decades in California prison history. But this isn't a prison memoir. And it's not a personal redemption story, though I've done all right on that front. This book is about camaraderie, commitment, and grassroots organizing. Prison introduced me to more brutality than any human being should experience. But inside those walls I also learned the art of critical analysis from revolutionary brothers. When I finally walked out, I made a promise to honor the unrecognized brilliance of those I'd left behind and the millions of others who would find themselves similarly situated. I made a commitment to fight for our collective dignity, for our liberty, and for the full restoration of our civil and human rights. I can honestly say that even in times of darkness I never wavered. The prison industrial complex would transform into a Goliath more damaging than any of us standing shoulder to shoulder in the trenches could have foreseen. But we fought like David. Like an army of Davids. As formerly incarcerated people, we insisted on speaking in our own voices, on becoming the architects of our own destiny. Our fight is not over. But we have changed the arc of history in this country. It's a story that needs telling. It is my story, and the story of a movement that keeps on gaining strength.

My search for a cowriter led me to Lee Romney, a former journalist for the *Los Angeles Times* who had covered my work over the course of a decade. She was there in 2005 for our first policy victory as a grassroots coalition of formerly incarcerated people, when we persuaded the city and county of San Francisco to remove the box that asks about conviction history from public employment applications. She kept track of our work, and in 2015 chronicled my trip to Washington, DC, with other formerly incarcerated leaders to meet with Obama administration officials. Lee's investigative skills supplemented our continuous conversation over three years by pulling in interviews and archival research. We collaborated on the writing and editing of my story to create this book you now hold, and I'm grateful to Lee for going on this journey with me.

I come from a family with a legendary capacity to string cuss words together and make them sound like poetry. I'm a formerly incarcerated Black man who has pledged my primary allegiance to people locked in cages and coming out of cages. I swear like a motherfucker. I've learned to rein it in. As the executive director of a nonprofit legal organization, I've had to. But I aim to use my authentic voice in my own memoir. You will encounter some choice swears. But trust us, we thinned them out considerably. Lastly, when I speak, I mostly speak Black English, unless I'm code-switching. When I write, I veer toward so-called Standard English. In this memoir, you'll notice those same shifts in diction. I hope that you find meaning, rage, and hope in the pages to come.

INTRODUCTION

O n a Friday afternoon in the spring of 2003, about fifty of us formerly incarcerated people filed with singular purpose into the high-ceilinged parlor of a Victorian house with peeling purple trim near Oakland's Lake Merritt. The drapes didn't match, the chairs didn't match, and neither did the sofas. To some, the people gathering might not have seemed to match either. But in our common experience, we were as one. The well-worn house was headquarters of the Center for Third World Organizing, which a local newspaper article had described as a "halfway house for hell-raising" that helps "communities take matters into their own hands." To us, it felt like home. Other than the kids who played on the royal blue carpet in a corner we set up for childcare, just about every man and woman who walked through the door knew what it was like to live in a cage. Most of us were from the Bay Area, but some had come all the way from New York, others from Seattle, and a few from Southern California. What brought us together was a paper I wrote and passed around to every formerly incarcerated person I could think of. I called it *Save Our Selves*, and it was, to a word, precisely about taking "matters" into our own hands—those being our fundamental and thoroughly trampled civil and human rights. I couldn't have known it at the time, but the weekend organizing marathon at that house for hell-raising would define the rest of my life, launching a movement of formerly incarcerated people acting and advocating on our own behalf that reaches from coast to coast and gets stronger by the day. It also answered in the deepest way possible a question that a prison elder had posed to me before I walked out the gates of San Quentin State Prison, one that weighed on my every waking hour: What are you going to do with your newfound freedom?

The work I'd been doing, first as a paralegal and then as co-director for Legal Services for Prisoners with Children (LSPC), was rewarding. As a civil rights legal nonprofit, LSPC was among the first to recognize that women, who the state was locking up at historic rates, were being denied basic dignity, health care, and other needs behind bars. What was missing was street-level advocacy from people who had the most at stake, those who'd been sucked into the prison system and spat out the other side. Us. We were an army for change, and that truth was sinking in as we deprogrammed our own minds and, leaning on each other, rebuilt our self-esteem. We were sick of being props in the hands of well-meaning attorneys and politicians who thought they knew what we needed, sick of having our stories treated like garnish on top of a motherfucking hamburger somebody else had cooked and planned to eat. We were ready to speak in our own voices.

Some gathered at the center that Friday, like George Galvis, were in their twenties, youngsters I would go on to mentor into powerful leaders. They sat shoulder to shoulder with the gray hairs—longtime freedom fighters in the Black liberation struggle that included Ronald "Elder" Freeman, a founding

2

member of the Black Panther Party for Self-Defense who many of us had looked up to on the San Quentin yard for his wisdom and strategy. Others were approaching solid middle age: me; former Weather Underground member and political prisoner Linda Evans, who'd served sixteen years in federal lockup; and Susan Burton, who had cycled in and out of prison herself before founding A New Way of Life in Los Angeles in 1998. Her safe houses were bringing stability, family unity, and recovery to women, most of them Black or brown, who were coming out of cages—recovery that would have likely kept them out of prison in the first place if they'd had the access so many wealthier, whiter women enjoyed. Every one of the people in that room would remain my comrades in the fight for our full human and civil rights.

I had just returned from a trip to Africa, and George and I draped Ethiopian cloth over a table to form an altar, placing sacred African earth on top. George, a big man with an uncompromising "I'm not here to make you feel comfortable" vibe that I like to think he modeled on my own, added an abalone shell and a ceramic vessel from Central America, filled with cedar and sage that he lit to smudge the room. We held hands while George opened with a blessing passed down from his Indigenous Colombian grandmother. An African libation ceremony followed. Each of the fifty or so adults in that room were standing in for hundreds of thousands of other formerly incarcerated people exiled by a society that branded us as the sum of our worst mistakes. We honored historical and intergenerational trauma, acknowledging the very first prisons in this nation as the slave plantation and the reservation. We knew it was no coincidence that people of African and Indigenous descent were disproportionately represented in our prisons.

We were full of love and trust for one another, but it was anger that brought us together. My relationship with anger had been evolving since I was a kid. Anger had proved essential to my survival, but the two of us had hit some rough patches and would navigate more. On this day, though, anger and I were joined in righteous purpose to demand justice. Our ancestors were in the room. Loved ones who had died behind bars and those still confined were there too. Yes, we were angry; as formerly incarcerated people, we had no control over our own agenda. And that's what we were there to change. Like George would tell me later, that erasure of our agency was like having a white driver at the wheel of the freedom bus at the height of the Civil Rights era, deciding which way to go. As the ones directly impacted by our incarceration histories, *we* were best situated to drive that bus. We were done asking permission.

4   The next morning, we arranged the saggy couches in a circle, set up long tables, and taped our white butcher paper to the walls. One by one, we shared stories of discrimination and stigmatization we'd experienced—*after* we paid for our crimes. The initial price was steep enough. We paid with years, decades. We paid with trauma, from violence done to us behind bars to violence that plenty of us had no choice but to bust out on others to survive. Then, when we finally walked to "freedom," we paid some more. We were locked out of any meaningful chance to participate in our own communities by too many laws and policies to count. Plenty of us were barely surviving.

Our main goal that weekend was to settle on a collective agenda. Our stenographers stood with markers at the ready as we called out each injustice that demanded reversal: Repeal of California's three strikes law. Public health effects of prison on the community. Harsh parole policies. Then we each got up and placed Day-Glo sticky dots next to the issues we wanted to prioritize. There were many to choose from: Family reunification. Prison abolition. Voting rights. An end to reentry barriers and discrimination against ex-prisoners. That last one won out. It was drowning in dots. We'd start by pushing local government to ban that box on public employment applications that inquires about conviction history—and lands our applications in the trash can before our qualifications are ever considered.

It took a while, but when we finally discovered a name for our organization, it fit like a glove: All of Us or None. It comes from a poem written by Bertolt Brecht in the 1930s and translated into English by H. R. Hays. We were hooked from the opening stanza: *Slave, who is it that shall free you? / Those in deepest darkness lying, / . . . / Comrade, only slaves can free you. / Everything or nothing. All of us or none.* It turns out the German dude wasn't just a poet, playwright, and theater director, he was a Marxist too. The poem is a call to collective action. It notes that only the downtrodden and enslaved can break their own shackles—by rising up together. Which is exactly what we were doing.

The poem became our anthem, and the ethos at the core of our name speaks to us forcefully of our duty to write the script for our own struggle and lift up every single voice among us. No education? No problem. Swear too much and don't care to code-switch? I hear you and don't give a rat's ass. Queer or transgender? Your fight is our fight too. When we gather to speak at public meetings or lobby state legislators, those who walked out of prison last week stand next to others who served our time decades ago. We now have chapters across the country. We've "Banned the Box" on public and private employment applications in cities and states from coast to coast, and that was just the start of our practical and political work to end the

5

ongoing oppression caused by mass incarceration. To expand our work, we joined with other organizations led by the formerly incarcerated to form a powerful national collective. Our demand is full citizenship.

After I've been traveling abroad, immigration officials often ask me, "Are you a returning citizen?" For me, it evokes a deeper question: "Am I an American citizen?" Because if I don't have the right to vote, if I can't sit on juries, if I can't run for office, I don't have the basic rights that come with citizenship. And if I can't land a job or secure a student loan or get a professional license or rent a home, I don't have the basic right to survival. Think about this: Have you ever told a lie? Now suppose I went around introducing you to strangers, year in and year out, "This is so-and-so, the liar." Could you ever expect to land a good business deal, a job, a place to live, or a decent partner who believes you every time you come home late?

As a proud cofounder of All of Us or None (AOUON), this is my fight. I'm now in the winter of my life. But the work is unfinished. So I keep on pushing in large and small ways that amount to big change. When that San Quentin prison elder who challenged me to be an asset to my community walked out of his cage—nearly four decades after I did—he came to my office. It was the first time he'd used local transit, and we were both proud that he'd made his way to me on his own. After we embraced, I showed him what my comrades and I had managed to build. *This*, I told him, is what I do with my freedom.

Chapter 1

INNOCENCE UNAVAILABLE, GUILT NOT REQUIRED

I was nine years old when I got my first bicycle. I came charging into the living room half-asleep to see a pile of presents under the Christmas tree. And in front of them, a bike so perfect it didn't need wrapping. It was deep purple with a banana seat. The handlebars, motorcycle cruiser–style, seemed to reach for the ceiling in a gesture of celebration. I could tell that somebody had tricked it out, bending the front wheel's chrome forks downward for that low-rider slope.

My sister Joyce, the eldest of us Nunn siblings, always said our parents met all our basic needs when we were kids. We had a father who worked two jobs to make sure we were fed and clothed, and a mother with a sweet disposition and a devout love of the Lord. Joyce is right. I never went hungry. But there were plenty of things I wanted that I may not have needed. That purple bike was one of them. And now it was mine. It was the cherry on top of my Christmas.

What Kind of Bird Can't Fly

We'd arrived in the Belle Haven neighborhood of Menlo Park from South San Francisco five years earlier. We called it "East Menlo Park" because even though we paid our taxes to that richer, larger city, our corner was the ugly stepsister, and getting uglier by the day. Just like railroad tracks cleaved cities in the American South and left Black families on the wrong side to sink into poverty, that stretch of Highway 101 to our west, known as the Bayshore Freeway, did the same. It was Northern California's first planned freeway, and it was erected like a border wall, hemming in our neighborhood's triangle of streets. There are all kinds of prisons in this world. Sure as shit I'd come to know one made of steel, concrete, and razor wire, filled with the stink of fear. But that highway helped turn our tract of small suburban homes into a prison of a different kind. A formative one. Where I learned to play by prison rules, where I gave up hoping and settled into plain-ass surviving. Everything to the west was a no-go zone for kids who looked like me. Whites only. There was no law against us being there, but we stuck out like black beans on rice, and the powers that be made us feel more than unwelcome. Turning to the east, as a young boy I found flashes of something that felt like freedom in the marshes of San Francisco Bay. The air left salt on our skin as we played hide and seek in the brush and built rafts from wooden junk that we found close to rotting in the briny mud near the railroad tracks. I was proud as hell when I shot my first rabbit. My older brothers clapped me on the back and high-fived me like I was a war hero. And damn straight we ate it, with wild greens that my sister Joyce gathered with Moms.

In some ways, it looked like the life my parents had in mind for me, Little League and all that. But by the time I was playing shortstop and second base, dreaming of making my break as a sports star, every kid on my team was Black except one. That shift wasn't slow. It came on like a runaway train. Even at nine years old I was on high alert to the changes. On practically every street, I could pick out the homes where Black families had moved in as whites sold in a hurry and left in droves. That's partly because we were already on our third house. My parents had managed to buy their first place in the Belle Haven neighborhood back in 1955, on Madera Avenue, before losing it when that low mortgage deal that probably seemed too good to be true turned into a balloon payment. At that house, I had learned with a racing heart to ride a bike on one I borrowed from some other kid. Onetta Harris was one of our neighbors. A devoted community activist, she made sure all our families were fed. Thanks to Onetta, we ate plenty of government cheese, because even working two jobs my father had too many mouths to feed. Harris is what Black descendants of that crazy time of transformation call a "root family" name, tethered in history to early Black settlers of my San Francisco suburb. Just like Nunn is.

9

Our second house, after the one on Madera Avenue, was four blocks away on a quiet, curling cul-de-sac called Henderson Place, and by the time we got there, there were a couple of other Black kids on the block I could horse around with long after the streetlights came on. By the time I woke up to that magic purple bike we'd moved yet again, a short two-block hop to Hollyburne Avenue. In retrospect, I believe that with all those whiplashing moves my father was chasing a better way of living for us kids, a safer environment. He was always aspiring to that community barely within reach, the whiter one, the one that didn't want us. Some moves were aspirational like that. Others were just damn necessary because my pops couldn't afford to stay where we'd been. Hollyburne Avenue was a good landing spot though, because that's where Nate Harrington stayed—three houses down. And he and I got tight as twins. Only a few more years would pass before we'd learn together to hate the pigs for thinking us thieves when we were just being boys.

But today was Christmas. I had just turned nine years old. Half of me might have been jaded already, but the other half still believed in Santa Claus. The neighborhood streets were good for bike riding, narrow and mostly residential, with rounded curbs and no sidewalks. My school, Belle Haven Elementary, was another solid place to show off on a Christmas Day so crisp I could see my breath. I felt loved. I felt happy. I felt damned proud. I took the bike out for a spin.

Maybe the memory sticks with me because I felt so on top of the world. Maybe because the fall from "have" back to "have not" came so quick and hard. One thing I do know: the experience marked the start of my war with law enforcement. I rode the purple bike every day of my winter break. Then, six days in, on the corner of Hamilton and Hollyburne Avenues, I heard a police car pulse its siren behind me. Two cops got out, and one told me to get off the bike. The bigger one hoisted it in the air and flipped it, searching for the serial number. He wasn't mad. He wasn't nice. I sure as hell didn't remind him of his own kids.

"It's stolen," he said, talking more to the air around him than to me. Then he popped the trunk and tossed it inside, and with a slam, they were gone. I felt invisible. I *was* invisible, and I didn't care for it. On the short, slow walk back home, my mind puzzled it out. The purple bike was borrowed, just like the one I'd learned to ride on. It wasn't mine at all. I never did find out if my father or one of my older brothers stole it, whether they bought it from someone who had, or whether the police were lying. But when they took it from me, they planted a seed of rage, a seed that would grow with me into a sharp-as-shit blade of grass that joined all the others sprouting in my neighborhood as our dreams dissolved. And that anger, that rage, it cut like a razor.

In that moment though, the seed of anger inside me was still dormant. I felt empty. Confused. Upset, but at who I had no clue. When I got home and told my family, nobody blinked. It was what it was. Gone for good. It didn't take long before I put my own spin on it. My father had loved me enough to procure that bike, however that went down. And that was something I could hold on to.

My family bounced around a bunch more in East Menlo Park and neighboring East Palo Alto, always on the wrong side of the Bayshore Freeway. Nothing seemed to last. Starting over was a form of hope. Many of those places were rentals, already turning decrepit. Then, in late 1968, my family bought the house I live in today. We managed to hold on to that one asset like a life raft, even as so many of the markers of success my parents had aimed for disappeared over the horizon. You might have expected to hear that we were moving up, to brighter homes with bigger yards. Living the suburban American dream. But the opposite was true. Buying into a neighborhood that ghettoized practically overnight doomed us to failure. Like most of the families around us, mine struggled with mortgage defaults and credit damaged beyond repair—just like so many other Black and brown families did in the aftermath of the 2008 economic collapse decades later. I know for sure that the bank snatched that first house my father bought, the one on Madera, and probably others too. The blows to his finances and his dignity turned out to be numerous. My parents were both dead by the time I learned that they'd only managed to buy the house I now live in by putting it in the name of one of my older brothers. As a kid, reality set in for me with each passing year: our slice of San Mateo County, meant to be a ticket to upward mobility, had a lot more in common with a cage.

MY PARENTS HAD migrated to the San Francisco Bay Area from Houston, Texas. My father served in the US Navy and got here first, during World War II. His own mother, who we called Big Mama, moved out to California with him. She raised our father on her own, naming him John Henry for the legendary emancipated slave of mid-nineteenth-century ballads, that self-possessed rebel known for extrahuman strength and a laborer's ferocious work ethic. The last part my father emulated, working long hours in the tannery and at a warehouse that stocked school supplies.

With my eldest sister Joyce in tow, my mother joined my father just after the war in South San Francisco. Lula Mae Nunn was a devout Christian, and she and some close friends founded Friendship Baptist Church, holding services in the community hall of a federal housing project before finding a building of their own. I was sixth in the sibling lineup. After Joyce came John Henry Jr., Ronald, Robert, and Patrick. David and Gloria followed me. My mother never talked much about the two other babies she'd lost. Joyce, twelve years my senior, was assigned the role of "assistant mom." As we younger babies came home from the hospital, Moms handed us straight to Joyce. We slept in her bed, and it was Joyce who changed our diapers, sterilized our glass baby bottles, fed us, and kept us clean. We had no bathtub in the South San Francisco place, so every Saturday evening, Joyce heated up the water and bathed us in a big aluminum tub before laying out our Sunday church clothes. Suits, boots, and hats for the boys.

My father wasn't especially religious, but he was an avid reader and an amateur debater. Even though he was a big drinker, he knew his Bible verbatim. On some Sundays, after an all-night bender, he'd show up at the church reeking of booze to correct the minister's use of scripture from the pews. He was always right. But rarely around. When he was, he sure put us in our place. He seemed to feel more at ease showing uncensored affection to his dog, Rover. When that sooner walked into the house, we had to get off the couch and sit on the floor. Rover would get the place of honor. When my father got sent to jail for being drunk in public, sometimes Rover would get picked up too, for not wearing his tags. That dog had his own stylish cap, just like Daddy's, and they'd set out together for private drives. That's right. The dog got to ride shotgun while we sat at home, wishing our father would show us half the same consideration. The memories of the times he did show up when I craved his presence are so rare I can count them on my hand. My sister Joyce had to remind me that my father made the drive all the way to Pescadero on the San Mateo County coast to watch me play in a Pop Warner football game—and I scored a touchdown. Joyce had been living out of the house for a while, having her own kids. But as my "assistant mom," she screamed her lungs out and ran down to the field to snap my picture. I have no memory of my father being there. Little League was where I really shined, and at every game I'd scan the bleachers—mostly filled with white parents who'd shown up for the other team—looking for my dad. I didn't expect to find him. Every time I saw the empty space where I wanted him to be, anger would cut a tiny notch. And that different kind of pain helped me practice not giving a fuck.

13

My view of my father would change as I got older. When I saw my brothers hauled off to jail for not paying child support when they were truly out of pocket and unable, an injustice I would later dedicate myself to fighting, I began to realize how much our father had sacrificed for us by working his ass off. Every month, he would give Moms his money two days after he got paid. He didn't care if the PG&E or the phone were gonna get shut off, he kept his money just long enough to feel some pride, to feel like a man who had earned something. It was hard cash, and he slept with it in his pocket for two nights, like clockwork, before giving it up to keep the rest of us alive.

These days, I keep a photo of my father tacked above my desk at work. He's wearing a cream-colored fedora with a pin-striped suit and his Florsheim shoes. He was dignified—when he wanted to be. But he wasn't soft. He was a hard man with hard language, and he didn't feel shit about calling you a bitch punk-ass motherfucker. By the time I got to school, that was core language in my household. During my first thirty-one years of life, anger was my primary line of defense, and it sure paired well with a creative string of curse words. Even today, when people comment on my cursing, I want to tell them, "You weren't raised in my home. You weren't with me when my world changed colors multiple times, not with me in juvenile hall, in jail, or on the prison yard. The coarseness of language pales in comparison with the coarseness of life. So, how about we get to the content of what I'm saying?"

Debt collectors and a bunch of delinquent sons were not exactly what my parents planned for. Before they moved the family to the peninsula, they envisioned a life of integration, education, and culture for their children. When Joyce was growing up in South San Francisco, there were only seventy-two Black families in town, and she was one of three Black students in her graduating junior high school class. She learned to play the piano and took in the opera and ballet in San Francisco now and then with our mother. Then, in 1955, when I was four years old, my parents started house hunting.

Agreements written down on paper in plain ink had kept Black people and other minorities from buying into certain neighborhoods since the beginning of time. And California had more of those so-called "racially restrictive housing covenants" than any other state. By the time my parents started shopping for a home on the peninsula, the US Supreme Court had called those covenants out as constitutionally bullshit. But that didn't mean much because it happened anyway, with a wink and a nod. Real estate agents only showed Black families houses in certain pockets, pockets like ours. And that went for Black school teachers, scientists, and other professionals with money in the bank. Meanwhile, they kept white buyers out. Sure enough, in the mid-1950s, those real estate men were drawing lines around my ghetto-to-be east of the Bayshore Freeway with every sale and every purchase. But I only learned more recently exactly how they abracadabra-ed Belle Haven and neighboring East Palo Alto from white to Black practically overnight: a technique called blockbusting. As my father might have described it, it works like this: "I'm gonna stir up some bitch-ass white people panic with my bullshit talk of a motherfucking Negro invasion and get rich." And that's what they did. They whispered to white homeowners that the Negroes were coming and warned them that property values were about to tank, fast. To save the shirts on their upstanding white backs, they better sell *now*, though yesterday would have been better. And sell they did. When my parents set eyes on that first house, on Madera Avenue, there were two Black families living on the block. By the time they moved in a few months later, there were only two white families left. That year, it turns out, at least a quarter of all the homes in Belle Haven were put up for sale. The US Civil Rights Commission even paid a visit to San Francisco in 1960, just five years after we moved to the peninsula, to hold a special hearing about all this racist master planning. One real estate operator, the commission learned, had sold sixty Belle Haven homes in ninety days.

My parents and plenty of other Black families were happy to have access to a slice of suburbia, but it came at a cost. In our early years on the peninsula, I heard my elders whispering about cross burnings. As Black families moved in, racist whites made their feelings known through intimidation and hate. That does damage, and I know my father hit the bottle a little harder because of it. There were other worries too. You don't just need a house with four walls and a roof to move up in this world. You need a job that pays more than dirt. The kind of work that would have helped a man like my father build some savings—an office job, or a customer service job in a bank—were off limits to Black men. And it was worse for Black women, because secretarial and sales jobs were off limits too. My mother learned that firsthand. When my father relented and allowed her to work, she wound up taking care of white kids at the nearby Air Force base and cleaning houses for white people across the freeway bridge.

As our invisible prison turned Blacker, more white families fled, and our schools turned to shit, which caused even more to get the hell out. By the time I was in third grade, only about a sixth of the kids at my school, Belle Haven Elementary, were white. The neighborhood kids called my father "Mr. John Henry," and thanks to his warehouse job, we all had plenty of yellow Pee-Chee folders, pencils, and other school supplies, even as the quality of our education tanked. Most of our teachers were inexperienced and didn't stick around long. Most didn't seem to care whether we learned to read or write. And a lot of us knew it. We threw shit in class, swore, ran around, and raised hell.

At age nine, I was already getting suspended and sent home for screwing around, the manifestation of my unconscious rebellion. I didn't want to disappoint my parents, but it's not like I attached being at school to my own self-interest. Willie Mays stayed over in Atherton, the richest white neighborhood on the other side of the freeway bridge. He was almost close enough to touch, but the white people over there had more access to the man than we did. Still, our teachers held up entertainers and sports figures like Mays as people we should want to emulate. If we got lucky, our icon was Jackie Robinson. Threading that needle was a one in a million proposition. I can remember the dawning realization that my weight wasn't of such a nature, and my height wasn't of such a stature that I could make it as an athlete. What was left was pretty much nothing. No teacher held up an example of any Black person who had achieved intellectually. It's a mark of the depth of my disinterest that I can only remember one who *did* seem to care. Mrs. Starris, in fourth grade, actually passed on some rudimentary reading and writing skills. When *Mary Poppins* came out, the teacher spent hours trying to teach us to spell that bizarre-sounding white people word: *supercalifragilisticexpialidocious*. She was showing us that we had intelligence. She also taught us science—and teamwork. She had seven of us squat in a circle and lift a classmate up above our heads, an exercise that helped us see what we could achieve together. Not one other teacher I can recall seemed to give a shit. I'd later attend Ravenswood High School in East Palo Alto. Black families had battled the district before that school opened in 1958, demanding boundaries that promoted integration. They lost. Until I got to prison, Ravenswood High was the Blackest institution I'd known.

If my own father was struggling to support us on two jobs, that didn't leave much hope for the crop of Black kids who came of age in our invisible prison. I knew that we'd been sidelined and subjugated. But until I got to prison, I lacked the language to express it. My lot was our collective lot. It wasn't like I was served up more or less dignity than anybody else who lived over here in this small-ass section of one of the richest counties in the fucking state. We were all equally insulted. By the time I was twelve, I was thieving on a modest scale, and so was just about everyone else I knew. That, I learned, is how you got what you wanted. It took me leaving for a life sentence in lockup and coming home again to recognize, consciously, that I'd even been poor. But subconscious knowledge often feeds rage. Every time a liquor store owner chased us off his property, every time an older brother got hauled off to jail, every time a cop so much as looked at me, that rage inside me got a sharpening. The confines of my ghetto had a lot to do with the man I would become, for worse and then for better, when I returned to give back.

THERE WAS ONE way over the freeway on foot back then—a narrow pedestrian bridge that dropped us onto Ringwood Avenue and into another world. That's how we walked the more than two miles to Burgess Park, in the heart of whiteness, to play some of our Little League games against the white kids from

Atherton and Palo Alto. But the larger thoroughfare of Menlo Park, Willow Road, lay to the southeast. One sunny Saturday when I was eleven years old, Nate Harrington and I took the long way home, looping through the open grass of Willow Oaks School. That's when we spotted a hunk of metal catching the sun on the schoolyard.

"Check that out," Nate said, in his quiet, lilting way.

Nate was tall, gangly, and uncoordinated as a kid. He was so quiet my sister Joyce thought he was touched. But I knew he was brilliant. A lot of us were, though there were few people around who seemed to recognize it, least of all ourselves. Both of us would have had trouble back then believing we'd even live another decade, but our bond—mine and Nate's—would last a lifetime. On that sunny day in 1963, though, we were just two boys in sync. Two boys exploring. The metal thing looked like a piece of junk, a cool piece of junk. We picked it up and made it exactly one block down Willow before a cop car hemmed us in at the 76 gas station. Then the interrogation began.

Did we know we had stolen public property? Did we know we could be placed under arrest? The thing, it turned out, was a sprinkler, though there'd been no hose in sight. The officer loaded us into the caged back seat. But instead of taking us to the station, he brought each of us home, reporting our breach of the law to our parents. That evening, each of us got a whooping from our dads. We met outside, bruised and indignant—anything to mask the hurt—and made a plan to run away. It was a fucked-up plan. We had no place to run to. But we got on our bikes—by this time I had one I could call my own—and we rode. We got as far as Coyote Point, a spit of a public park in San Mateo that juts into the Bay about fourteen miles north of our ghetto. The fog rolled in and the cold broke us down, leaving us shivering on the

19

concrete floor of the public bathroom. That marked the end of our childish quest for escape. But it was just the beginning of our strident relationship with the law. We were learning how disrespect can harden a person to the point that consequences mean nothing. Soon we figured out how to use the black-and-whites as a taxi service, courtesy of the taxpayer. When we got tired after a day of exploring, we'd just make ourselves visible. And sure enough, some pig would load us up and drive us back to the ghetto. America's finest. Keeping the streets safe, for some.

Two years after Nate and I got screwed over by the cops and worked over by our dads, my family moved to Baylor Street in East Palo Alto, part of a housing tract called University Village. We'd pack up and unpack our meager shit a couple more times before my family bought the house where I now live. The move to the Village stood out though. It was one of my father's attempts to do better for us, to reach for the kind of refuge that too often seemed to involve neighbors who wanted to lynch us. The Village was the latest front in our community's storm of ghettoization—with enough whites left to make things uncomfortable. One of them lived next door. I was tossing a ball with my younger brother, David, when it went over the fence. So, I hopped it. David and I were back in our yard playing catch when a sheriff's deputy rolled up. The neighbor had reported me for trespassing. Our parents weren't home, so this time, he took me to the substation and scared the shit out of me before letting me walk home. It was the first of many visits. I was thirteen years old, and that suspicion and disrespect cut another notch inside me. If this was how the cops were going to see me, this was what I would become.

My childish trespasses began to grow into the kind of thieving expected of me as a Black teen. My parents may have given us everything that we needed, but there was a whole hell of a lot more that I wanted. But I hadn't fully spread those wings when my older brother Ronald gave me a beating to remember for whining about some ten-dollar Converse sneakers I wanted from the mall. Shoes my parents couldn't afford. Ronald was reminding me, just as Joyce often had, that there are needs and there are wants. I made a pledge that day never to take from my own family. Since my community had so little to offer, most of Belle Haven was also spared contact with my sticky fingers. I'd do most of my taking on the other side of the Bayshore Freeway. If the cops weren't depositing me back on my side, I got around on a bike. A whole series of bikes that I stole myself. I remember my first—a three-speed Schwinn I nabbed from the Stanford campus. From then on, I did all my bike shopping at that elite institution.

As white families drained away like water down a bathtub drain, our schools were turning into a Black version of *Lord of the Flies*, cheating us out of an education. Stanford University was just three miles away, but the only endeavors I envisioned myself accomplishing on that storied campus involved thieving. Still, I *was* getting an education—on what it meant to be Black in a ghetto created by white realtors. Soon, a buddy and I were smoking weed that we'd steal from our fathers as they hung out drinking and getting high late into the night. It was some damn good weed. I started shoplifting from "the Big M," our code name for the Macy's at the Stanford Shopping Center, and relieving people who didn't look like me of their cash. I wanted clothes to impress the girls, one girl in particular. Money for the pool hall down the road in East Palo Alto, and for gas when I finally got access to a car. Brief stints in juvenile hall followed, so numerous that I lost count. At least they served pancakes.

21

Yes, my parents were disappointed. But my dad was getting hauled off to jail himself for his drinking, and every now and then for knockdown fights with one of his boys. A few of my brothers were already jail regulars. As our world shrank, so did our ambitions, and we became what the law expected us to be: robbers, vandals, burglars, addicts—but then, in some cases, eventually, revolutionaries.

That same summer that Nate and I almost got arrested for picking up a sprinkler, the Watts riots burned and shook Los Angeles. The news was not lost inside our cage of a neighborhood. A few days after the fires quelled, my brother Ronald was arrested with a group of other so-called "hoodlums" on arson charges, for tossing Molotov cocktails through the plate glass windows of certain convenience stores. They were the stores that shortchanged Black youth and called the pigs to chase us off for "loitering." Ronald was laying the foundation for my political education, though I wouldn't fully realize it until I got to the prison yard. I'd been rebelling since third grade. And every year, I turned the volume up. Our whole community was raging at the cops for holding their knees on our collective neck, always jacking us up, never showing an ounce of respect for our humanity. White folks in nicer neighborhoods saw them as partners in a two-way social contract. The way I saw it: They were outsiders, trying to do me at every turn. I was trying to survive the experience. That's no contract I would ever sign, so I relieved myself of any responsibility to abide by their terms.

The mid- to late 1960s brought honorable efforts by some of our Black elders to feed our minds with something other than white-centered imperialist bullshit. Gertrude Wilks, who came from an East Palo Alto root family, founded the private Nairobi Day School for Black kids when she figured out her own son was barely learning how to read, and went on to create the Nairobi High School too. Her choice of name inspired. There was even an attempt down the road to change the name of East Palo Alto to Nairobi. Onetta Harris, the Belle Haven neighbor who'd kept us all fed with government cheese, also stepped up to teach us pride in Black brilliance. She became a community counselor at Belle Haven Elementary, and she successfully pushed parents to get involved in their kids' education. She also rallied the 'hood to demand services from Menlo Park city leaders who rarely crossed the freeway to visit the eastern side of town. As Onetta noted, our tax dollars were as green as anyone else's. Thanks to her, we got a community center and swimming pool just around the corner from the house where I still live, so we wouldn't have to trek deep into the world of white wealth for such basic amenities. In 1983, a year after Mrs. Harris died, the Menlo Park City Council voted unanimously to name the center after her. All the root families in East Menlo Park and East Palo Alto remember her contributions. Unfortunately, Facebook doesn't. The tech giant moved into Menlo Park in 2011 and within five years started buying up our side of town. Not long ago, the company teamed with the city to fund a massive remodel of Mrs. Harris's hard-won accomplishment. They're calling it the Menlo Park Community Campus. It's not clear if Onetta will even get a plaque. But back when my elders were working to teach us pride in our African roots, the idea of Facebook was more than half a century off, and my personal notion of Black brilliance was a solid burglary on the rich side of town. Twice, I dodged police bullets as I ran off with some stranger's bounty. One night, as I played it cool at a party, I saw for the first time what a gun can do to a young man up close. He dropped right there, blood

23

pooling, though he'd wind up surviving. It was ugly and it stayed with me, but it sure as hell didn't deter me. Crime made the world accessible to me. I was finding my place on the streets. I was getting laid. I was dressing fine. It was the only kind of respect I'd felt.

I never did set out to cause harm: I was searching for pleasure, the high of a joyride, the thrill of a beautiful girl looking my way. I was enrolled at Ravenswood High, but I was a happier brother when I took my regular class breaks to smoke, and every now and then sell, weed in front of the Dairy Belle across the street. Those were my office hours. Playing dice in the bathroom also suited me all right. The vice principal was a Black man from the South who went on to become the first Black high school principal in San Francisco. He'd write a letter on my behalf when I was facing life just three years later. When he was the man policing the hallways, I never went out of my way to disrespect him. He was decent to me, even as he hauled me into his office for my misdeeds. The man saw something in me, something I didn't. However, we agreed to disagree on one major matter of practice. He wanted me to name names. Who was selling? Who was fighting? Who was breaking into school lockers and burglarizing those fancy houses on the sweet side of town? *That* was a nonstarter. A few years down the road, my "no snitching" stance would cost me a lot more than the consternation of a vice principal. But I abide by it today. Taking responsibility is a personal act. I don't do it for others. Here's the thing, though: back then, I had no idea what else might be possible for me in this life. Sitting with my juvenile probation officer one afternoon, he asked me what I saw myself becoming. What did I want for my future? To me, those were paint-by-numbers questions that I could color in without much thought: More money. More drugs.

More pool hall. More sex. I got sent to continuation school in nearby Redwood City. Incarceration Prep. I never graduated.

By now, there were plenty of us who couldn't see a way out. We were an army of razor grass, looking for any opportunity to express our unarticulated rage. That's why so many of us showed up on Henderson Place in the spring of 1969. Henderson Place is the curling cul-de-sac where my family lived for a hot second when I was small. By now, there was only one white family left. I'd known them in those earlier years, but never paid much attention, because white and Black kids didn't try to mix. On that day in the spring of 1969, that white family was in deep shit. A friend of their grown son had beaten up a little Black kid—a much smaller kid who was recovering from brain surgery—and when that line got crossed, all hell broke loose. It was like a mini-Watts, suburban style.

The whole neighborhood flooded into that cul-de-sac to vent. 25
We were sick of motherfuckers treating us like shit on a shoe. Ronald was getting busted left and right, not only for selling weed, but also for taking on the fucked-up, repressive, ever-tightening chokehold of injustice we were bucking up against but didn't fully understand. I loved Ronald for that. Rebellion against any and all rules was the only way I'd seen a brother maintain any sense of power. And I followed Ronald's example. Law enforcement swarmed in and came down on us hard. They called it a "riot." They maced me in the face. A woman I'd never met was right there with a bottle of water, washing out my burning, weeping eyes. That's when a part of me realized: This is necessary anger, community. It wasn't just people like my brother tossing Molotov cocktails. There was a cross section of our whole community. Even the church ladies came out to protest. I was seventeen. I had already fathered two kids, and

I was afraid I wouldn't be able to give them a future. We were all sick of it.

Still, whatever sense of community bond I felt, I had no language to express it yet, no way to further it. With no concept of a better future, I slid into the gaping hole that took its place. Within two years, I participated in an ugly act that left a man I knew nothing about lying dead on the floor of his liquor store. Before the echo of the gunshot left the room, I knew that my life had changed forever. I was drowning in a place where nobody I knew had the power to save me.

Chapter 2

GLADIATOR SCHOOL

Our keepers herded us into a dimly lit room with a cold-ass bench in Receiving & Release, where the key turned in my cuffs and the chains dropped. I had learned the routine, and I'd repeat it so many times over the next decade that I felt the pull of history deep in my DNA. The dance of the slave. Pull off your clothes. Stick your tongue out. Let me see what's behind your ear. Lift up your nuts. Spread your legs. Cough. Squat. Show me the most intimate parts of your body on demand. It could have been any auction block anywhere in the country when they were getting ready to sell my ancestors. Let me see if you got good teeth. Let me see if you're capable of reproducing. Let me see how you're hung. Let me see if you're clean. Dignity erased. But on this sunny morning in April of 1972, we were just getting started.

I walked into Deuel Vocational Institution in leg irons and waist chains, if you can call the convict shuffle walking. I was short and skinny. I hadn't started shaving, and I was still

sporting baby fat on my cheeks. I'd marked my twentieth birthday in a county jail cell four months earlier, contemplating the
life expectancy of the average Black man as I waited on my
retrial. It didn't go my way. That made today the first day of
the rest of my life sentence, and this was not the place I would
have chosen for the mission.

Most people called the concrete complex out in the middle
of farmland DVI or just Tracy, for the Central Valley town two
and a half miles down the road. It's where a lot of young prisoners who caught serious cases got sent. That bought us time
to prep for San Quentin or Folsom state prisons, the state's
aging fortresses from the nineteenth century. DVI was newer,
but *vocational* and *institution* in the name were ghost words that
stirred up dying ideals of rehabilitation. State-sanctioned rehabilitation is definitely *not* what I would be receiving, but I was
about to get one hell of an education. Because not more than a
few years before the armed guards marched us young people off
the prison transport bus, DVI had earned itself another name:
Gladiator School.

The Gray Goose, as the transport bus was known, pulled into
DVI and dislodged five of us into the last of the morning light
before continuing with its human cargo to other California prisons. My street clothes were gone. I'd given them up to the trash
heap as soon as I was moved from jail to Vacaville, where the
California Medical Facility served as the state's main reception
center. That meant pretty much every homie went there first to
kick around for a while as white men in suits picked apart our
criminal histories and decided which hell to ship us to for the
longer stay. Other than ten pounds of chains, I'd gotten off the
bus wearing nothing more than borrowed transit overalls and
prison-issued boxer shorts. After the strip search at Receiving

& Release, we sat in a row on the cold-ass bench in our underpants and waited on our next set of prison gear, blues this time. Tension was starting to play on my skin like electricity. I could smell my fear and the fear all around me. I tried to ignore it, to make it familiar.

DVI's reputation was no secret to those of us coming from Vacaville. Sure, there was racial tension there, but guys who knew had warned us it was like a Disneyland vacation compared to Gladiator School. That's in part because Vacaville's reception center was temporary, a kind of DMZ for racial warfare. At DVI, though, racial gangs were congealing like spilled blood. The Aryan Brotherhood and La Eme, or Mexican Mafia from the southern part of California, tended to back each other up. Meanwhile, the Black Guerilla Family (BGF) was burning up with justified rage. A full year hadn't passed since San Quentin prison guards gunned down George Jackson, whose book of prison letters, *Soledad Brother*, had transformed him into the voice of the militant prison movement. He was a Black Panther, a Marxist, a brilliant thinker whose call for uprising led to the creation of the BGF. He was shot full of holes during a so-called escape attempt that all Black nationalists and the entire radical Left viewed as a setup, a state-sponsored assassination. But everyone needs allies, and when the shit hit the fan at DVI in riot mode, BGF would join forces with Nuestra Familia, Mexican dudes from Northern California. I'd learned at Vacaville how the lines cleaved. But once the DVI goon squad guards handed us our new uniforms and flimsy woolen blankets, the real orientation started.

Honor prisoners, inmates with good disciplinary records, were tasked with walking new arrivals to J Wing, where each of us had been assigned to an eight-by-six-foot solo cell. That would change as soon as the prison "classified" us—judged us according to our supposed risk level and sent us off to the worst housing the facility had to offer. My guide was a light-skinned brother with a limp, and he gave me a quick and quiet tutorial as we walked. Lesson 1: Big Bertha. That was the tear gas gun the COs used to blast inmates when riots broke out. Lesson 2: Where you land in that poison fog makes a huge difference in your prospect for survival, because the pigs slam those gates closed to break up the party.

"Be sure you be conscious of what side of the gate you on," he told me in a dull voice, like a bored guide at a run-down amusement park, "so you don't get caught up with too many whites or too many Southern Mexicans."

What it came down to: Know which Mexicans to trust. And *never* trust whites. In time, I'd deviate from that advice. But it wouldn't take me more than a week to grasp DVI's bigger power picture: You can't have a gladiator fight without a Roman in charge. And true enough, it was DVI guards who stirred up the shit, spreading rumors, passing whispered lies and truths in the ears of prisoners like unpinned grenades. Then they'd sit back and watch, firing plenty of shots along the way and orchestrating the throwing of a motherfucker or two off the tier.

I'd done OK at Vacaville. I'd even learned to stand my ground—which I did after a beef with a man named Juan Corona. He was a serial killer who'd buried twenty-five migrant farm workers in the peach orchards of Sutter County. I was a Black kid from Belle Haven. But when Juan and I got into it, we managed to work it out without a physical fight. DVI was something new. The violence among prisoners was racial, political, and off the fucking hook. Beyond that was the larger war, of keeper versus caged, and despite our obvious disadvantage, we were determined to fight—to the death if we had to. Our common enemy was the closest we got to harmony. There was no question that my childhood was gone. Soon, I'd get used to the idea of kissing my adulthood good-bye too.

THE LIFE THAT got me here was standard in the invisible cage of my ghetto. I'd been to juvenile hall for burglary, weed possession, and for just being incorrigible, that crime of "we don't like your fucking attitude." The visits blurred together, but I *do* remember my first stay, and I have to say, I dug it. I'd never had a room to myself. I'd never had dessert on a regular basis. And then there were the pancakes. Back home, I shared a room with my younger brother, David, when I cared to come home. The house was crowded because Moms always had room for cousins, nieces, nephews, and neighborhood strays. Still, year by year, hope drained from my parents' outlook. Ronald and Pat were already cycling in and out of jail. Meanwhile, in the space of a few years, Lula Mae Nunn and John Henry Nunn Sr. lost two sons. The third oldest, Robert, died of sickle cell anemia in December 1968. My eldest brother, John Henry Jr., died in September 1970. He and a neighbor had gone fishing off the coast of Half Moon Bay; they both drowned when their boat capsized. My life sentence came just sixteen months later. It nearly broke my parents, but it didn't surprise me. My circumstances had been pointing me to prison like a neon arrow.

As a younger teen, weed was my drug of choice as it was for all of us, and we were doing fine with that. Buying it. Smoking it. Selling it. But one year, in the late 1960s, the supply dried up almost overnight, and heroin came flooding in. It was a cartel move with US government approval, if you ask a lot of us who lived it—an attempt to wipe my ghetto off the face of the earth.

And it was a nationwide phenomenon. When it didn't quite finish the job, the powers intent on keeping us down gave it a second try a couple of decades later with crack cocaine. We were expendable subjects of a twisted marketplace experiment. If marijuana is a gateway drug, what our oppressors did was either close the gates or take them completely off the hinges.

I walked into the pool hall one night, and there it was, a line of horse spread out on one of my favorite albums, *The Electrifying Eddie Harris*. That brother put the funk into tenor sax. It was sitting there on the fraying green felt of the pool table, calling my name. Everyone else was snorting it, so why not try? After I threw up, I developed a taste for the stuff. I was sixteen years old. For me, though, getting high wasn't the motivation for burglary or robbery. I had plenty of friends who shared their dope. For me, the taking had more to do with babies and ladies. For some people, sex marks an entry into adulthood, but DVI carried me across that threshold. My first sexual partner was a girl named Jackie. I was thirteen, and after we got done, I truly believed my dick was broken. My first child was born three years later, to a girl named Alma who was just shy of her sixteenth birthday. Alma had swept me off my feet not long after I lost my virginity. She had the most beautiful big brown eyes, a smile that knocked me out, and a serious side that would pay off for her down the road with a stable job in the square world. As youngsters, we pulled off our first burglary together, raiding a candy warehouse behind an East Palo Alto park and stuffing our cute little faces for weeks. She was quiet and smart, and her mother cursed like a sailor, just like my father. My friend Fred was sweet on Alma's older sister, Dolores. He got her pregnant first. Then, one day, the phone rang at my house.

"Dorsey," Dolores told me, "Alma had a baby boy."

I was standing in the kitchen, and she must have thought the line went dead. Being that I didn't have a clue I was going to be a father, I posed what might just be the most insulting question a male can ask: "Is it mine?" Alma hadn't told me a fucking thing. Alma told nobody. Not her mother. Not her teachers. Not any doctor. She'd carried that child to term in her hips because she was scared, and she probably wasn't too eager to let her momma know who planted the seed. In those days, if girls risked taking me home, and most didn't, it wasn't like their fathers figured this is the kid they wanted their daughters to marry. I was striving for the streets, emulating pool hall dope fiends. I'd already seen my brother Ronald and a whole bunch of people from my community go to prison and come back home. It was becoming obvious that we had a shared destiny.

By the time I learned that Alma had a baby boy named Anthony, her mother had moved the family to San Francisco's Haight Ashbury. I suspect it was an attempt to keep Dolores out of the clutches of Fred, who we all called June Boy. I didn't get up that way much to see them. Besides, being a clumsy Romeo who was horny as hell, it didn't take but a minute before I hooked up with Alma's old friend and soon-to-be nemesis, Faydell—and got her pregnant too. This time, I was in on the details. I swooned all over that growing belly. I even got mad at my own moms for not showing up at the hospital when Faydell gave birth to my baby girl, Denise. (It was December 5, 1969, and I'd failed to recognize that my moms was marking the first anniversary of Robert's death.) I was, in theory, maturing toward adulthood. I should have been a provider who could protect my family. I felt like a little man, and I wanted to be respected as one. That's how I rationalized my taking. Years passed before I admitted to myself that what I wanted most of all—more than to responsibly provide for my babies—was the attention and affection of women. I stole because I wanted to dress fine, to look good. I had a street life, with street taste. My choice in fashion made that clear. I wore a fucking purple crushed-velvet suit to both of my trials. But the truth is, if my attorney had told me how I *should* dress, I wouldn't have owned the shit he talked about. That purple suit *was* my nice clothes. I looked like a cross between Barney the dinosaur and a peacock. That's the way it was, because Black men in my ghetto had no access to the things that truly measure manhood, like a decent education and an equally decent livelihood. Many still don't.

THE EAST BAY town of Newark is a straight shot across the Dumbarton Bridge from East Palo Alto. My homies and I made that drive a lot, to take a break from the pool hall, expand our horizons, and scout new territory. But on the night that changed my life and took another's, we had no plans to rob. Zig-Zags, English 800, and Colt 45 were what we had in mind. I'm not saying we weren't robbers, and we were definitely high, but the three of us who walked into that establishment that night didn't do it thinking this was the lick we were gonna hit. Then, all that rage in us we didn't have words to define, the rage at our limited circumstances that had turned us into razor blades of grass, came rising up when the store owner behind the counter made the choice to service a customer who was white before he serviced us. That night, you couldn't have told me somebody hadn't wronged us. We were in the fucking store first. And although I personally had no eloquence yet, no language of analysis, Black people around me were loudly, finally defining what their oppression looked and felt like. The Black Panther

Party had come through the neighborhood, as had the NAACP and SNCC, the Student Nonviolent Coordinating Committee. I wasn't listening too closely, but I grasped the basics. My take-away: we didn't let whites do this or that to us. Over time, my idea that white people were by their very nature arrayed against us would change in a fundamental way. A few key white allies helped me on that journey. For now, though, I was expressing my anger. We all were.

Through both of my trials, I denied I set foot in the Newark liquor store. But I did. On a Monday night in April of 1971, one of us drew a gun. We demanded money. The liquor store owner refused to open the register. I jumped the counter to persuade him. He reached for the alarm button. Then, the one who drew the gun fired two shots. It wasn't me. But I was there, and the felony murder rule is clear. All three of us were equally respon-sible for his death.

The store owner's wife and a lady who'd been driving by that night picked me out of a lineup. My first trial was a shit show. Both witnesses had botched other identifications, and they were all the prosecution had. I tried to make my best impression. My purple crushed-velvet suit jacket had wide lapels, and I dressed up the ensemble with a satin shirt and purple-and-black pat-ent leather shoes. Looking back, I did myself no favors. Friends who'd come to watch the trial wore crushed velvet too, lime green and Day-Glo orange. The bailiffs and judge kept warning them to settle down. Pretty fast, I got a message to them: Man, stop! Just send me some money.

The judge was Lionel Wilson, who went on to become Oak-land's first Black mayor. But when the jury in his courtroom found me guilty of first-degree murder in September 1971, it made no difference to me what color he was. I was a small person, but when my rage and fear kicked in, I picked up the counsel table and flipped it into the jury box, where it crashed in splinters. The bailiffs had to pile on to get me cuffed. I knew I was guilty. But the system that had led me down this path without giving me any avenue of escape seemed guiltier. Judge Wilson called me into his chambers and spoke to me calmly.

"Son," he said, "you tore up my courtroom."

He seemed to recognize in me a young Black man who was kicking for his life, to understand my rage without excusing it. He wasn't the first brother I'd encountered in a position of power. But to get that far you had to be squeaky clean and stick to the script. Judge Wilson, and the vice principal at Ravenswood High who tried to turn me straight, may or may not have understood the underpinnings of systemic racism. But from their seats of power, they weren't able to do much about it. Still, I apologized to Judge Wilson and meant it. Not long after, he granted my defense attorney's motion for a new trial on grounds of insufficient evidence. And three months later, we were at it again. Trial #2. Judge Wilson couldn't preside over that one because the Alameda County Superior Court needed him for a high-profile Black Panther Party case. But before he handed my case to another judge, he appointed me a new defense attorney: Wilmont Sweeney. Sweeney was the first Black man elected to the Berkeley City Council. He was serving as vice mayor when he represented me, and he'd go on to become a prominent juvenile court judge. But even Wilmont Sweeney couldn't save me from myself.

I'd sworn up and down to my mother and father that I wasn't in the liquor store that night. I was starting to believe that shit. My mother, the cofounder of a church, a woman sustained by her beliefs, got up on that stand as my alibi witness and swore on the Bible she believed in that I'd been home, sleeping. My pops did too. But it was my mother's sacrifice that stayed with me. At first it was a seed of discomfort, a knowledge I'd asked too much. But it grew into a colossal tree of regret. I knew my mother loved me, and I knew she lied for me. It killed something inside her. As for my father, when I told him I wouldn't snitch, he wept. It was the first and one of the only times I saw John Henry Nunn cry. But I never once considered turning state's evidence. Becoming a snitch was worse than a life sentence. It was a death sentence. And besides, every rule I lived by dictated that I stay silent.

Ten days after my second trial started, it was a wrap. The prosecution managed to match my fingerprint with one on the greasy liquor store counter, something they couldn't pull off the first time. The verdict: Guilty. Again. On sleepless nights before my sentencing date, I got on my knees on the floor of the cell and prayed. That was something my moms had taught me. I'd come to believe that God doesn't show up all the time when you want him to, but he generally shows up when you need him to. Lying there in the dark, listening to the sounds of other men snoring, I pondered one question: How long does a Black man live? I made an assumption right off the top that my moms and pops would be dead by the time I got out.

I had no idea how fast my prayers would be changing. In the weeks, months, and years after I walked into DVI, I prayed to live. I prayed that I wouldn't have to kill. And if I did, I prayed that I didn't kill somebody I liked. I prayed for a parole date too. I prayed for some real good shit.

ALL THE DVI wings in East Hall and West Hall—J Wing included—were off the mainline. Getting placed in any of those indicated some type of restriction. But when the prison brass really wanted to punish you, they'd send you to K Wing. That was solitary confinement, what we call the Hole. In K Wing, you only got out of your shit-infused cage to take a shower or get a quick bit of exercise alone on the tier. Since we were new arrivals who had just gotten to Receiving & Release, it would take a few days before we were "classified." For Black arrivals especially, that's when the mind games ramped up. "We don't like who you associate with." "We don't like your attitude." "We don't like your color."

I was in my temporary cell when the chow hall bell sounded. That's when the fucked-up ballet began, an invisible hand guiding us through each steel gate that buzzed open and slammed closed behind us. We were the fish, fresh bait, swimming with sharks. I kept my head down as much as I could. I smelled the dead air, the sweat and piss and fear. There was way too much movement for my comfort. Glancing around, I recognized how muscular everyone was, bulked up past the normal parameters of nature. Lines painted on the floor dictated where we could walk—one on each side of the hallway corresponding to the direction of foot traffic. The space in the middle was a no-go zone, or at least it was supposed to be.

As we approached the chow hall the flow of men slowed, and we formed a line, shoulders up against the wall on our right. That's when I saw the scuffle, a quick frenzy of motion in front of me. Before I knew it, a wide-eyed brother was coming toward me, straight down the no-go zone. I saw his raised eyebrows before I saw the shank sticking out of his back. As new arrivals, we were marked by the color of our jail threads. We were supposed to play it cool. But I was barely twenty years old, and I was scared. I turned to the guy behind me.

"Did you see that?" I asked him, my eyes gone wide. My neighbor kept his fixed on some spot on the wall, real or imaginary. When he answered, his voice was hard.

"I didn't see no motherfucking thing," he said. "And neither did you."

Chapter 3

COMMITMENT TO KILL

I lived in prison for many years, and when I try to explain my time inside, violence can dominate my stories—because memories of violence set up house inside me and never left. That's the toll that trauma takes. In California prisons during the 1970s, the prospect of violence was constant, and at DVI that was true even in the Hole. Almost all the other cells had solid sliding doors painted a faded green, each with a fortified glass window for the guards to look through. At least those solid doors closed, giving us some privacy and temporary protection. Not so in K Wing. There, the punishment of solitary confinement came with the bonus of open bars that left us exposed to attacks. In fact, a white Nazi motherfucker shot me in the chest that way with a prison-made zip gun. It hurt. It also taught me how to make a zip gun—and never to hang out at the front of my cell for more than a minute. After I witnessed the stabbing on my first day of Gladiator School, that kind of violence became a way of life. I saw men thrown to their deaths off the tier and pierced by bullets that screamed down from the guard towers. I watched them shank each other with handmade spears. And the violence that I didn't witness I heard about, strangulation and burning included. But I don't want to bring you prison porn. I want to take you deeper, to show you what happens when the prison system sets human beings up to lunge at one another like starved beasts. DVI's violence was orchestrated. It divided us along color lines in order to destroy us. It not only exposed me to constant danger, it compelled me to make a commitment to kill. That takes a toll on a human soul. Perhaps more remarkably, I want you to see that despite the violence and destruction, it remained possible to find love and community, even to grow. That was the miracle of prison. We did not let the system break us.

Vacaville, where I'd spent my first few months at the reception center, had been manageable in part because of the unspoken and imperfect truce among race-based gangs, and because of the company. Thanks to two measly joints, my older brother Ronald was there when I arrived, like a Wal-Mart greeter giving me the welcome rundown. As my big brother, he looked out for me, helped orient me and ease me into prison life. When the day came for me to transfer out, Ronald even managed to get some money into my canteen account at DVI. But as soon as that Gray Goose took me away, I never had a big brother again. The next time I ran into Ronald and my other older brother, Pat, together on the San Quentin prison yard, everyone thought I was the eldest—based on the hardened man I'd become.

I went to prison for first-degree murder committed during the commission of a robbery, and I was legally responsible for murder. But I'd never fought with anything other than my fists. I'd never so much as contemplated taking a life, and I sure as hell had never flat-out asked myself the question, would I kill? At DVI, the prospect became intellectually acceptable overnight. Yes, I would kill, if I had to. The questions of when and who ran through my head on a loop. You didn't have to have a beef with anyone to be subject to violence. You could be on your way to the canteen to buy you some soap, and a riot would pop off around you. The short distance from the cell to the chow hall, any distance at all, became a potentially deadly space to navigate. It plunged us all into a state of primal fear, our animal brains whispering, *survive, survive.* Every time I walked out the cell door, I asked myself if I would be willing to fight. And would I be willing to fight even if it wasn't *my* fight, just because shit broke out? Once I'd answered the question—would I kill?—another one gnawed at me: Would I die well? I didn't think I would die from a disease, and I was almost certain I wouldn't die from old age. If I was going to die by violence, I promised myself I wouldn't run from it. I wasn't going to die cowering in the back corner of my cell while some motherfucker stabbed me. DVI schooled me that if I was fitting to drop, I'd do it in the doorway. *That* would be an honorable death. So would stabbing a pig while he was shooting me or denying him the pleasure of killing me by taking my own life first. These were scenarios that were suddenly rampaging through my head at the age of twenty. It sure marked a shift in tone from a year or so earlier, when I spent my days dressing in Barney purple, looking to get laid.

Prison would test me, and I didn't always pass. But in the end, I held on to the thread of my own humanity. Not only that, I came to recognize and value the humanity of every person living in a cage and coming out of one. Despite the violence inherent in the system, prison helped make me the man I am today. It doesn't define me, but it sure as hell shaped me.

What Kind of Bird Can't Fly

I'D BEEN AT DVI less than a month when I landed in the Hole for the first of many stints. The Hole was mostly reserved for those of us the pigs assumed were involved in gang warfare, or even loosely allied with racial gangs. In the early 1970s, that made it a crowded place. The layout meant that guards didn't have eyes on us at all times. Even when they did, they were willing to look the other way when homemade projectiles took flight or a prisoner on the way to the shower shanked an enemy standing too close to the bars. K Wing might as well have been named Z for Zoo Wing, except we were treated with less dignity than most zoo animals. No yard time, infrequent showers, and no access to programming. We weren't even allowed reading material. And perhaps because of that deprivation, camaraderie crept in. We'd talk—to, at, with one other—often without knowing each other's names and not bothering to ask. The mere sound of the human voice was like caramel on candy. We brothers tended to find each other that way. In the darkness of night, one particular voice wove stories about a desert land populated by a superfly dude. It took me a while to figure out they were Bible stories, because the brother didn't refer to Jesus as Jesus. He was Jerusalem Slim. You know, "Jerusalem, he's a good dude. He stopped someone from getting stoned to death." When I finally got to the mainline, or general population, I'd take a Bible study course, inspired by that silk-voiced brother.

On one of my first nights in the Hole, I heard the sound. A relentless, rhythmic grinding, stopping and starting for hours. I couldn't place it. But it kept me up. The next morning, I mentioned my shit night's sleep to a neighbor. "Man, that scraping noise is a motherfucker."

"Sharpening," he answered. I couldn't see him, but I imagined him tipping his head back a bit with a slight nod. "You know," he added, in case I was dense, "sharpening knives."

The scraping of steel on concrete was powerful language. It meant, *nowhere is safe.* It meant, *you better get working on your own weapon.* So I did. I learned how to soak a shoestring or rare piece of wire in cleanser and use it to cut out pieces of the goddamned bunk. I learned how to sharpen those pieces on the concrete cell floor and fashion them into a spear that could pierce the flesh of another human being. Prison ingenuity was something wild, and the knowledge got passed along in the old-fashioned oral tradition. But for most of us—most certainly for myself—violence was compelled, not innate. We were gladiators, forced to entertain the Romans. And the Romans were the pigs and the entire system that put them in charge. Those motherfuckers used their power to stir up racial conflict throughout the prison—but especially in K Wing. After all, they had sent most of us there *because* of our racial alliances. The Gladiator Games were on, and they brought us low. Pretty soon, I found myself shitting in a cup for the sole privilege of throwing it in the face of another human being, a white supremacist whose racial slurs had launched my rage into the stratosphere. With each dehumanizing act of aggression or transgression, I got closer to becoming a man I never wanted to be.

FROM DAY ONE, I knew my size was going to be a handicap. To have any shot at survival, I had to change physically. That night I started running in place, doing pushups and sit-ups, serious as shit. I worked up to a thousand pushups a night. And when I wasn't cycling through K Wing, I'd hit the iron pile on the

45

yard. The first time I walked out there, I saw men lifting 300, 400, even 450 pounds on the bench press, so much weight the goddamned bars bent. I was struggling to lift 165. But soon, I felt my body changing into something I never knew I could be and never really wanted to be. By the time I walked to so-called freedom, I weighed in at 210 pounds, all muscle. I could bench press 395 and tear a phone book in half with my hands. I was a certified product of the state's carceral system, a freak guaranteed to turn violent in self-defense. The outside world did not react well. I could hear the click of car doors locking as I walked down the street.

Blacks and Latinos never worked out at the iron pile at the same time. That was a sure way to get your skull crushed. But as the weeks turned to months at DVI, I found brothers I could trust—plenty of them I knew from back home—and we acted like the young bucks pumped full of raging hormones that most of us were. One thing that was top of mind when we gathered at the pile was getting strong enough to be attractive to women if we ever got out and to protect the households and community we were returning to. The other was tearing the heads off our keepers. And when I say keepers, I mean guards, correctional officers, fascists, hogs, pigs. Choose your term. We preferred the last three. We even had a Hog's Club. To be inducted, you had to push at least three hundred pounds. Because that's what it would take to kill a pig, in theory at least. Our size and strength turned us into such formidable opponents that in the 1990s, the state banned weights at prison, along with rescinding plenty of other rights prisoners managed to win in the 1960s and 70s. These days, you might see prisoners lifting bags or buckets of water on the prison yard. But unless you're enslaved at a fire camp, you won't see iron.

Commitment to Kill

Other than plain survival, our main objective in blowing our bodies up was flipping the script and fighting our oppressors. Some of the brothers I worked out with were good company, simple as that. Others were becoming comrades in a deeper endeavor—contextualizing our collective confinement in revolutionary terms. There was a rising consciousness in California prisons regarding the conditions that had channeled so many Black brothers into cages. Men who became my greatest influences were locked up for acts of Black militance on the outside, and we fully considered them to be political prisoners. They helped radicalize a generation of us. Even those of us who didn't yet understand the underlying historical, sociological, or political context of prison's racial and economic disparities knew something was fucked up in a serious way. The previous September, just two weeks after George Jackson was gunned down at San Quentin, and one day after I lost my shit in Judge Wilson's courtroom, the Attica Prison Uprising went off in upstate New York. Of the twenty-two hundred prisoners, more than half participated, taking forty-two guards and other staff hostages. Just like our brothers in Attica, we didn't think of our DVI keepers as "guards" or "correctional officers." My experiences on the streets of my real estate–created ghetto had primed me in that direction when it came to any kind of "law enforcement." Thanks to some revolutionary schooling on the yard, it wasn't long before I identified every pig working for the prison system as the fundamental enemy of conscious people. I was in good company. Every awakening Black man and woman in America, along with a growing number of white revolutionary leftists, viewed them as a military force that was oppressing us. Their very purpose was to break us, divide us, defuse us, destroy us, and remind us that they held the power. We were fully committed to fighting back.

We knew we were on to something, because the more politicized we became, the more we were punished. You could be a Crip or a Blood who engaged in gang warfare that was violent as shit but *wasn't* political—and the system would let you walk around all day on the yard. But if you affiliated with the Black Panther Party or associated with anyone remotely connected to the Black Guerilla Family, we quickly learned, you'd get sent to the Hole every time you sneezed. The wiser we got to the injustice of it, the deeper our rage.

It was hard to riot in K Wing, each of us alone in our open-barred cells. But we did it anyway. One afternoon, we started rattling those bars, first a few of us, then an orchestra of shaking steel. When the guards came around, yelling for us to shut up, we spit on them. We wanted them to know they couldn't break us. We wanted to own them. We were determined not to be the only ones who were fearful. By banding together, we realized, we could cause *them* fear—even from the fucking Hole.

"Tear gas! Tear gas!" we hollered one day, shaking the bars until the rattle was deafening. Our goal was to show them we were unbreakable, so we made a demand: "We need some tear gas down here. What y'all motherfuckers doing? Give us the tear gas, you punk-ass bitches."

We wanted to show them their tools of destruction couldn't keep us down. In time, they answered our call, turning Big Bertha on us with force. That's when we yelled some more.

"Man, this ain't killin' me," one voice cried out. "It's just making me stronger."

"Can you give me ten pushups?" another voice joined in, as the poison mist settled on our clothes and on our skin.

"Hey, I can give you a hundred, dawg!" someone else yelled back.

48

We got down on the ground, dozens of us, counting out those pushups. Letting those motherfuckers trying to kill us know, you don't even have us. You can't touch us. We don't care if y'all never give us a book. We can tell Jesus stories and *make* this shit revolutionary.

LOSS OF HOPE doesn't do favors to a person's sense of humanity. I'd been guaranteed a legal appeal of my life sentence, and an attorney filed one on my behalf. But about eighteen months into my stay at DVI, I got the news: denied. That made my life sentence real. And survival mind took over, making those parts of me that were soft and joyful and playful far more difficult to access. It put real distance between me and my parents.

"Dorsey, be a good boy," my mother had pleaded with me on one visit after my appeal was denied. But it's impossible to be a good boy when you're in the middle of a war zone. In a man's prison, being good was equivalent to being a little girl. I'd never cussed around my moms, not on the real. But when she told me during that visit that a high school friend I'd grown up with had died, I shot back at her, "I don't give a fuck." I *can't* give a fuck would have been more accurate. Prison was forcing me to compromise myself in ways I never could have anticipated.

When I wasn't in K Wing, I bounced around between East Hall, West Hall, and the mainline—general population. It was on the mainline yard that I failed a litmus test of my own humanity. Lee was a little dude I liked to talk to and occasionally play chess with. He was a brother, kind of timid but easy to joke around with. A truly good-natured guy who, we'd learn, wasn't fit for prison. One day, I finished playing handball in the yard and was standing by myself when I saw Lee coming toward me. His eyes were panicked, and he had his hand cupped over the side of his head. When he got closer, I could see a chunk of his ear was gone. Lee wanted my help, needed my help. But I'd already been sent to the Hole once just for having Kool-Aid on my towel. So when he staggered over to me, the only thing I knew how to do to protect myself was to plead back, "Man, don't bleed on me, please don't bleed on me." I've thought about that a lot over the past five decades, with shame and regret.

The gaps in the story filled in a bit later: Lee had joined a prison gang. He probably needed the protection. He got an assignment and didn't live up to the directions he'd been given. So, two guys hunted him down on the yard and busted him in the head. The KKK didn't have to hang every Black person in the south, they just had to carry out a couple of very public lynchings. The attack on Lee sent that type of message. It reinforced the danger all around us. I never did see him again. But

the way I responded was a barometer of how far I'd fallen. It marked a line I wished I hadn't crossed, one I feared I would cross again. It would be a while before I could share those fears with anyone. That kind of talk was off limits to men in cages. But there were absolutely men at DVI who became my saviors in a different way, radical brothers who would set me on a lasting path. And by the time I sidestepped Lee and his bleeding ear, they were already blowing my intellectual world wide open.

Chapter 4

MAO'S LITTLE RED BOOK

I hadn't been at DVI but two days when a friendly voice called out, "Hey, Dorsey!" It was the best sound someone in my circumstance could hope to hear. After Vacaville I was feeling the loss of my big brother. I was lonely and scared. But here was someone who could make out who I was, and even sounded happy to see me. I was walking the hallway that led from J Wing to the chow hall, trying to keep my head down, and when I heard my name, I turned around to see Nate Harrington's smiling face.

Nate, my childhood friend. Nate, who got harassed by the pigs with me for picking up a sprinkler on the wrong side of the freeway. Nate, who ran away from home with me and chickened out with me damn quick when we got cold and hungry. Running into Nate was sure as shit a better welcome surprise than watching a brother get stabbed in the back. Still, my first response was confusion. Because even when Nate was young, I knew he was brilliant. Seeing him here, locked up, gave me cognitive dissonance. I recognized that *I* might have been an asshole. And when I later reflected on my life up until that point, there were many instances that could confirm that opinion of myself. Nate, though? I had fully expected him to be someplace else in life. Nate had promise. It wouldn't be long before I'd learn that a lot of the other brothers locked up with me did too.

Nate's presence at DVI added a piece to the puzzle my mind had been working since I arrived. As soon as our escorts marched us to J Wing, I noticed all the Black faces in the yard that separated East Hall from West Hall. I saw them in the chow line, and on the tier. "Damn," I mumbled to myself, "it's more Black men here than everybody that went to high school with me." More Black men than I'd seen in church. More brothers than I'd stood shoulder to shoulder with at a packed concert infused with the sweet smell of weed. Nate's presence seemed to provide the answer: we were *all* destined for prison.

Racism was not surprising to me, given my childhood. But the composition of DVI shocked me. It's how I imagined Jews might have felt in Auschwitz or Dachau. They may have occasionally seen a Gypsy, or a gay person, but they knew *they* were target number one. Because they were *all* there. It'd be like, "Fuck, you the doctor!" "And *you* was the baker!" DVI established one fact for me fast: prison had a color scheme, and it didn't match the larger society.

A couple of weeks later, the prisoners organized a baseball game on the yard by hometown. Oakland gathered in one spot, San Francisco in another. When East Menlo Park/East Palo Alto grouped up in our corner of the yard to represent, we looked around and recognized our whole Little League team was there, reunited—everyone but the one white kid. And that was the tip of the iceberg. I'd soon run into kids I'd seen in continuation school, guys I'd hung out with in the pool hall, and just about everybody else from my youth. There was William Charles, a solid brother and a decent burglar too. And Tommy Moore, who'd learned to sing and play the piano at the Nairobi Cultural Center in East Palo Alto and boogied right next to me on dance nights. Tommy had a political consciousness before he arrived. DVI was a mix like that. There were those of us whose opportunities and ambitions had been limited by racism and the poverty it engendered, so we'd turned to taking other people's shit and getting high. Then there were brothers already affiliated with the Black Panthers who'd broken the law in the service of their ideals or had straight-up been framed by the FBI. Black Panther Party members Arthur "Tha" League; Jalil Abdul Muntaqim, who I knew at DVI as Anthony Bottom; and Geronimo Ji-Jaga Pratt were all politicized before they came to prison, and when they hit the yard, they brought that with them. They seeded the global prisoner rights movement and cultivated us newcomers to fight for justice.

WHEN I ARRIVED at DVI, my political consciousness was still nine parts rage to one part reason, and there were plenty of others like me still flipping through the pages of girly magazines. When we'd get lonely, we'd turn to each other and ask, "Hey, you think I could write your sister?" Still, I could *feel* revolution in the air, even if I couldn't articulate it. Nate would help with that. Even as the system stole my physical freedom and trampled my humanity with its impossible choices, he and some other brothers gave me the key to intellectual freedom, and that was a lasting gift. They helped me understand structural racism so I could strategize ways to blow that shit up and put something better in place.

Nate never spoke from a place of ego, and he never dished out bullshit. A lot of guys you run into in the pen are more than happy to have pretend conversations. "Man, when I was out there, I was moving pounds of dope. I don't know how in the fuck I got caught. Some snitching-ass motherfucker told on me, you know?" *That's* a bullshit conversation. But Nate and I weren't going there. That day we first reunited, we sat down with our trays of cold mac 'n' cheese at one of the steel four-person tables bolted to the floor. Nate was even taller than I remembered, thin as a green bean with long limbs that each seemed to march to their own tune. He was keeping his big warm smile in check – that's what men in prison do – but I could sense love for me in his liquid brown eyes. We were as tight as if no time had passed.

"What happened to you, homeboy?" I asked him. "Where did you go?"

54

Nate's family hadn't been healthy. As dysfunctional as my own household felt sometimes, his was worse. So much so that the county had dumped him in the foster care system. The last time I seen Nate, I rode one of my stolen bikes fifteen miles down El Camino Real to visit him in a group home in the city of San Mateo—and fifteen long miles back. Sitting in the chow hall, Nate caught me up. He'd wound up in San Francisco and even attended the same high school as Alma for a while. Then dope came into the picture, just like it had for me. Nate got busted for selling smack and here we were, in the same grim space at the same fucking time, together again. Nate wasn't about regrets though. He was only nineteen years old, a year younger than me, but he was intellectually more grown, inquisitive, analytical, and generous with his mind. As we picked at our food, he changed the subject.

"Have you read Eldridge Cleaver's book, *Soul on Ice*?"

Nate consumed books like a chain smoker consumes cigarettes. He didn't have time for girly mags. He wouldn't just teach me *how* to read, he would teach me *what* to read. Thanks to Nate, big boobs got boring even for me. He would walk up to me in the yard and without so much as a "What's up?" start breaking down dialectical materialism for me. He'd read Karl Marx, and soon I would too. Nate also turned me on to Ralph Ellison, talking about the *Invisible Man* in such a way that I had to find out what was exciting him. The system had eyes though, and our revolutionary fervor landed both of us in trouble, for hanging around too close to the BGF and for raging at the pigs. There were weeks, even months, when I didn't see Nate because I was locked in K Wing. Back on the mainline, we'd seek each other out and pick up where we left off, sitting in the bleachers on the yard.

55

"Come on, man," Nate would coax, "read to me a bit."

My ghetto education had brought me into prison at a third-grade reading level, but Nate never judged me. He was a gentle teacher who helped me embrace knowledge without feeling shame about my lack of it. Nate could tell right away I was grasping stuff. It wasn't that I was just mimicking. I was having real opinions about the shit I was consuming. And he appreciated that. After giving me a book to read, he'd wait around like an expectant father for a couple of days, then jump at me with questions: What did I see in there? How did I arrive at my conclusions? Was I willing to pass the book on?

To be honest, the quest to deconstruct Western capitalism was not the only thing that motivated me to step up my literacy game. I wanted to be able to write my own love letters. And I wanted to read my own mail. I was trying to woo Faydell, hoping she and my baby daughter, Denise, would stay in my life—and my first solo attempts were horrible. "I love you. Do you love me?" Soon I was paying people in cigarettes to write those love letters for me. And *that* shit always has a chance of going bad.

I got good at stringing words into sweet poetry, though I'd wind up practicing my eloquence on someone other than Faydell, someone I never successfully romanced who as a result helped me redefine what friendship with a woman could be. She'd come along soon. For now, my forays into the written word helped me understand the roots of oppression. If the conditions of society had dictated my life's course, I reasoned, then I could become a warrior in the struggle to change them. It brought me self-empowerment. I'd had some exposure to the ideologies I was about to embrace, because while I was busy getting high, big-name brothers like Eldridge Cleaver and Huey P. Newton were blowing through my community. I'd heard both speak when they came to East Palo Alto looking to start a chapter of the Black Panther Party. By the time I went on trial in late August 1971, Huey was a hero to me, even if I didn't quite sweat the details of why. I remember crowding around a window at the Alameda County jail, craning our necks to get a glimpse of the apartment near Oakland's Lake Merritt where we'd heard that Huey stayed. The Black Panther Party was consolidating power in Oakland then. Six years later, Judge Lionel Wilson—that same judge whose courtroom I trashed—would win the Oakland mayor's seat in large part because of backing from the Black Panther Party. No joke. He'd serve three terms.

NOTHING GAVE ME a stronger appetite to learn how to read than being told certain books were prohibited. That made them sexier than all the *Hustlers*, *Playboys*, and girlie calendars in the pen. Censorship came in waves for people caged in California prisons. Before 1968, people sentenced to life were considered "civilly dead," which meant you had no civil rights at all. If you wrote shit down, you didn't own your own words, because legally you more or less didn't exist. As for reading material, the prison chose all of it. Prisoners couldn't even write confidential letters to lawyers and lawmakers. What became known as the Prisoner Bill of Rights changed a lot of that. In 1968, long before I knew where I was headed, it deemed prisoners undead, limited prison censorship, and expanded what people locked inside could read. Governor Ronald Reagan signed that, believe it or not. In 1975, right after my transfer to San Quentin, the law changed again under Governor Jerry Brown, giving us prisoners a list of new and specifically enumerated rights, including the right to own property, make a will, marry, and have conjugal visits with spouses. If prison brass wanted to withhold those rights, it was on them to cite specific security reasons. They threaded a lot of bullshit through that loophole.

We had some intellectual freedoms when I was at DVI. But with more of us behind bars getting hip to notions of revolution, Marxist or otherwise, plenty of reading material was on the contraband list, broadly interpreted as anything that might incite violence. *War of the Flea: The Classic Study of Guerrilla Warfare*, for example, was definitely on the unofficial syllabus. I had two educational tracks at DVI. I managed to get my high school equivalency degree, studying for the exam through clouds of tear gas. I also learned how to put a timer on a bomb. At the *very* top of our contraband list, though, the book that was like water to a man on a desert island, the one the goon squad guards and prison bureaucrats least wanted us to have, was George

Jackson's *Blood in My Eye*, the book he'd finished writing just a few days before San Quentin guards gunned him down. It was in equal or higher demand than *Soledad Brother*, Jackson's first book, which the *New York Times* had called "one of the most significant and important documents since the first black was pushed off the ship at Jamestown colony." It prompted a generation of white leftist radicals to take up our cause. If that's how large the brother's impact was on mainstream notions of prison oppression, imagine how important it was to us. Jackson was one highly relevant motherfucker.

One night when I was back in K Wing, I got my first chapter of *Blood in My Eye* by special delivery—folded up in legal paper attached to fishing line and banked through the open bars of my cell. Some brother I never did lay eyes on had copied Jackson's words in longhand in a blend of pencil and ink. (When I finally got free, I bought a used copy of *Blood in My Eye*, just to make sure the dude in that cell down the hall hadn't made shit up.) I stayed up for hours reading and rereading those pages, and by the looks of the smudged ink and graphite, a small army of us had done the same. This was how real men made love to each other in lockup, not through force or violence, but through the sharing of information and dreams about what we *could* be.

The next night, I leaned up against the cell bars like I was hawking rugs at a Turkish bazaar and made my pitch. "I've got chapter number one. Anybody got chapter number two?"

Eventually, it came to me, sailing across a floor that smelled like piss and shit and sweat and right into my cell—thanks to fishing line and prison ingenuity. Over the coming decades, I'd insist to anyone who would listen that you can't lock up millions of people without locking up genius. The person who taught me geometry may not have been able to read, but he

Mao's Little Red Book

had serious skills when it came to banking books off the wall to pass a note three cells down. He taught me the importance of a fucking triangle. By the time I got to San Quentin in late 1974, prisoners who could afford one were allowed to get their own televisions. I'd get a nice little mirror instead and rig it just right to catch Gladys Knight and the Pips on my neighbor's set.

THE BROTHERS IN DVI gravitated to a variety of ideologies, all of them responses in one form or another to intolerable oppression that stretched back to the slave master. I had a lot of respect for the Nation of Islam, but religion didn't float my boat. Revolution did. There were a lot of Black Panthers locked up at DVI, and the Black Guerilla Family and Black Liberation Army were growing. One afternoon, while smoking some weed on the mainline yard with three comrades, I committed to taking part in political readings and discussion groups. That yard contained a football field, basketball courts, a track, a weight lifting area, and more. It was huge. It was also surrounded by gun towers, and we knew the pigs were looking down on us, identifying us, trying to pin us down by affiliation. I never did join the BGF or any other group inside. I have never been one to limit my options in that way. Today, I'm an abolitionist by principle. My first answer will always be to let more people out of cages. But I don't let ideology get in the way of pragmatic measures to help human beings who are suffering. Purist abolitionists don't want any dollars flowing into the carceral system. That would mean no litigation to improve medical conditions or to end the torture of solitary confinement. At DVI, I was learning to think independently. So I engaged in political education with anyone whose ideas resonated. I also made alliances in order to survive.

I was fortunate to be at DVI during the height of radicalization. Small and large study groups convened at different times, and we used them as an opportunity to discuss readings and probe the philosophical questions of our circumstance. One day, I brought up something I'd been pondering while reading Eldridge Cleaver's *Soul on Ice*. Most of the brothers were enamored with the man. I thought he was all right. I also thought his book glorified rape. He'd written it before he joined the Black Panther Party and became its minister of information. In it he called raping white women a revolutionary act, one he'd practiced on Black women. The brother was even doing time for rape. I hadn't been exposed to any kind of feminist ideology at this point, but I wasn't OK with any of that. I stepped up and offered my analysis: Cleaver was a fucking rapist. Then I laid out my reasoning. I thought they'd kick me out of the club. But after we wrapped up, the group leader approached me.

"Dorsey," he said, "I think you ready to lead the next session."

BIG LESSONS CAME along at unexpected times. Even before I'd been at DVI a full year, I was noticing brothers getting out and cycling right back in as if they'd taken a leave to run a quick errand. William Charles Gibson was one of them. I'd known William Charles since childhood. So one afternoon, I pulled him aside on the mainline yard.

"Man, if you hate it so fucking much here," I asked him, "why you coming back?"

William Charles didn't have to think long before he gave me an honest answer. It was the heroin, he said. Plain as that. Heroin was addictive in a way that most of us, myself included, hadn't yet realized. People who'd been introduced to it on the streets of East Menlo Park and East Palo Alto in the late 1960s when the weed dried up were throwing away their lives. They'd earn their release, get out, and celebrate. Before they knew it, they were in addict mode. They'd get caught holding drugs or committing crimes to support their habit.

The truth is, I had started selling heroin inside DVI not long after I got there. I had a few contacts willing to bring it in, and I wanted the currency and power that came with dealing. Every now and then, I'd partake. After William Charles spoke that plain truth to me, I never used heroin again. And the more I thought about it, the more I recognized that I had to stop selling it too. I could see I was poisoning my own community—and so were other revolutionaries who were dealing heroin inside and outside of prison to raise money for the cause. That made for another intense discussion I brought to the yard: What is our responsibility to our own community? If we're going to deal smack, can we justify the destruction that's landing brothers in cages? What kind of a revolution are we gonna have if we poison everybody back home? I was processing what I was reading and calling myself and others out on our hypocrisy. That marked the beginning of my ideological practice. What William Charles told me about recidivism turned out to be more prescient than I realized. I wish he'd had a crystal ball, so he could have warned me to stay the fuck away from crack cocaine.

ON A TUESDAY in November of 1973, about nineteen months after I walked into DVI in waist chains, the war between caged and keeper ramped up exponentially. A CO named Jerry Sanders was filling in on the second-floor mainline tier on a shift he normally didn't work. He wound up stabbed to death with two prison-made knives. It's not like guards hadn't been killed before: In the four years before Sanders was shanked, a dozen others had died violent deaths in California prisons—along with one hundred inmates. But this time, prison officials pinned it on the BGF rather than some prisoner's personal gripe. Political violence. If there were witnesses, they weren't talking. Still, the prison zeroed in on two young brothers—one younger than I was—and the state charged them with murder. They happened to cell right next to and across from me on the mainline, and that fact was enough to fuck me up for a good while. The brothers maintained their innocence. They wound up being tried four times over the next seven years, at one point sentenced to death, before they were finally acquitted. The younger one was sent back to prison to serve out his indeterminate life sentence for killing another prisoner while he was locked up at the California Youth Authority. Indeterminate sentencing means you get hit with a range—one year to life, five years to life, or seven to life in my case. It leaves all the discretion to the parole board. The system can play you out, deny you for any and all reasons, load you with new offenses, real or contrived, without due process. It's what we called "the silent beef." That younger brother wouldn't taste freedom for multiple decades.

My proximity to those two men, their BGF involvement, the fact that we knew each other even a little, did me no favors. State prison officials ordered a massive lockdown across DVI, San Quentin, Folsom, and Soledad State Prisons. No recreation, no education. Those of us with *BGF associate* stamped on our files fared worse. It wasn't long before the prison started shipping young revolutionaries out without warning to more restrictive facilities. Among them was Paul Jones, or PJ, a towering, quiet man I knew as kind, giving, and sincere. He disappeared behind concrete and steel for more than half a century, but never lost his political convictions. While PJ and other politicized men were buried alive, back at DVI, the rest of us landed in a repurposed maximum-security "management control unit" the prison slapped together on the third tier after Sanders's killing to contain conscious people who fought back. There with me were other prisoners deemed superagitators, strikers, ultrarevolutionaries, or dissidents. Hard-core killers and even snitches who were no longer productive to staff joined us too. The violence was pronounced and understandable, given the composition of our little population. And the guards had taken up the habit of firing their weapons from the gun rails to break the shit up. Sometimes the prisoner they killed was the one who'd gotten attacked in the first place, not the one who started the fight. Meanwhile, our keepers wouldn't give us a mop, broom, or rag, so I used my dirty underwear to clean my cell walls and floor.

The vigilance was exhausting. But my mind was free, and with that new awareness came an indescribable high. Plenty of men decorated their cell walls with pictures of loved ones, girly calendars, and centerfolds. Mine were covered with images of Mao Tse Tong, Che Guevara, political philosopher Frantz Fanon, Marx, Lenin, Emma Goldman, and Malcolm X. Mao's *Little Red Book* was like the prison Bible for revolutionaries. I held on to my copy, but other books came and went, since we were only allowed twenty-five at a time. Reading had become my channel to hope, hope of a changeable world. Still, I wondered whether I would ever be allowed on the mainline of any prison again. If I wasn't, physical freedom would be unattainable. Then, on November 18, 1974, a year after Sanders's killing, I got a funky two-day notice to pack my shit. The California Department of Corrections and Rehabilitation (CDCR) policy, at least up until then, had been to keep young men at DVI until we were at least twenty-five years old before shipping us off to harder prisons. But because state officials maintained that Sanders's death had been a planned political assassination, the age policy went out the window. I was a few months shy of twenty-three, and I was headed to San Quentin State Prison.

In my first two years at DVI alone, there'd been 102 stabbings, seven of them fatal, and one fatal strangulation. And I'd been forced to come to terms with the fact that I'd rather let a friend bleed out than go to the Hole. We all knew San Quentin was worse. I had no idea how I was going to break the news to my mother. It was like telling her I was about to get gassed.

TWO DAYS LATER the Gray Goose pulled up at DVI, and six of us shuffled on for the short drive to San Quentin. We crested the Altamont Pass and cruised into the Bay Area, passing Oakland and crossing the Richmond-San Rafael Bridge before pulling up at a nineteenth-century fortress with a million-dollar Bay view. That looming menace was associated with a long history of pain and violence. In retrospect, I believe prison officials were setting us up, sending us in as human chum. Within a month, two who'd ridden that bus with us were dead. Little Arthur, a friend, got took immediately, stabbed in the chow hall.

At San Quentin, the cells were damp as fuck. They were smaller, lacked hot water, and all had open-faced bars. The yelling, guns firing, bars clanging, and gates slamming created a symphony of terror that could drive a person insane. At DVI, we'd been proudly unafraid of the guards. All of us prisoners hated them so deeply we found ourselves with a common enemy. That mentality didn't exist at San Quentin, but the racial divisions were even more pronounced.

I'd been under the impression San Quentin was the tip of the spear of California's struggle for prisoner rights, a West Coast Attica. In some ways it was. I'd eventually meet my allies and continue my political education there. But the unity and trust were absent. That came as a shock and a disappointment. I had left Nate, my closest friend, behind at DVI, and I wouldn't see him again for years. I felt unmoored and lonely. Then, on my fourth day, I was sitting in the chow hall with some brothers when I saw Mark, a white dude I knew from DVI who'd been a solid and reliable ally. When Nate organized a prisoner strike of the mainline movie night to demand entertainment that was more culturally in tune with what Black prisoners wanted, Mark was all in. All I had to do was explain the situation, and he promised to boycott until I gave him the word. Mark sat tight, despite pressure from other whites. And we won. The next movie on the calendar was *Superfly*. I knew Mark wasn't a racist. At DVI he and I had traded ideas, talked about current events, used each other's books to study, even played a little chess.

From the table where I was sitting, I called out his name. He didn't look my way. When he got up to get some more coffee, I followed him. I asked him to come share a smoke with us, and he shook his head without making eye contact.

"Man, why are you shining me on like this?" I asked.

Mark's eyes were on the move, scanning left to right, but he sighed and opened up. "The shit is different here," he said. "I'm sitting over there with a bunch of hypocrites, bigots, and racists, and you should steer clear of them. Because they will cross you."

Mark explained that it wasn't safe for us *not* to shine each other on. Besides, he didn't trust some of the brothers I was sitting with any more than he trusted his own crew. His head was still in the right place, he told me. But openly associating with each other at San Quentin wasn't gonna happen. I felt hurt, and that manifested as anger. But I knew Mark. Whatever had caused him to change up like that, I concluded, had to be a motherfucker. And it was. Gladiator School helped prepare me for San Quentin. But I would have to get a lot harder to survive it. Meanwhile, to come out the other side with my humanity intact, I had to learn to keep giving a fuck. When I didn't, I failed to consider or care about consequences, and that would mean death in a cage. Threading that needle was the challenge of a lifetime. There were, however, a few special people who made it possible. Two were women from the outside who kept me tethered to hope, dreams, love, family, and community.

Chapter 5

LIFELINES

B y the time the transport bus dumped me at San Quentin, I'd had a pen pal for four months. Her name was Kathy Labriola, and she was a nineteen-year-old anarchist, bisexual, polyamorous, radical feminist. She was also white. Kathy came from a struggling working-class home in New Jersey and became a young nurse at a county hospital that exchanged education for labor. Then she high-tailed it to Berkeley to live in a feminist commune. When I met her through the US mail, she was working nights at a nursing home and studying at UC Berkeley by day. She didn't have a lot of time on her hands, and she was juggling lovers too. But she was a committed antiwar activist and prison abolitionist, so when she saw a flyer on the student union bulletin board listing prisoners who needed allies, she wrote down my name. How it got on that list, I'll never know. But Kathy became a lifeline. For seven years of my confinement, she was my intellectual sparring partner, object of my annoying unrequited lust (I was at the mercy of raging hormones), and teacher on the nature of platonic love. That was new for me. Growing up I always said if girls weren't fucking me, we weren't as close as we should be. But Kathy's kindness, warmth, and brainpower were just what I needed at a time when the racial politics of prison were screaming in my ear that white people were evil. I had already started to distance myself from that line of thinking at DVI, finding solidarity with prisoners like Mark, speaking out about Eldridge Cleaver's rape habit. Something in me knew it didn't compute. When the Symbionese Liberation Army kidnapped Patty Hearst in February 1974, a bunch of us gathered around the radio to take in the news. Then a brother suggested her captors burn her with cigarettes. It was a flavor of Black rage that made me deeply uncomfortable. I was already beginning to recognize I wanted solidarity against the system, not revenge against individuals. Kathy's unwavering friendship helped me recognize that my gut instincts were righteous. The fact is, most brothers inside talked shit about all women—not just white women. It's as if they were silently screaming, "Let me stop feeling for something I can't have." If you really loved chocolate and were completely denied chocolate, pretty soon you'd be saying, "Fuck chocolate. I like vanilla."

Kathy was clear from the start that our relationship would never be romantic, but she expanded my notions of what a romantic partner could be. Meeting her was a lightning strike of revelation, even if the practice of becoming a decent man wasn't. Not long after we started writing to each other, I was falling all over myself to share the news of my transformation. "At first, I was only looking for a nice body and pretty face, but now I got to shop for someone with consciousness," I wrote to Kathy. "Someone to talk with me late into the night, someone who won't look at me strange when I ask her to put on some pants and come to a protest with me, someone to fight with me for the people, and someone who won't expect the world from me so I won't have to suffer when I see the disappointment in her eyes when I'm not able to give it to her. See, before meeting you, I too was one of those men that thought a woman's place was in the bedroom, but now I see that she is more beautiful when she stands beside a man instead of in back of him. Would you say that I'm learning about 'Women's liberation?'"

It was one of several hundred letters I'd send to Kathy over seven years, letters she was kind enough to save. She'd mail them to me four decades to the year after we started writing.

After I got to San Quentin, Kathy came to visit. She had to jump through all kinds of hoops to get on my visitors list. She had to take Bay Area Rapid Transit to the end of the line in Richmond, then hop a bus to the Greyhound station in San Rafael. The last leg of the journey came thanks to volunteers from the House at San Quentin, who fed family members lunch and gave those without cars rides to the prison gates. The fact that Kathy was willing to do all that was the biggest compliment I'd gotten in a long time. When the day came, I stared at the young hippie with long light brown hair and airy confidence sitting at that visitors' table in front of me and was struck dumb at my luck. Kathy was fine-boned and skinny enough to look frail, which made her inner strength seem all the more remarkable. I wanted her to come every week and told her that, but the woman knew how to set a boundary. For any man to oppress her, I once joked, would be a full-time job! She made it clear, twice a month was the most she could do, and there were times when her schedule kept her away much longer. Still, her commitment and regular flow of letters reminded me that someone wanted me to make it. She sent me packages of chocolate bars, cigarettes, and reading material—mostly books on political theory, though I did talk her into a copy of *Players* magazine, soft-core porn that exclusively featured Black women. Kathy was no prude. But as a feminist, she wasn't a fan of pornography. Still, she understood how hard it was to be locked away without access to sexual touch, or any loving touch at all.

At DVI we had radios, and at San Quentin there was TV. I soaked up all the news I could, and searched out every newspaper, from the mainstream ones to the ones prisoners started putting out, filled with plenty of liberation viewpoints. The radical papers fed my intellect; the mainstream ones let me know how fiercely we were hated. Kathy was down to talk about all of it: the plight of California's Central Valley farmworkers, inflation, South African apartheid, the Cuba embargo, and whether or not Huey P. Newton was a sellout. I relayed my views on the two-party system, political repression, poverty, police brutality, poor education, inadequate housing, lack of medical care, lack of nutritious goods, and the overabundance of addictive drugs that had been in existence in my community ever since those realtors carved out our ghetto boundaries. All my conversations with Nate and other brothers on the DVI yard had primed me for this dialogue, and my ideas were springing forth like popcorn at the movies.

I hadn't been at San Quentin but a month when I floated by Kathy my concept for replacing the carceral state in one of my letters: Since the vast majority of people in prison don't pose any real threat, why not send them back to their own communities? Tax money diverted from incarceration could go to building apartments for families, which would keep the families of prisoners from being broken up and destroyed. I was only twenty-three, and I was posing the same question to Kathy that I'd repeat decades later in city halls, the state legislature—even the White House: How can incarcerated people pay their alleged debt to society if we're kept away from that very society? Instead of working for three cents an hour in prison slave jobs, I told Kathy, we could be fixing up houses in the ghetto. Once a prisoner's sentence was done, if they chose to stay, the community would come together to find them an apartment and a job.

"This is just a wild suggestion," I wrote, "because prison has no valid reason for existing until they correct a lot of ills in this society that put people in a position where they have to take things from other people to survive."

Meanwhile, Kathy planted seeds in me that would become central to my life's work. Take voter disenfranchisement. Two months after I got to San Quentin, she asked me whether any prisoners I knew were voting. I hadn't given that any thought, and when I poked around, none of the other brothers had a clue what I was talking about. It took me two years to get back to the question. By then, I was becoming a better strategist when it came to making change inside San Quentin. What I really wanted, I decided, was to play a role in bringing about change *outside* the gates, where I'd eventually have to survive along with everyone else spat out by the system with two hundred dollars in gate money and a burden of trauma. I wanted a say in what that outside world looked like, so I sent away for a voter registration form. The San Mateo County clerk wrote me back soon after to set me straight: No. Not while I was in prison. Not until I got off parole. It pissed me off. "I haven't had a voice in the past and they still refuse to recognize that I'm capable of rational thinking," I told Kathy.

Probably the most important thing Kathy did for me, though,

is provide a space where I could be vulnerable, where I could practice warmth. "Share with me your thoughts so I might grow closer to you," she wrote to me, quoting a poem she'd read somewhere. "Reveal to me your hopes and dreams that we might travel together a ways. Tell me why you cry so I might comfort you, for loneliness has touched me too." I took her up on it. I had learned not to smile inside prison walls. It signaled weakness. But in the visiting room, as other men focused on sneaking a kiss with wives or girlfriends or beaming at their kids, I was able to smile wide at Kathy. I could even laugh. And with pen in hand in my cell at my darkest moments, I opened my heart fully. I even told Kathy how I cried the night I got to San Quentin, something I never would have admitted to another caged man. I'd walked through the yard scanning frantically for a familiar face without finding one. About the time I hit the unit and the cell door closed behind me, I leaned my forehead against the cold concrete wall and let the hot tears flow. Crying came as a release. So did confiding in Kathy that I'd done so. I truly believe this avenue for softness allowed me to walk out of prison as a man still capable of love.

There was one other person who shared that gift of warmth and safety with me during my time at San Quentin, and that was my god sister, Shirl Miles. I met Shirl when I was six years old, even before I got that purple bike for Christmas. She lived on Madera Street, right across from our first Belle Haven house. She was a couple years older than me, a gap that seemed to grow smaller as we grew older. But there was still a distance between us, because Shirl's family was much better off than mine. I think she actually got a 1965 Mustang in 1965! Shirl became my god sister when her moms took me to get baptized—for the second time. I guess she figured from the way I was acting that the first one didn't take. Though Shirl and I didn't hang out much, once I landed at San Quentin on a life sentence, she started coming to see me. Her younger brothers were both addicts by then, like all my brothers, and in retrospect I think Shirl came—and kept coming—because she believed she might make a difference for me where she hadn't been able to do it for them. And she did.

My older brothers each had a network of outside support when they were in prison, people who sent canteen money and came to visit, even wives who came to make love to them once the law allowed for that. I didn't—until a certain arranged marriage brought me that pleasure at the tail end of my sentence. As for my father and my moms, letters and visits from them were rare gold. With all their surviving sons sucked into the world of addiction and incarceration, they were focused on keeping the family together, letting whoever was "free" at any one time lean on them much too much. Shirl bridged my longing for home, family, and community. She was someone I could reminisce with and catch up on news of the neighborhood. She was also a reminder of the strength and human potential that existed beneath or despite the poverty and drugs that were crushing my community. She helped me see that I could be something other than what I'd been. After all, we'd more or less come out of the same shithole. She had to travel farther than Kathy, but being there for me never did seem to burden her. I shared a lot of my fears with her. Just like Kathy, Shirl was a lifeline for me.

Both of these powerful women helped me grasp that freedom is more than a physical state. It derives from being at peace with oneself. The love and consistency they showed me was infinitely more important than the tear gas, more lasting than the beatings, stronger than all the oppression the system was imposing. Without it, I doubt I would have emerged from more than a decade of persistent dehumanization with the core of my humanity intact. Beaten but unbroken.

THE SAN QUENTIN goon squad wore olive jumpsuits adorned with the American flag and, two months after I got there, they started carrying M14 machine guns. The paramilitary mother-fuckers would watch us from each tier like they were fitting to play a carnival arcade game, and they were quicker to shoot into a crowd than the pigs at DVI. San Quentin even had a fifty-caliber machine gun in its arsenal, and every month when they cleaned the barrel, we'd hear it blasting into the Bay. That sound raised the hair on my arms. As I suspected when I left DVI's management control unit for troublemakers, San Quentin brass delivered me straight to another secure housing setting—in South Block. It's where all new arrivals cooled their heels while our keepers decided where to place us. That meant no school, no job, no yard, no clubs, no movies. We did get out of our cells to eat, but not when stabbings and other racial violence triggered lockdowns. And those were constant. Even later, when I made it to the mainline, lockdowns still took a toll. Sometimes the whole fortress would be locked down for days, weeks, even months, and once again I'd find myself eating peanut butter sandwiches on my bunk and sucking down a tiny carton of picnic milk.

I never got a parole board hearing while I was at DVI. My first came four months into my stay at San Quentin max security, and it landed like a punch in the chest. Quick as a rabbit dashing for the brush, they handed down three more years. I wouldn't get to make another case for my freedom until 1978. "I don't know how I'm going to do this time," I wrote to Kathy, "but I do know that I've got to grow more indifferent, apathetic, and ruthless, because sensitivity and concern can kill you in here. I have a choice to make, either compromise my humanity or die, and I want to live. But what is life like when one can't be humane?"

I couldn't see much of a way to solve that dilemma, and within a week, the guys on my high-security tier could see I was changing for the worse and told me so. I brushed them off. But the next thing I knew, I was saying "fuck it" in ways that would come back to bite me. I found myself standing at the bars of my cell, arguing with a pig because he'd returned a letter I tried to send to Kathy along with two birthday cards I'd mailed to my brothers Ronald and Pat, each now in a different prison. Writing to other prisons, the guard told me, was against the rules. So I threw the letter and cards into the shitter and told that pig to kiss my ass and suck my dick. Sure enough, he wrote me up for language. Those disciplinary write-ups were exactly the weapon the system used to set us back with the parole board for eternity.

My years at San Quentin weren't linear when it came to my relationship to anger. I was able to contain it when I wasn't under threat, but I had no control over those circumstances. My keepers bounced me from tier to tier, cell to cell, leaving me confused and at their mercy. They'd give me props for good behavior and loosen my restrictions, then suddenly reclassify me as max security. During my first seven months, it just about guaranteed that I couldn't make close connections. Meanwhile, the label of "BGF associate" had shadowed me from DVI, so as violence ramped up in those early months, the goons took the opportunity to punish me along with other brothers they considered politicized. Their imposed torture: forcing us to visit in chains, behind plexiglass. Ankles locked in the convict shuffle and wrists shackled to the waist. No welcome hugs, no touching Kathy or Shirl's hands. The routine wasn't just inhumane, it also put prisoners in danger, because some of us were shackled and others weren't.

To make matters worse, the brass was making new rules for prisoners. We'd have to be clean shaven for a visit. We couldn't wear hats. There were all kinds of ways a pig in a mood could use these rules to make us late or blow our visits altogether. Soon, a prison memorandum laid the news on us that visitors would have to start scheduling appointments instead of just showing up. Once the slots filled, they'd be out of luck. It put a burden on poor families who relied on others for transportation and on working families with limited schedules. I knew it was wrong—and all of it became fodder for my activism down the line. The fact is, the prison system manipulated visiting, used it as a tool of coercion and punishment. At DVI, I would have never done a motherfucking thing any pig told me to do if it hadn't been for the promise of a family visit with my young daughter. That was the carrot that motivated me to "behave" for six long months. And it was worth it. More often, though, visiting was used as a stick, to deny any form of human touch that wasn't suspicious or violent. My longest stretch at San Quentin with no-contact visits was still ahead of me: one full year. One year of being touched only with hatred, disgust, or indifference. When I was finally allowed to walk into that visiting room unchained, with no plexiglass barrier, Kathy greeted me with a hug. Out of nowhere, my entire pelvic area started to shake. The only experience I'd had that even came close was when I was pushing weight at my maximum capability. I knew that I was experiencing sexual deprivation. I didn't need a telegram on that point. But this was more about foundational humanity than the urge to fuck. Kathy had touched me in a gesture of love, something I hadn't experienced for a year, and my body was absolutely confused. What about thirty years? I'd later wonder. What about twenty? I tried to hide my seismic convulsion from Kathy. I never did share the experience with her. I was too embarrassed.

AFTER I GOT that first dose of bad news from the parole board, I spent a few months in a funk. I even stopped reading. Television and depression can do that to a brother. Plus, the tensions of regular stabbings and occasional shootings were so high, it felt almost impossible to focus my mind elsewhere. But one day, I made a commitment to myself that helped free my spirit at least a little. I wasn't gonna brownnose to system rules to impress my keepers in hopes of a shorter sentence. It was unmooring me from my sense of self. "I get the feeling they are trying to train me like a dog, break me like a slave, domesticate me like a horse," I wrote to Kathy. "They want to fashion me in their degenerate-ass image and trade my reflection for a reflection of another man's. They might just as well castrate me and put my nuts in a jar."

77

They could kiss my natural dark ass and punish me, I decided, but I was done keeping my head down. To feel true to myself, I needed to take part in constructive struggle. I just wasn't quite sure how yet—especially since I was still locked down so tight. But in June 1975, I caught a break: I got moved to the mainline. After twenty months of harsh restrictions at two prisons, it was a relief—and deeply disturbing. I was used to being locked in my cell most of the time. On the mainline, it seemed like everyone was running around like chickens with their heads cut off, coming and going from every direction, even lounging on their beds watching TV with the cell door wide open. I'd seen too many people get hurt or killed, even by so-called friends, so these new freedoms gave me a bad case of the jumps. But the mainline brought me some semblance of a daily schedule. It meant a slave-wage job in the kitchen that had me up at 5:30 a.m. Men who were hungry practically begged me for extra food. I couldn't give it to them, and that was an uncomfortable position to be in. I'd hoped for a job in the printing shop, where I could learn to put together leaflets and newspapers, a marketable skill. But then, as now, Black prisoners seemed to get the worst jobs. The harshest labor. A later job in the prison's detergent factory left me with chemical burns on my hands. Still, being on the mainline meant I could watch a movie for the first time in nearly two years. And my increased freedom of movement allowed me to start a little weed business, small enough to fly under the radar of Al Haysbert, San Quentin's widely respected drug supplier.

78

Best of all, I started spending time with some wise brothers who had a lot to teach me. Arthur League, or Tha as we called him, had been tight with Nate and me at DVI, and as a Black Panther Party member locked up for his political actions, he was an important brother when it came to cultivating revolutionary thinking inside. I remember the first day I walked into the San Quentin educational building to go to a SATE meeting. SATE, or Self-Advancement Through Education, was an African culture club that doubled as a deep study group on Black history and the nature of our contemporary oppression. There was Tha, and next to him was Kalima Aswad. Decades later, Tha would wind up serving on my board of directors at Legal Services for Prisoners with Children. Kalima became my lifelong mentor. That meeting was my first encounter at San

Lifelines

Quentin with brothers who had a high intellectual engagement with the struggle. There was an electric energy in the room as they helped me trace a line directly from chattel slavery to nineteenth-century prisons in the American South that had turned from white to Black overnight, and then straight on through to the fortress we were now sitting in.

It felt good to have allies who shared common goals of liberation, and every now and then we had something to celebrate. A Friday morning in August of 1975 marked one of the sweetest of those occasions, as the news spread about Joann Little's acquittal. The sister had become a national civil rights cause, and a jury had just declared her life and freedom worth saving. Little was twenty years old when she broke out of the Beaufort County jail in North Carolina and disappeared into the night. Her white jailer, Clarence Alligood, was found stabbed to death the next morning with his pants around his ankles and semen on his leg. He'd been the only jailer on duty that night. She'd been the only prisoner in the women's section. When she turned herself in with Black civil rights leaders at her side, she filled in a key piece of the puzzle. What happened that night was exactly what it looked like: her jailer had tried to rape her. The evidence was as black and white as the two characters involved. But the sister was charged with first-degree murder and was staring down a mandatory death sentence under North Carolina law. Her defense, that she'd stabbed Alligood to protect herself from sexual assault, wasn't a winning argument in courtrooms back then, no matter what your race or class, and this was an incarcerated sister. Legal defense committees for Joann sprang up all over the country. Damn, even Rosa Parks started a chapter in Detroit! Most of the brothers inside San Quentin knew the case in detail. Many of us also knew the jury was half Black and

79

half white. When we found out they'd united to give Joann the justice she deserved, it was worthy of spontaneous celebration.

A few of us had heard the verdict on the radio and were out on the yard talking a mile a minute. Then more guys showed up. We greeted each new arrival with an excited, "Have you heard?" And since most hadn't, we got to keep getting high off the spirit of the moment, recounting the story of Joann and the people's victory again and again. There were about eight of us gathered when one brother slipped away and came back with a couple of gallons of wine in a plastic bag, stuffed inside a pillowcase to look as innocent as dirty laundry. We drank it slow, settling into a mellow joy none of us had felt in a long while. Another brother named Gilbert, who none of us had met before, joined too, and when we passed him some wine, he broke out the skinniest joint you ever wanted to see. It set everyone right. It seemed like even the hardest core among us had decided it was time for their annual smile. It was a golden moment, the first time I'd witnessed my new San Quentin comrades so jovial at one time. The party broke up when an officer came to tell us the work bell had sounded, and we were half an hour late to our job assignments. The good feels couldn't last. But our little party was a welcome reminder that we were more than just captives in a place of violence. We were humans, deserving of fellowship, and on this day, we felt safe enough in our common convictions to practice our humanity together.

Not long after, I made it onto a semi–honor unit. I even had a key to my interior cell door—the first key I ever had to any door I could call my own. The guards locked the outer door at night and during lockdowns, but otherwise I was able to protect my property while I was in the classroom, at one of my shit jobs, or working my side hustle. I was in a good headspace, or so I thought. Then one day, something happened that showed me just how thin that tether was to my own humanity. Some jive motherfucker broke into my cell and stole my TV, and I was prepared to wage war. "I hope that the goon squad find it, because if I run across it first, I will be visiting you through the plexiglass again," I wrote to Kathy, adding that me and twenty other brothers were looking for the thief. I was willing to fight and die for that blue Panasonic television, even start a riot in the process, because if the motherfucker didn't give it back, I decided he'd have to kill me to keep it.

As days turned to weeks my anger just kept building, threatening to derail me and everything I'd worked for. When I first started inquiring about my TV, I asked people if they'd *seen* it. Now I was flat-out asking them if they stole it. I couldn't seem to back up when I knew I was pressing someone or playing them too close. I was putting my own life in danger, and I didn't seem to care. I started punching my cell wall. It hurt. And worst of all, I became obsessed, not with getting my television back but with hurting or killing anyone I found holding it or selling off parts. I knew I was in danger. "Kathy, all of a sudden I find myself feeling anger like I have never experienced before," I confided. "I need help mentally, and I think you are the only one who can lift my spirits or break this mental lock."

This is what prison does to the human nervous system. That stupid key had given me an illusion of autonomy. I was led to believe I had some control—over my possessions, over my schooling, over my confinement, over my body. It was all a sham. We were locked under tons of concrete and steel without hope or dignity, at the mercy of violence from our keepers and one another. Why *not* kill? Sometimes, one small incident can unveil the truth of a situation, and the truth was we were fucked. How could I respond with anything but rage? My primitive brain was steering. And my rational brain was scared. Kathy tried her best to remind me of my better self. So did Shirl. But finding my way back was easier said than done. I held on to a kernel of anger about the TV. Twenty years later, someone told me who took it, and I almost did a detour to Bakersfield to pay him a visit. But by then I knew better. I could take a breath and control the beast, even laugh at myself. At San Quentin, I had no alternatives to anger in response to violation—until someone else from the outside came along and showed me another way.

Chapter 6

THE LEGAL AVENUE— A DIFFERENT WAY TO FIGHT

The skin searches were humiliating at first and became more humiliating. It didn't take us long to recognize that our keepers weren't really looking for contraband, they were trying to break our spirits. When I got to DVI, the pigs called us out of our cells one at a time to go through the motions: Lift. Squat. Cough. Spread. But sadism doesn't tend to hold steady, and soon they stepped up the degradation, lining us up together in a twisted choreography. We hid our pain behind stupid jokes. "What you think they looking for up that asshole, a TV?" We avoided eye contact, and whatever shame we felt we refused to admit. I got good at that game, or so I thought. But I was unprepared for what happened at San Quentin. It left no room for humor.

I'd been bounced around so much in that fortress, I felt like I could write the tour guide. I'd been in a max-security cell with no electrical outlet and a leaky shitter that left piss puddles on the floor. I'd been bumped to a cage in East Block so cold I had to wear socks on my hands. When I finally thought I was in a box I could call home, at least for a while, I spent three months decorating my wall. I wasn't a great artist, but I practiced through tracing, and it paid off. The day I finished I was damned proud. There she was in chalk and pencil, a naked woman twice my size with a dove on each shoulder. As if on cue, the goons showed up the next day and moved me again. No matter what I did or didn't do, I kept traveling deeper into the madness of the place. It was like quicksand: the more violently you struggle the faster you sink, and if you don't struggle, you sink anyway.

Despite all the moves, by mid-1976, I was still hanging on in the semi–honor unit. Even though my television was a goner, I woke up on a foggy Saturday morning in July feeling like a million bucks. I was scheduled to get the prison's very first visit of the day—on a weekend no less. It was reason for some small cheer. Of the three thousand motherfuckers of every race and shape locked up with me, I would be the first to pass through the sally port to the visiting room. And there would be Kathy Labriola, waiting on the other side. I was beaming like a pig in shit. But I was about to learn just how much harassment can come under the auspices of "security of the institution." I was a Black man, and my name was first on that visiting log—to see a white woman. I'm convinced that was at least *one* of the reasons why a particular guard by the name of Morrieira chose to mess with me.

Generally, if you're gonna be strip-searched around a visit, it's likely to happen when you're returning to your cell—in case your visitor shared something you chose to tuck away. This morning, Morrieira came at me as I was waiting to be cleared.

"B-39669," he barked, "routine body search." Then he jerked his head, motioning for me to stand up and strip down.

The Legal Avenue—A Different Way to Fight

Privacy is out when you're doing this dance, but the others in the room ignored us until I'd done the squat and spread. That's when Morrieira told me he saw something. Something white. He told me to pull it out. There was nothing up my ass, so I refused. He marched me over to the hospital for an X-ray. I let them take one. As we waited for the results, I decided I'd had enough. I had an important visitor waiting on me.

"See ya later," I told him. And I stood up to leave.

A sergeant blocked my exit. Then the two of them dragged me kicking and hollering to the emergency clinic, where a medical technician tried and failed to stick his hand inside me. The beating that followed seemed to last forever. There were three of them now, and every cell of self-preservation in me was screaming, *resist*. Later, I imagined that's how Joann Little might have felt. I could bench press more than three hundred pounds, and I fought like my life depended on it. But I couldn't keep it up. They got me onto a table face down. One held my legs. The other two each took an arm. Then the technician went in with a vengeance and no lubricant. Every muscle in my body was clenched, so the pain was searing. They found nothing. But it wasn't over. They dragged me to hospital security, where a doctor went through the whole routine again with a similar result. No stash. No contraband.

Back then we had to wear denim blue pants. That was the uniform on the mainline. Other than that, you got to wear your own clothes. I had put on a fine button-down shirt for my visit, red with wide lapels. It was ripped at the sleeve. My nose was bleeding. The sergeant shrugged. "You can go to your visit."

Kathy had been waiting for two and a half hours when I sat down across from her. It was obvious I'd been beaten. I was sweating and shaking, and before I knew it, the tears were rolling. Kathy took my hand. It was the only time she'd see me cry. She took a big breath. And she tried to work me through it.

"There doesn't have to be a penis involved for it to be a sexual assault," she said. "Going for your asshole like that, with everything that means in prison, is abusive. It's humiliating and demeaning. It *is* an assault. That's why this feels so terrible."

My whole body was trembling. I couldn't control that. But I was listening.

I FELL INTO a darkness. I vowed after I witnessed my first jail rape that I'd die before I got punked. I felt confused. Getting strapped face down to a table against my will so someone could shove their hand up my ass may not have been explicitly sexual. But it felt like a direct attack on my masculinity. And it was unquestionably a violent abuse of power. When I took issue on the DVI yard with Eldridge Cleaver's approach to ultramasculinity and ultrafemininity, I was working on instinct. It was clear to me that he was rationalizing rape. But I didn't know shit about the fundamentals. I didn't know rape was an act of dominance, a power trip. I didn't know it *wasn't* primarily sexual. Kathy and I had been discussing this topic even before my assault, because she was working with Bay Area Women Against Rape, or BAWAR, a new women's organization run out of Berkeley helping women who'd been raped. Now that I'd been violated by men who exercised near total control over my environment, my access to food and safety, and my freedom, men who were armed with machine guns, I was feeling the shit she'd taught me on a gut level. In the month after the assault, I kept picking up the pen to share my ongoing despair with Kathy, but I couldn't. Instead I took out a sheet of paper and addressed my plea for help to BAWAR. They never did respond.

The Legal Avenue—A Different Way to Fight

Depression was one way I handled my feelings. The other was the same blind rage that tripped me up when the jackass stole my television. Then some principled friends on the yard who knew and respected me told me I needed to chill. This time I kept my thoughts to myself, and they blew up. I wanted to use my bare hands to kill the guard who lied about what he saw during that skin search and forced me onto that bed face down. I wanted to see terror in his eyes. My murder fantasies were eating me alive. For another month, I held it in. Then, when I was sitting across from my moms on one of those rare gold visits, it came spilling out. She looked at me with a mixture of compassion and uncompromising ferocity. "Dorsey," she said softly, "what you need is an attorney."

My mother connected with Kathy, and thanks to the two of them, soon I had a visitor. Michael Satris was running the Prison Law Office out of a former hot dog stand right outside the San Quentin gates. He was a white dude with a full beard and bright eyes that were innocent, but full of knowledge and mischief too. Years later, he'd admit that he should have sued the prison system on my behalf. I'd tease him hard about that. "They stuck they whole elbow up my ass and you didn't get a dime out of the deal for me? I would have made more money being a ho." Michael was a fresh young attorney at the time, and instead of fishing for a payout, he negotiated for system-wide administrative change. The result was a new director's rule regarding the so-called "body cavity intrusion." From then on, instead of forcibly tying us to a bed face down and violating us after they beat us, they'd put prisoners on potty watch. Cuffed at the wrist, you could sit on the can all day or all week until you took a shit. The guards could wait. Not only was it less violent, it was more effective, because when there *was* contraband passing through a prisoner's system, it was often too far up for them to reach. Michael gave me tools to respond with logic, not just emotion, with long-term planning instead of short-term gratification. He helped me see that nobody else should be subject to the humiliation of being degraded the way I'd been. He introduced me to the notion of commitment to a greater cause, even though I was in pain. He allowed me to be driven by love and not just by anger.

THE DAY I met Michael, I thought the man was out of his mind. I was fixated on strangling a motherfucker, and this bright-eyed hippy was talking about law and policy. At first I was like, "Man, why don't you buy me a soft drink, some potato chips, and get through your speech," because I had shit to do. I was psyching myself up to commit an act of maximum violence for the first time in my life, but Michael just kept talking sense. It worked. In years to come, whenever shit *didn't* make sense, when my primal brain was leading me wrong, I turned to Michael.

I don't think he ever fully appreciated that he almost surely saved two lives back in 1976: mine and Morrieira's. He also gave me another lasting gift by opening my mind to an alternative to violence. For me, negotiating with my oppressors had always been out of the question. I saw it as capitulation. I was subjected to racism, orchestrated economic deprivation, and police violence before I even hit Gladiator School, where "kill or be killed" was a nonnegotiable formula. Fighting without uncontrolled rage or violence was not part of my repertoire. Michael showed me how effective it could be. Plus, I learned you didn't have to respect the motherfuckers you were negotiating with in order to sit down at the table.

The Legal Avenue—A Different Way to Fight

AS MICHAEL'S WISDOM sank in, Kalima, Geronimo, and Tha were teaching me equally useful lessons about building movement inside and outside the prison walls. Geronimo and Tha were Black Panther Party members before they got locked up, and as the feds framed one brother after the next, shredding the party through infiltration and deceit, Geronimo went underground to join the revolutionary Black Liberation Army. He'd get framed on a false murder charge and battle his conviction for twenty-seven years before winning his release. Kalima's story was closer to my own. His birth name was Robert Duren. He'd grown up dirt poor with no opportunity and no hope and started taking other people's shit, ultimately landing on San Quentin's death row for killings committed during some robberies. That's where he was when he had his awakening. Right after the shootout that left George Jackson, two other prisoners, and three guards dead on August 21, 1971, the state went batshit crazy looking to punish other human beings in cages for what went down. They targeted the San Quentin Six—Fleeta Drumgo, David Johnson, Hugo Pinell, Johnny Larry Spain, Willie "Sundiata" Tate, and Luis Talamantez. Death row was two tiers up from the Adjustment Center, and the ancient prison architecture meant Kalima could hear screams coming up through his toilet as the pigs beat these brothers and burned them with cigarettes. He tried getting word to a federal judge but got no traction. The man was in despair when he had a vision that called him to the struggle. He wound up on the mainline after California abolished the death penalty—at least temporarily—in 1972. And in 1975, the year I met him, he converted to Islam and changed his name to Kalima. Geronimo and Jalil had changed their names too. All three got deep into African history and joined a movement called the New Afrikans. It was an era when prisoners were evolving intellectually in all kinds of ways. Plenty took on new names only to leave them behind. That's what I did at DVI. For a while my prison name was Ajamu—until the pigs started looking for Ajamu. Then I became Dorsey again!

Kalima took a vow to fight for liberation and dignity. He started keeping detailed handwritten notes on prison conditions that made their way through the fortress. He understood that our slave masters kept us in the dark on purpose, isolating us in separate blocks to foster ignorance of our collective circumstance and keep us from rising up as one. After George Jackson's death, those tactics of isolation had escalated. It's why I felt so unmoored those first months in East Block. The system also tried to prevent us from unifying with our brothers and sisters in other prisons. I'd gotten a firsthand view of that MO in the fall of 1975, when I joined a correspondence network of prisoners around the country—or tried to. Our biggest goal was to reach women prisoners. We didn't know yet that crack cocaine would drive the incarceration rate for women, Black sisters in particular, through the stratosphere. But we already knew women's prisons lay in the shadow of men's. They hadn't had their Attica yet. They weren't on the radar of radical reformers. We hoped to harness radical female input through a grassroots letter writing campaign and draw attention to their plight. The plan was for each network member to write the head of any institution identified for questionable treatment of any other member in network—especially to women's prisons. I took on working conditions in North Carolina. But it was a short-lived campaign, because almost immediately, San Quentin leadership blocked our letters. Then I got fired from my job. Captain's orders. I took it in stride. It was a shit assignment, probably my worst—not physically as harsh as burning my hands on chemicals, but emotional torture. Prisons are full of sally ports, middle spaces with locking gates on both sides. Prisoners pass through one, then get searched before they pass through the next. I was the keeper of the middle space. Kind of like Cerberus, the three-headed dog in Greek mythology that guards the entrance to Hades, but with no power. I was just the brother who opened the gate from the chapel yard so guys could get to the visiting area or Receiving & Release. In that role, I had to watch guards search my fellow prisoners in denigrating ways all day, and I felt twice as uncomfortable when they made a bust. It was like watching the pigs throwing a raid on the house across the street from yours. It hit me hard to see some of the San Quentin Six come through, dragging pounds of chains, made to squat, cough, and that whole routine. They were my heroes.

Kalima was wise to the damage done by censorship and forced ignorance, and he came up with a solution. In 1977, he started a newsletter called *Voices from Within San Quentin*. It was mimeographed under the radar, and we devoured it like candy. His writings were reaching brothers in the Hole, East Wing, the Adjustment Center. They even made it into the wider world, with journalists who were allies of the movement reading some of his essays and articles on the airwaves of KPFA 94.1 FM. Meanwhile, I started working on other ways to achieve unity. Michael had brought about change for me and countless others through negotiation—coupled with the threat of litigation. I took note of that. But I was learning that we could only press for meaningful change on our own behalf if we were speaking in numbers. We'd never gain traction if too many of us were sheep waiting for slaughter. San Quentin had a Men's Advisory Council (MAC) in place, with an elected president and executive committee. You had to be on the mainline to run for those offices, but the MAC represented *all* prisoners, at least in theory. MAC leaders were tasked with taking complaints and grievances of the larger prisoner community to the warden, department heads, and guards. I started paying more attention to what the leadership was up to, and I didn't like what I saw. They were almost all white, and it seemed to me they were there out of self-interest. They were managing up, trying to put a gold star on their prison resumes and score themselves an easier path to release. The shit they pushed for didn't exactly rock the boat: Can we organize a dance? Can we host a Mother's Day brunch? I joined the MAC, watched, and learned, with Michael in one ear and my prison mentors in the other. And slowly, I became a leader.

Chapter 7

STEPPING UP MY GAME

As 1976 was wrapping up, I learned my custody status had been lowered to medium. I finally seemed to be shaking off the stamp of "BGF associate" that had followed me from DVI. I was in an honor section on the mainline—and I was obsessed with completing a B.A. degree by the time I got out. I was searching for a major that was conducive to social progress once I hit the streets, like communications. I took speech, psychology, archeology, history—just about anything other than chemistry, which our keepers found too instrumental to bomb making for their comfort. But San Quentin didn't exactly cater to student needs. At the ass end of things, I only wound up with enough credits for an A.A. or associate's degree, because prison schooling came with constant interruption. Every time I got caught with weed or cash from my side hustle, I'd get sent to the Hole or another high-security tier and have to skip class. School was also a no-go when we were on lockdown due to violence, and during my final years in prison, with overcrowding on the rise, those instances were too numerous to count.

In 1977, a frenzy of racial violence had me in my cell eating peanut butter or baloney sandwiches for four months straight. It started with the April stabbing of a BGF member by the Aryan Brotherhood. Over the next month, three white prisoners and one Black brother were stabbed. Cells had always been segregated by race, and among Latinos by geography, to prevent Northern and Southern gangs from mixing it up. Now, the system was trying something new—locking us down by racial group whenever racial violence went down. You could have a halo on your head, but if you were Black, you'd be denied basic privileges and robbed of your humanity every time some other brother was involved in violence, as perpetrator or victim. That practice would get challenged in court many times over the coming decades. When my section finally came off lockdown in July, the peace didn't last. Exactly one day later, I was on the upper yard, pulling the cool San Francisco Bay air into my lungs, when a swarm of neo-Nazis hit my buddy Charles Captain, filling him with stab wounds. He wasn't even BGF; he was a Black Muslim. A couple of other brothers and I carried Captain to the prison hospital without a gurney as he whimpered in my arms that he was dying. It's another one of those moments that never left me, because my response was so hard: "Man, quit sniveling."

Later that day, the Black Muslims retaliated. I watched them toss a white supremacist to his death off the tier, heard him land three floors down. It's not a sound I'll forget. Meanwhile, I learned, Captain bled to death. By the time I walked to freedom, he'd be one of three men I carried to that hospital only to learn they didn't make it. The violence and tension at San Quentin was doing me damage. But I had to shut down my

94

emotional responses to keep moving forward. I was doing well in school when I could get to class. I had a better slave job as the work furlough counselor's clerk, and right after we got off lockdown that bloody July, I got some seriously good news: Al Haysbert had paroled. That left a vacuum in the weed supply, and I slipped right in like a thief in the night.

DEALING WEED INSIDE prison was a felony, but I felt I had no choice. I got caught plenty of times, but for possession of weed and of cash, not for dealing. Those disciplinary actions nevertheless set me back. So why did I do it? First, personal access to sweet-smelling grass helped me survive some of the tensions of prison. Most important, if I was ever gonna have a prayer of surviving on the outside, I needed money. This was true for those of us who didn't come from wealth and just about everyone who wasn't white, because with a conviction history we were sure to face the most discrimination when it came to employment and housing on the outside. Prison was an economy of scarcity, which spelled opportunity. Right after I got to San Quentin, our keepers started rationing shit paper. Just about overnight shit paper pushers were selling rolls for a buck fifty each. That was a lot back then, especially considering the merchandise. I had no access to outside product at the beginning. So I started my hustle by making Pruno. Once I fermented a batch of that fine prison wine, I'd trade it for cigarettes. Then I'd take those cigarettes and trade 'em for cash, or enough weed to get me high. At five bucks for a Chapstick capful, it wasn't cheap. Next, I got a loan to bring a small amount of my own weed in to sell. I sure couldn't save money working prison "jobs." Even at thirty-two dollars a month for nearly forty hours a week of work, my highest wage, I made just enough for soap, snacks, and stamps from

95

the canteen. Al's departure gave me new hope for my nest egg, just as the prospect of another parole board hearing loomed large.

Al grew up just north of us Nunns, in a housing project at Coyote Point in the city of San Mateo. He was the same age as my older brother Ronald, and they came up together, kicking and scratching. They ended up in prison at Soledad, and that was the beginning of the merry-go-round for them both. Al was what you'd call a seasoned entrepreneur. He started dealing in stolen liquor when he was a kid, and by the time he was thirteen he was buying cars. Just like me, he did what he could to seize the same quality of life white folks had access to on the other side of the tracks. But he played a bigger game. To become a major dealer inside San Quentin, the man was nonpartisan and apolitical. He got along with Latinos, Aryans, Blacks, and everybody else who was a potential customer. He also managed to score himself a job as the captain's clerk. As a two-finger typist with big ears, he could hear the pulse of San Quentin from his desk chair, gaining insights into where and how to get product in. My own miserable job as a witness to degradation manning the sally port had similar advantages. I was as close as a brother could get to watching people make smuggling moves.

At seven years Al's junior, I was like a baby brother to him. He welcomed me as family, showed me love, and once I made it out of max, we spent part of just about every day together. We smoked weed on the lower yard, and always seemed to have a pleasant high. Back then, Al sported a healthy Afro and beard. "Big Dog" to us, he was six-foot-four and over two hundred pounds, with a slow, deliberate way of speaking that made every word out of his mouth sound like it was baked to perfection. We ran the track, talking like old friends, mostly steering clear

96

of revolutionary shit; it wasn't Al's thing. "I'll be so glad when you leave, man," I told him more than once while toking on his generous gifts, "'cause nobody can make no money with you here."

The timing of Al's parole didn't just match up with my mounting anxiety over getting out, it also paired nicely with my rising political awareness. Because if a man is looking to build a grassroots movement, it doesn't hurt to make friends. I never was able to deal as much volume as Al. I didn't have the contacts. But working the parts of the prison I could access in the second half of 1977 allowed me to chat up my customers and hear what was ailing them. They complained about jacked-up visiting rights and canceled parole board hearings, about weevils in their food, rats in their cell blocks, and power outages that blackened whole sections of the tier when too many guys fired up their homemade stingers to heat up the ice-cold water coming out of the tap. There was so much that needed changing, and I was a listening ear.

It was an interesting time. When I got sent away, the Black Panther Party was riding high, and the comrades inside who politicized me absolutely believed change was possible through struggle. As I stepped up my side hustle, I noticed the new arrivals were all complaints and no context. They only seemed to come together after shit had deteriorated past the point of return. Sure they felt the system's racism, but their response manifested as apolitical violence, not organizing. I learned a lesson right there: if you want people to exercise their rights, you have to give them political context, a reason to care, a reason to act. I had fought for the right of inmates to acquire personal TVs, and that right there might have been part of the problem. Now guys were lying around watching *Days of Our Lives* instead of enriching each other's minds with good conversation and book exchanges. But the outside political climate was changing too. Huey Newton had taken over the Black Panther Party and consolidated power in Oakland, marking the beginning of the end. Meanwhile, gangs were cohering in communities with nothing much to lose, police were turning into occupying forces in Black and brown neighborhoods, and California's prison population was on the rise.

The Uniform Determinate Sentencing Act of 1976 was also to blame. We'd all been cheering that change in the law. It put the question of sentence length in the hands of the state legislature, which seemed a lot fairer than letting some pig with a grade-school education screw you on paper when the spirit moved him. Senate Bill 42, as it was known, also recognized—implicitly if not explicitly—that racism baked into the system was leading to major disparities: it was Black and brown people who ended up serving the longest sentences, partly because whites had more access to doctors, lawyers, and bankers who could write letters to the parole board offering them a job and a place to go when they got out. But determinate sentencing wound up being a shining example of good intentions turned to shit, because state legislators and the rabid public turned out to be even more formidable enemies than the goon squad and the parole board. For starters, the law did not apply to murder sentences, like mine. We could live with that. Worse, the legislature started approving a whole lot of sentencing enhancements almost immediately that once again hit Black and brown people the hardest. A shit show of ballot measures followed, locking judges into imposing more and more time in cages. Over the next two "tough on crime" decades, the prison population in California would grow ninefold, like it was powered by rocket fuel.

Stepping Up My Game

BY CHRISTMAS OF 1977 I'd been elected to the executive committee of the MAC. That gave me the freedom to go to other prison blocks to take the pulse of prisoners, and into the industry area too. As a MAC executive committee member, I also had a seat at the table with the people I'd been calling hog, pig, and goon for years—guards, program administrators, and on occasion the warden himself. I learned to temper my language and sit back and assess their tactics. I came to conclude the MAC was little more than a pressure valve prison administrators could work to release a bit of tension when it was rising too high. They'd grant us small victories. When it came to larger, more substantial proposals, they would never outright deny us. Like hostage negotiators, they played like they were gonna capitulate, then appeased us by tossing us the equivalent of a couple of pizzas and some beer. That's how they allowed hope to linger. Because people who have no hope are hard if not impossible to govern. If they haven't got shit to lose, they might just blow themselves up to make a point. The MAC taught me a lot about negotiating. I learned better control of my emotions. If you're playing poker, you shouldn't produce a massive smile when you got two aces, and you shouldn't do the opposite.

The MAC was an imperfect vessel. But serving as a prison leader gave me purpose and lifelong direction. It helped me channel my anger into a strategic fight for constructive change. I found myself effectively helping people with basic stuff. I pushed prison leadership to expand access to computer classes and increase the number of packages we could receive each year from one to four. All that shit is negotiated, and it really didn't cost the state anything. I also scored moderate victories around visiting. I helped persuade them to build a larger, more modern visiting room that didn't look like it came out of a dated prison movie.

What Kind of Bird Can't Fly

My influence inside was growing. But being a man of the people and a brother who was trying to improve my own education turned out to pose complexities. The more "successful" I became at making my own voice heard with prison officials, the more I risked alienating the very people whose interests were at the heart of my purpose. Language played a part. I signed up for that speech class because I wanted to learn how to present a cogent argument and defend it. It wasn't easy. I'd learn when I got out how much work I still needed to do when speaking to potentially hostile audiences. I also took speech to learn how to code-switch, to say "we were" instead of "we was," to find a way to insert passion into my oratory without dropping a trail of f-bombs and MFs along the way. I was getting there, but my feelings about the whole endeavor were mixed. I didn't want to change to such a degree that I sounded like a freak or lost my ability to relate to people on a day-to-day level. What I was learning was slipping into my conversations on the yard. I had one foot in each world, not an easy act of acrobatics. I was seeing how easily the white man's educated speech could alienate me from brothers who didn't have that ability or hadn't taken the classes like I had.

One day I was working the lower yard, making myself available to homies who had issues. Gilbert, who'd joined our circle on the day of the Joann Little acquittal, had been framed up on his cellie's weed charge and landed in the Hole for what felt like an eternity. I was talking to a brother we called Seven about how to push for Gilbert's release. Seven was a boxer—a cool boxer who did his training in platform shoes. He was a dude who only had seven fingers, because someone shot the other three off. He was chill, and we'd spent plenty of mellow times with Gilbert toking on his too-skinny joints. On this day, I caught Seven looking at me funny. "Dorsey, man," he said, half teasing, "you startin' to sound like you think you better than us."

I didn't think that. But my own personal growth sometimes made itself known in conversation. It wasn't something I wanted to hide. Still, I heard what Seven said as a friendly warning, because I didn't want to become disconnected from the people I cared about most. With every passing year, I was more committed to the community where I grew up. I was intent on dedicating my freedom to changing the structural racism that had landed me in chains, barely able to read—the same forces that landed Nate Harrington, brilliant to his core, and every Black face from my Little League team in the same situation. If I lost the language, I feared, I would lose touch, not just with others but with myself. I found myself questioning whether higher education was a process of conditioning designed to strip a person of culture and integrate them into some whitewashed master-class notion of Americanism. On the other hand, I was feeling the benefits of education and digging it in a deep way. It had pushed me into new territory of abstract theory and logic that was inaccessible to me when I was thinking and acting from a place of pure emotion. I guess the best way to describe my state of mind is to say that I was examining my identity, questioning my value, working to define my priorities, and wondering how to bend language to my will without letting it overtake me. My conclusion: I would have to become a lot more motherfucking intentional when it came to code-switching.

WHATEVER I WAS doing for the MAC seemed to be resonating, even if my language sometimes sounded white. Because in January 1979, I was elected MAC president. It was a big endorsement from the prison rank and file. I had a suspicion the rest of the MAC leadership viewed me as too radical for the organization, a force to be controlled. But I wasn't about to let down all the men who voted for me by catering to bullshit institutional status quo. A couple of days after the election, I pulled the MAC vice president aside and made it clear I couldn't act in a way that was at odds with my core personality. It would be a slap in the face of our electorate. Ten minutes later, we came to a reasonable understanding of the roles we each would play for harmonious development of the organization. Mine was populist, truth teller, and shit stirrer.

One Saturday, after I'd been president for a while, I ran into Geronimo on the yard. I had a meeting scheduled with Warden George Sumner, so I asked him if there was anything in particular he wanted me to bring up. Geronimo was a husky brother, well built and powerful. A group of us was sitting in the bleachers on the lower yard. "Tell him to pay us minimum wage for our labor and demand his resignation," Geronimo answered without missing a beat. Then we all just kept on talking.

I did what Geronimo suggested—and that was my last meeting with Warden Sumner. But I never forgot where Geronimo was coming from, and what it felt like to work for nearly nothing. Paying captives pennies on the dollar, compelling prisoners to work or face denial of parole, amounts to slavery. And the state and federal constitutions explicitly allow it.

Being on the outs with Warden Sumner didn't interfere much with my rising power because I had other ways of making change. Since I was MAC president and had close ties to the Prison Law Office, I became an unofficial media spokesman on behalf of the prison population, showing up regularly in the *San Francisco Examiner*, the *San Francisco Chronicle*, the *Sacramento Bee*, and on the *AP* newswire. Meanwhile, I helped Michael Satris search for prisoners willing to sign on to class action lawsuits as named plaintiffs when his negotiations with prison officials fell flat. One of the most significant cases involved overcrowding that had led to double-celling—two men jammed into cells made for one. The brother I helped select as lead plaintiff was Don Wilson, a tall man with a deep baritone voice who was serving on the Men's Advisory Council with me.

With arrest and conviction rates on the rise, our keepers started pushing prisoners to pair up. In 1979, when word came down that it was gonna be mandatory, William Charles and I decided to volunteer to move in together, that same William Charles who told me back at DVI that it was heroin driving brothers like him to cycle right back into prison. We figured, better to be trapped in a cage with the devil you know. Still, it was hard going. Our cell was four and a half feet by eleven feet, so skinny only one of us could be standing at any one time. Our toilet had no lid, so we couldn't tamp down the fumes after dumping a load. I liked the radio, William Charles liked the TV, so we'd often have them going at the same time. My seniority gave me first crack at the shitter and dibs on the lower bunk, and William Charles didn't cause me any big problems. But I had other cellies after him, and the prospect for violence was built into the arrangement. Double-celling made you responsible for your roommate's business, whether you were in on it or not. If my cellie was bringing in drugs, bringing in knives, if I wasn't controlling that person on the top bunk, whatever was happening in that cell would become my beef too. Since I wasn't gonna do any snitching, dominating the cell became imperative to freedom.

That constant tension meant no downtime. No privacy. No place to process. It was driving some prisoners to mental health breakdowns. Once again, determinate sentencing was partly to blame. When the parole board held all the power, it was no doubt bad for a lot of brothers. But it also gave the state a useful tool. If tensions due to crowding were running too high, the board could quietly step up releases. By 1979, that option was off the table. Meanwhile, all those laws increasing mandatory sentences meant prisoners were staying longer. The class action lawsuit filed by the Prison Law Office argued that double-celling was cruel and unusual punishment. It was Michael's baby, and he teamed up with two bigshot law firms to file the case in June 1981. While they were at it, they brought up the weevils and cockroaches in the kitchen, rats and mice in our cells, and nineteenth-century ventilation that spread disease, boiled us in hot weather, and froze us in cold. The goal of the litigation was to shut the whole decrepit fortress down, and if that wasn't possible, significantly reduce the population.

Warden Sumner welcomed the media in to cry about the inhumanity of our cramped quarters. He put on a dog and pony show, but he sure as hell didn't want to set us free. He and the state's soon-to-be all-powerful union of correctional officers demanded more prisons. And they got their way. California state researchers would call what came next the largest prison building program in the history of the world. But even that building boom couldn't keep up with the thirst for locking us up. I thought we'd had problems in my day. I never could have conceived of what was to come: prison gymnasiums packed with triple bunks so close together prisoners could have held hands to sing "Kumbaya." It got so bad that three decades after I got out, a federal appeals court ordered the California prison

104

system to cut the population in *half,* calling overcrowding the main cause of a massive crisis in prisoner medical and mental health care. The US Supreme Court agreed. California was violating the Eighth Amendment rights of prisoners to be free of cruel and unusual punishment.

BY LATE 1979, the board finally gave me a parole date. You'd think I would have been doing a happy dance. But I was overwhelmed by anxiety. My father's health was in serious decline, and I wondered if I'd have to support my parents. I thought of becoming a youth counselor. I'd spent a few years at San Quentin working with a program called SQUIRES that brought in kids from juvenile hall to listen to the wisdom of elders like me who'd gone wrong. Then I remembered why I'd quit SQUIRES. A young brother asked how I expected him to go straight if nobody on the outside would consider giving him a job. He had a point. Youth counselor would pose the same philosophical dilemma. To be true to my ambitions, I needed to make change on a deeper level—to create a world where that young brother *could* get a job. But how would I do that if no one would give me a legal means of survival?

"Once I'm out, I feel as if I'll finally get the opportunity to see what I'm made of," I wrote to Kathy. "I want to see if I have the heart to hold fast in regards to my goals and direction."

At least I had a roadmap—drawn by my mentor. Kalima Aswad was full of ideas about brilliance behind bars, brilliance that could be transformed into a labor force for healthier and more just communities on the outside. When he was serving as executive secretary of SATE, he crafted a message to the Black community outside the gates on behalf of all us brothers inside. It was a powerful call for mutual aid. Imprisoning us and cutting us off from the neighborhoods where we'd grown up was a failed experiment. How were we supposed to make it when we'd been isolated in the racist cesspool of the prison system for so long, when our ties to home had frayed? "Black-to-Black" was a treatise that called on churches and other community organizations and community leaders to step up, visit us in prison, get to know us, and help us when we got out with housing and education so we could strengthen our own communities as free men, so we could be assets instead of liabilities. I never did see a copy until four decades later. We'd passed it along inside the walls in the African oral tradition, committing its core principles to memory. They informed my answer the day before I left San Quentin, when Kalima looked at me with his liquid brown eyes and asked, "What are you going to do with your newfound freedom?" I didn't answer with words. Instead, I lived it. I would become an asset to my community and not a liability, and fight for justice for every human being living in a cage or coming out of one.

I was leaving friends and mentors behind who would go on to serve years, even decades more while I worked from the outside to make their lives bearable, better, and ultimately, free. I never forgot them, and when they did finally get out, they hadn't forgotten me either.

Chapter 8

FATHERHOOD

On October 22, 1981, I left San Quentin. I'd dreamed of this day for nearly eleven years, even planned it. I wanted to go for a ride in a two-seat Corvette, eat me a Winchell donut, drink a Henry Weinhard beer, smoke some weed, and have sex with my shoes off. I had my measly two hundred dollars in gate money in my pocket and nearly a thousand dollars in proceeds from my side hustle stored where the sun don't shine.

But my plans didn't go as expected.

The first thing that surprised me was my tears. As I passed through those gates to hug Michael Satris on the other side and wait for my ride, I cried for all the times I stayed silent when people in my circle were planning acts of violence. For the hardness of my heart. For Lee, who I begged not to bleed on me on the DVI yard. For Captain, who I snapped at when he was dying. I cried for the humanity I'd lost, and the fear I carried about the journey to regain it.

Kathy had found me a studio apartment in East Oakland

with a key of my own, and no outer door controlled by keepers. She even had a phone hooked up. I could have called up some homies and gotten the party started. But I didn't end up chilling in the safety of that space or having wild sex in a cloud of weed smoke. Instead, I spent the next two days on a singular mission—to find my son.

MY CONCEPT OF fatherhood was underdeveloped when I got locked up. I was a kid when I had kids, and to me those babies were appendages of their moms, like an arm or a leg or a titty. If I was mad at the mom or giving her the cold shoulder, I'd ignore the arm or the titty too. It took me a while to view the kids as their own individual components, as real people, and then they became a part of me—"Shit, that's *my* leg!"

I complicated matters with my choice of girls. I picked two friends who, because of me, became enemies. I hurt Alma deeply when I took up with Faydell. But I loved them both, and my heart and head and hormones always seemed to be pointing me in different directions. About a year before I was charged with the crime that would earn me a life sentence, Faydell found herself another boyfriend, got pregnant, and gave birth to another girl. In my heart, I felt I was still in love with Alma anyway. As the police were closing in on me, poking around my circle of homies from the pool hall, I got in my mother's car and drove to San Francisco for what I thought would be my movie moment—beautiful, quiet Alma running into my arms, swearing her allegiance to me forever. Nope. When I got there, she was holding our son, Anthony. "Alma," I told her, almost breathless, "I really do love you."

Everything in her body language told me she'd had enough, that she thought I was an asshole, that she figured I was lying. She was right on the second count. But I wasn't lying. I just didn't have the words to persuade her, and I didn't have the time to win her back. Then, before I left, my immaturity landed me deeper in the doghouse. Anthony was three years old by then, but to me, he was the arm, the leg, or the titty, so I acted like he didn't have ears.

"Why the hell you got my son dressed in white tube socks? Those ain't cool," I said. "And why the hell didn't you name him Dorsey?"

It would be a long while before Alma and I saw eye to eye again. She came to visit just twice during my eleven years in prison—without our son. But she would absolutely return to my life. With Anthony, I didn't know we were having a baby until he entered this world. It was different with my daughter. I felt her kick through her mama's belly, even sang her dumb songs. When I got arrested, Faydell came to the county jail, bringing Denise and her other baby daughter, Shelby. And for the first bit of my time at DVI, our relationship was back on. It didn't last, and the brothers inside told me I'd been a fool to expect Faydell to stick around longer than it took my fingerprints to dry. She told me she couldn't wait for my freedom, not with two babies. I couldn't blame her. I'd come to accept this notion, and with that acceptance recognize that extreme loneliness would visit more often than people.

But Faydell made me commit to taking responsibility for my daughter. I will always be grateful to her for that. Denise became a powerful motivator. For six long months, I followed institutional rules at DVI to secure a family visit with her. My mother and father brought her, and feeling her warmth for a few days, hearing her laugh, it was powerful medicine.

When the relationship with Faydell ended, my mother helped negotiate my visitation rights. Faydell was on board. When I got to San Quentin, she kept on bringing Denise and Shelby to see me. Shelby's dad was in prison by then too—still is—and I treated her like my own. These visits meant the world to me, but I knew they had to be hard on Denise. Starting at the age of six, she had to watch her father walk from the sally port into the visiting room in chains. I tried to make a game of it. San Quentin was painted in some bright colors on the outside, and I played like it was Disneyland and Mickey Mouse and I were messing with each other. It was a hiding game, I told her, and he couldn't come out. It didn't make sense, and even as a little girl, Denise was probably thinking, *You lying dog.* It wasn't long before Denise called me out, breaking my heart and mending it all at once. "I know you're in prison," she schooled me in her strong little voice, "and you have to be good so you can get out, because I want you to walk me down the aisle at my wedding."

Denise was a forward thinker, a planner, because she had to be. She'd been diagnosed at a young age with sickle cell anemia, and she understood what that meant a whole lot better than I did. I didn't have the privilege of raising her, but thanks to Faydell, at least I got to watch her grow. In my cell, lying on my bunk, I'd imagine what it would be like to watch her playing in the schoolyard, unaware of my presence. I wanted so badly to be in her world, but instead I had to bring her into mine. The pay phones arrived in 1976, and those costly collect calls helped. We could talk just the two of us. She'd tell me about all the places she wanted me to take her when I got out, like the amusement park Great America. I was getting a taste of fatherhood, feeling deep love, and harboring regrets. I was doing my best to show Denise how much I cared. But the fact was, being a father to my son and daughter entailed a degree of responsibility my situation couldn't permit. It got me thinking about my own father. Despite, or maybe because of, the physical distance, the thick stone walls and steel bars between us, and all the things we'd left unsaid, I came to a new understanding of John Henry Nunn.

ANGER WAS MY response when my father pushed me to get involved with sports and then barely showed up for games. But prison put new lenses on my history glasses. I thought about how many people around me didn't have a father who was present when they were growing up. Plenty didn't know who their father was. The reason mine was so absent, I came to recognize, was because he was working to put food on the family table. He loved to party just like me and my brothers, and he knew his way around a pool hall. He likely would have enjoyed a life of getting high, playing games, and pretending to be a man, just like I had. But he didn't choose that life. He stayed. He was a complex man—a hardworking man who drank heavily in his off hours. Sometimes kind, sometimes violent. Doing his best to love his family and keep us above water.

When I managed to grab hold of his attention, he made me feel like a million bucks. I'd learned how to drive on stolen cars, and that came in handy when I was fourteen years old and my father put me behind the wheel of his Studebaker Lark on a trip to Los Angeles to meet my grandfather, a Shriner who lived clean and owned a couple of barbecue places. He was married to a woman who wasn't our grandmother, so being a true dad to our father, let alone a grandpa, was never on his agenda. That stung my father, and surfaced whenever he told us in anger that we should feel lucky he stayed with us at all. The Studebaker Lark had a skinny gear shift sticking out of the steering column, three on a tree. I felt like a big man driving

111

down Interstate 5 with my father passed out drunk in the backseat, snoring like a French bulldog. In my teenage mind, we were complicit in a grand adventure. When you're a kid who craves intimacy, you grasp at straws. A couple of years earlier, I had met my father's mistress by accident. I happened to be friends with her son, and when I went to his house one day, there was Daddy. We agreed to keep it between us. It felt like he was taking me into his confidence.

My warm feelings didn't last. When I was little, my father had taken a lot of anger out on my older sister Joyce, our "assistant mom," even burning her arm with a steam iron. With Joyce long grown and gone, he found other targets for his frustration. I'd seen him beat my little brother and slap our mother. I was frightened of him, and when I got larger and stronger, I felt compelled to act. One evening I laid in wait for him behind a bush near our driveway, and before he even got out of his car, I was on him, attacking. I was barely fifteen years old. It was the first physical fight we had, but not the last. It took the benefit of distance and age to recognize that violence wasn't foreign to our household, that the word *dysfunctional* applied to us. But none of these facts canceled out my father's constancy. He worked his ass off all his life, and I don't think he nearly got out of it what he could have if he'd been a selfish man. He was burdened by grief, with two dead sons, three already property of the state, and the sixth, my little brother David, heading that way. His two daughters were his only surviving children who escaped criminal records, and the youngest still wound up addicted to drugs and violent men.

My father had come to visit me not long after I arrived at DVI. Then nearly three years passed without a single letter. I was starting to wonder if he even remembered the date of my birth. Then, to my surprise, in 1974, he sent me forty bucks along with a short birthday note. I appreciated it. Here I was, imprisoned for a crime that took a life, surrounded by men convicted of similar actions, and with each passing year I became more convinced human beings are not the sum of their worst mistakes. I would repeat that truth all over the so-called free world once I got out. It was at the core of my convictions. If I was applying that principle to all of us in cages, didn't my father deserve the same consideration?

All this reckoning about John Henry Nunn also helped me contemplate my own responsibilities and desires as a father. In prison, I couldn't be a provider for Anthony and Denise, and that was the closest feeling to being emasculated I ever want to experience. It was familiar ground. I remembered my older brothers hiding from social workers because they couldn't pay child support—and as they got deeper into the system, they became even less able to pay. I'd seen plenty of men so frightened of the workers that they would deny the child was theirs. It was a line I wouldn't cross. And it was weighing on my subconscious when I walked free. I hadn't seen Anthony since the day I threw shade on his tiny tube socks. Sitting in my new studio apartment, he was suddenly all I could think about. Next thing I knew, I was on a bus to San Francisco. My singular two-day mission to find him was on.

I KNEW ALMA was living on Baker Street, and I remembered the address because the number matched my childhood house on Hollyburne. But Baker is a funky street. It dead ends and starts up again. When I got off the bus that first night of my freedom, all I did was walk, wearing holes in the cheap Naugahyde shoes I'd been given courtesy of the California prison system. I could feel the cold seeping up from the concrete into my bones, and

I shivered like a dog in a rainstorm—because the one thing the motherfuckers hadn't issued me was a coat. It took connecting with some homies from San Francisco on Day Two to set me straight. When I finally found the place, it was close to dinnertime. I hadn't told Alma I was coming. I hadn't known I was coming. But there I was, ringing the bell. They lived up on the third floor, and soon I heard the voice of a young teenage boy come out of the speaker, asking who it was. "Dorsey," I said.

When the voice answered, "Dorsey who?" my stomach dropped. I felt like I'd been disappeared from my kid's life like an old photo snipped with scissors.

"Dorsey Nunn," I answered. There was a pause that felt like a small forever. Then the footsteps came like thunder. Anthony running down the stairs. It forever changed my association with that sound. Anthony Nunn, my son, was running to *me*. He was thirteen years old, and his dad was home. That's when I knew Alma hadn't poisoned the water, hadn't turned my kin against me. Standing in the fading light, I promised myself I would do everything in my power to be a decent father to him—and to make sure he would never wind up in prison like I had.

I had ten dollars in my pocket. I pulled out the folded stack and gave the kid nine. It was the least I could do after so many years of nothing.

Chapter 9

WHAT KIND OF BIRD CAN'T FLY?

I walked into the pen as a young man who hadn't started shaving, doing time for a murder I hadn't anticipated. I emerged as a man who'd witnessed too many stabbings to count, who stayed silent when I *knew* deadly shit was about to go down. But even though I cried on my way out those gates for the man I had become, I had no idea that trauma could cast such a long shadow. In my first years on the outside, in between moments of joy and pleasure and during my attempts to make plain sense of a changed world, reminders would drop like boulders from the sky.

There was a joke going around back then: "What kind of bird can't fly?" The answer: "A jailbird." I could never smile at that.

Before my release I confided in Kathy and Shirl that I didn't think I could handle a group living situation. After watching my back for nearly every second of every day, I craved the safety of solitude, or so I thought. Kathy picked out the studio apartment from the classifieds. The price was right for a place without rats and roaches, and it was on East Oakland's Foothill Boulevard, a thoroughfare for bus lines headed across the Bay to San Francisco and south to Cal State Hayward, where I was planning to study. Kathy paid for the first few months. Shirl helped out too.

Plenty of brothers leave prison without a ride and no clue where they're headed, but thanks to Gilbert of the too-skinny joints, the day I got out of San Quentin his wife, Julia, pulled up in a station wagon to soften my transition. That mediocre car felt like a spaceship after eleven years in cages. When we stopped for gas, the price came as a shock. So did the bulletproof window where I slid my cash. Before I got locked up, gas station attendants would not only pump your gas, they'd hand you free dishware, S&H green stamps, or blue chip stamps just to thank you for your business. If you went to the bank and opened an account, the manager might offer you a toaster or some glassware for your kitchen. In my new neighborhood, I'd find out, even Kentucky Fried Chicken was passing the bucket of bird though a bulletproof spin window. It wouldn't take me long to realize I was living in a society that didn't trust. It felt similar to the vibe I'd get two decades later when I set foot in South Africa and wondered where those motherfuckers got that much barbed wire. My conclusion: American society in the early 1980s didn't care about the young, the old, or anyone in between.

Before Julia delivered me to my new digs and I set off to search for my son, we took a ride to my childhood home in East Menlo Park. I hadn't told my family I was out, and as soon as I walked in, I could see in their faces that they were making mental calculations that didn't involve love or welcome. They were wondering whether they would have to support another grown man when their resources were already challenged. My brothers had more or less taken over the house, letting friends come and go to get high. My father was in a wheelchair. He'd been cut loose from his warehouse job of more than nineteen years before losing both of his legs to diabetes. He and my moms seemed to be making themselves small as they tried to hold on to some of their dignity. None of this was about me, but it stung. Who doesn't want love and welcome? If I stayed, I told myself, I'd feel obligated to obey my parents' rules even though my brothers didn't. And that would be more restrictive than parole. I was too old, too changed.

In the coming weeks I'd learn that a lot of other things had changed too. The slide at the school playground looked smaller, the girls I'd known looked less attractive, and all the places in the marshland where we used to hunt and play had been paved over. Meanwhile, some of the shit that should have changed hadn't. My homies down on the peninsula seemed frozen in time, aging in place on a sad-ass hamster wheel.

On my second night of freedom, I caught a ride to East Palo Alto and headed for the pool hall on University Avenue. My old office. It smelled the same—like piss and beer and Clorox bleach. What shocked me was how many of my friends who *hadn't* lost years of freedom to cages had fared. I was brimming over, eager to share what I'd learned. I told them about Guinea Bissau, about Cuba. I explained that I'd arrived at a philosophical conclusion: I didn't necessarily see taking people's shit as wrong. If done under righteous circumstances, I called it by a different name: expropriation. The prison system had stoked a race war inside the walls that had bled out into the streets, I relayed, my voice urgent. It was crushing our communities. When I looked up, I saw blank stares. My intellectual development was alienating me from them just like my speech classes had when I was using Standard English with Seven on the yard. It was sinking in just how different I'd become from so many of the brothers I grew up with. The violence of prison may have leaked onto the streets, but the revolution sure hadn't.

My old homies talked as if the best part of their lives had happened in high school. The brother I knew who had a Cadillac when I went in was driving the same Cadillac when I got out. I would bet money the farthest he'd traveled was to San Francisco. Life in a thirty-mile radius. The invisible cage. It was sobering to realize I'd left prison with my dreams still intact, while many of my homies didn't seem to be dreaming at all. None could tell me where they were going. They could only tell me where they'd been. Then there were the drugs. A couple of weeks later, I took a ride with an old friend, a dealer named Charlie who'd risen in the ranks. He pointed out every addict he could spot, including members of my own family. I'd come out to a world that seemed smaller than the one I left. Heroin was everywhere. And Colombian cartels were flooding the state with cocaine that would soon be transformed into cheap and plentiful crack.

A couple of days after my visit to the pool hall, I walked into the unemployment office with a confident stride, as if I was wearing an invisible purple suit. I grabbed an application and filled it out, listing my terminated job as file clerk to the assistant warden at San Quentin. The prison system called it "work," not slavery or involuntary servitude. So even if I'd earned no more than thirty cents an hour, I considered myself eligible for unemployment. No one I knew who'd come out of prison had tried to apply, but I gave it a shot.

What Kind of Bird Can't Fly?

WORK WAS TOUGH to find, but the stress and rejection were tempered by the sweetness of friendship. One day I was kicking it at my place in Oakland with the stereo on when I heard the phone ring. It was Michael Satris, calling from the bar across the street, a mostly white joint I'd never set foot inside. He'd tried my buzzer, he told me, but either the Smokey Robinson was playing too strong or he hit the wrong button. My place was one of five apartments on the second floor above a run-down store that sold used furniture. The neighborhood was depressed, but right up the hill was Mills College, a private women's liberal arts institution covered in trees and the green grass of privilege. When I brought women home—and before Alma and I got serious again, I tried to make up for lost time— I mapped out a workaround. Instead of driving down Foothill Boulevard, I detoured north past Mills and slipped down to my place from the rear.

I counted Michael as a friend, and that shit was mutual. I'd hugged the man outside San Quentin's gates before stepping into that run-down station wagon that felt to me like a gold-plated limo. But we'd never kicked it on the outside. Now, on this Saturday in early December, one day after my thirtieth birthday, I could see him squinting into the winter sun on the other side of Foothill. I waved. He answered with a dorky salute. Then he jogged across the street and hugged me *again*. Prison trains that urge right out of a man, so that tells you how much I trusted Michael. It was his first visit to my apartment, and I was happy for the company. Kathy and Shirl had done me a solid by securing my privacy, but I wasn't used to sitting alone under my own lock and key, and it felt like solitary confinement more often than I cared to admit. My thoughts would get to spinning—about the job I hadn't found, the homeboys who were getting me too close to trouble for comfort, and all the close calls with my own motherfucking anger—those reminders of the residue of my trauma that fell like boulders from the sky.

My hair was styled in tight braids, and Michael looked me over and gave his nod of approval. I like them too, I told him, but I'd be taking them out soon as an ass kiss to potential bosses. As a Black man, finding any kind of job was hard. As a Black man with a felony record, it was nearly impossible. It would be decades before a campaign to change that would gain any kind of traction. I'd be at the heart of it. For now, these roadblocks weren't budging. My East Oakland studio was small, but class A luxury compared to a cage in an overcrowded medieval shithole. Michael waved his right arm around real slow like he was surveying a kingdom of riches. "Where'd you get all this stuff?" "All this stuff" was a pea-green couch, a coffee table, stereo, TV, desk, and a stool. A pretty good haul for a man six weeks out of the pen.

"Out of storage," I told him. Some unlucky dude hadn't kept up his payments and offered everything he'd stuffed into the unit to the first person to clear his debt. I took the deal, grabbed what would fit, and left the rest behind. A friend with a truck helped me haul it all upstairs, everything except the stereo. That came from my brother Ronald. It was a fine component set. Probably stolen. I didn't ask. I was old enough not to believe in Santa Claus. As for the bed, I pulled it down at night out of a gizmo in the wall that looked like a spinning closet. A James Bond trick—except more low rent. Now, though, with a visitor by my side, my private refuge felt mighty fine. Lived in, with a jar of weed on the coffee table and a couple of bottles of wine I hadn't made myself sitting on the shelf. Michael looked kind of amazed. "How'd you find this place?"

"I didn't," I told him. "Kathy did. I'm telling you, man, I've had help."

We sank into the plush couch, and I filled him in. I'd given my TV to a brother who needed one, just about an hour before I walked out of San Quentin. It was the last prison rule I broke. Michael had a big laugh that made you feel like his best friend, and one came busting out of him now. If anyone knew about my run of prison rule-breaking it was him. I hated the system when I was shackled by it, and I was becoming less of a fan with each passing day. My litany of complaints came pouring out. Every day I was out searching for work, walking, knocking, asking. And every day I got the same answer: No. No. And no. I reached for the weed and some rolling papers. "They got me going down and talking to parole once a month and peeing in a bottle every week, but all that stuff ain't gonna help me make it."

Michael didn't seem to mind that I was venting. He knew I had to. Several of my homeboys had already offered to set me up in business with a quarter pound of cocaine and a .357 Magnum, but I was holding my ground. I'd promised my father I'd die of pneumonia looking for work without a coat before I'd go back to the pen. The amount of hustle required to keep that promise was substantial. When I left San Quentin carrying that secret wad of ill-gotten gains, I thought I'd taken the risks for a reason. I imagined myself sitting pretty with those savings. In my first week of freedom, I even took a stroll near San Francisco's Marina to see if I could upgrade my living situation to one with a waterfront view. I hadn't accounted for inflation. Neither had the prison system, which set that gate money at two hundred dollars back in 1973. Half a century later we'd still be fighting for an increase. As you can imagine, that gate money disappeared fast. So did my ill-gotten gains, which I sprayed with Hai Karate aftershave before loading up my wallet.

Just a few weeks earlier, I told Michael, I was down to my last three dollars. I was making my rounds, begging for work, when I came across a man standing in front of a property piled high with junk. I offered to clean it for fifty bucks. He haggled me down to thirty-five. I attacked that motherfucking mess and the rats started running. Dirty work. But I was proud I found a job, even if it was just for a day. Michael pumped his fist in the air, a combo move that seemed to say "congratulations" and "fight the system" at the same time. He had ordered a Bloody Mary while waiting for a gal to get off the pay phone at the bar and had a midday buzz going. He was doing more listening than talking. That was his style. He cared about the circumstances that made surviving on parole so hard. He cared about me.

On the surface, the two of us were as different as tofu and chitlins. He was a Marin County hippie poet who surfed in the moonlight and had probably never cheated on a woman. He was white and hadn't grown up stealing other people's shit. But those differences fell away easy. By now I'd rolled two fat joints—not the skinny-ass kind I scraped together inside by the Chapstick capful. I handed him one and turned up the music. I'd just had a birthday, and Michael's visit alone was a reason to celebrate. It felt good, two friends relaxing and getting high on some damn good weed. For a few hours, inside those four walls, the stress melted off.

I was thrilled when California's Employment Development Department approved my claim for unemployment, as long as I didn't collect General Assistance at the same time. The eighty-seven dollars I would soon start receiving every two weeks covered my rent, with fourteen bucks a month left to spare. It helped. Still, the obligations of freedom were foreign to me. I didn't know how to pay a utility bill. Kathy was working night shifts as an intensive care unit nurse while sleeping days. I woke her up too often, calling to ask for help. Once, I almost got evicted when I missed a rent payment—not because I didn't have it, but because I'd never had to pay monthly rent. I made dates to meet Kathy for coffee and forgot to show up. One day, she made it clear she couldn't do it anymore. She couldn't afford to keep giving me so-called loans. More than that, responsibility for my success seemed too high a price for friendship.

"Dorsey," she told me one day, "I'm willing to be, like, one of five people who are supporting you now. I cannot be the *one*."

Kathy backed off for her own sanity. But she also did it for me. She wanted to give me space to grow my own pair of wings. To fall if I was gonna fall. And to get back up. We didn't talk for about a year. By then I had hooked back up with Alma, and I had a job. To this day, Kathy and I remain close. Not in an everyday kind of way, but our love and respect for one another has never diminished. We both see it the same way. There was a place and time when I needed her support the most, when despite all our differences we bonded like glue on glue. Her stepping back was just life running its natural course. The same goes for Shirl. As my god sister, she will always be family. She moved to Sacramento and our catchup calls became less frequent. But our love has lasted. When her grandson died not long ago, I was there at the funeral. Shirl kept bugging me later to read the program, and then I saw it: she had listed me as honorary pallbearer.

As Kathy and Shirl shifted their roles from primary to perennial support, almost like runners in a relay race, a few others stepped up to see me through the next leg of life.

OLD FRIENDSHIPS ARE like well-made furniture—they hold up across the reach of time. My bonds with Kathy, Shirl, and Michael each supported and sustained me through some of life's deepest trials. The same was true of my bond with Nate Harrington. Our love went deep, and like an angel of conscious analysis, he always seemed to turn up when I had questions that needed answering. All the lack of trust I'd encountered in my newfound freedom, the empty stares I got when I was hoping for revolutionary brotherhood, signaled that times had changed in ways deeper than I could fully comprehend. Nate would step up to enlighten me.

124 By the time I left San Quentin, Nate was on his way to becoming an attorney, studying at the New College of California School of Law in San Francisco's Mission District. It was a progressive school that sprang up while we were filling our minds with Mao and George Jackson at DVI. Its singular purpose was to churn out public interest lawyers to join the fight for justice, and Nate would rise to the occasion. The last time I'd seen him was the day I boarded the Gray Goose in shackles for my ride to San Quentin. But a couple of months after my release, we had an unplanned reunion. Our collective prison experience left fingerprints of violence and fear all over it.

I was living in the studio apartment on Foothill—at least officially. But by now my struggles for survival and Alma's own needs had thrown us together. I was back in her arms, on a fairly short leash, spending nights at her apartment in San Francisco's Western Addition while lying to my parole officer about it. Alma's sister had died while I was in prison, and so had her man, my old friend June Boy. So Alma was raising their three kids in addition to our son Anthony, and her son by another man, Mingo, who I'd come to view as my own. She needed help with all those children and protection from the abusive brother she'd been seeing. I was tearing phone books in half with my bare hands—a natural fit for the job. Meanwhile, I turned to Alma to meet some needs of my own. I was craving human touch—and partial to the sexual variety. Beyond that, Alma had her head on straight and was helping me navigate postrelease existence. The woman worked for a goddamned bank! Besides, we'd known each other since we were practically babies. We spoke the same language.

I was headed to Alma's on the day Nate and I reconnected. I'd taken the BART train to the city from Cal State Hayward, where I had enrolled as a criminal justice major, trying to finish that B.A. I hadn't quite got in prison. It was a cold day, and when I stepped out of the Embarcadero Station at the foot of Market Street, I could see my breath. I squeezed myself into the back door of the 21 Hayes bus, rubbing my hands together, and spotted tall, lanky Nate before he saw me. He was sitting in a row seat toward the back of the bus. I picked him out right away: that stylin' beard, that warm, open face, those round glasses that showcased eyes that were alert and curious even when the brother was exhausted. Seeing Nate sent a good vibe rushing through me, a feeling of home in a world where I felt more like a stranger than I had when I got locked up. When Nate caught my eye, I expected him to see me as a refuge. But his first stare indicated that the refuge was compromised as fuck. His body flexed. I could see his eyes darting to the back door, then the front, like he was calculating an escape. I called his name and made my way over, smiling. I could tell he was on high alert, and I gave him a look, eyes wide, like "What?!" Nate nodded toward the door. We got off together at the next stop so we could debrief without a crowd pressing in on us. We walked in silence in the dusk for a while, up the wide sidewalks of Market Street, past a patchwork of T-shirt shops and strip clubs. Then Nate spoke.

"I thought you were out to kill me, man."

Me. His homeboy. His childhood coconspirator. Nate, who had given me not just the gift of reading but the gift of reason, thought I was out to murder him. That's how unstable the ground underneath us had become. The movement for Black liberation that sprang up in prisons across the country during our time inside was in chaos. Splintering and fragmenting from internal strife. A lot of brothers had come out with plans to be shot callers, not soldiers. Too many. Bodies were dropping. I was committed to returning to the community an asset instead of a liability, but I had no idea what that would look like. I'd spent years of confinement literally assuming some radical brothers would take me straight to a forest clearing for weapons training so I could take up arms with them and fight for control of our own communities. It turned out changing times and utter disarray in the movement made that impossible.

Nate had been deeper into the politics of the Black Guerilla Family when he was inside than I was. That explained his fear. In the months before I paroled, I heard about a couple of BGF-connected killings on the outside. Nate filled in the blanks: The BGF was cleaning shop, beefing with known enemies along with former members who in their view had betrayed or dishonored the mission. White intellectuals had already started to flee the movement a few years earlier. A tipping point came on

What Kind of Bird Can't Fly?

Memorial Day in 1979, when a brother who'd just paroled alleg-edly walked into the Berkeley home of attorney Fay Stender and did something that would scare the shit out of white leftists for decades to come. Stender had represented many high-profile clients, including Huey P. Newton and, notably, George Jack-son. It was Stender who arranged for the publication of *Soledad Brother*, and she stood by Jackson for years. But they'd fallen out. Prosecutors said the brother who entered her house was out for revenge. That he tied her kids and her partner up inside the house and made Stender say out loud that she'd betrayed George Jackson and the whole movement. Then, they said, he shot her six times. She wound up paralyzed, in a lot of pain. She testified against the man a year later. Then, about eighteen months before I paroled from San Quentin, Fay Stender com-mitted suicide. By now, plenty of white radicals were cowering under their bedsheets, becoming less radical by the minute. The movement was fracturing from the inside in ways that made it difficult to tell who was friend and who was foe, who was cool and who wasn't.

It felt good to be out in the air, and as we walked, Nate filled me in on the chaos. I'd already witnessed some of it. On my first visit to the parole office in Oakland, a book fell off a desk and hit the ground with a crack. Before I knew what was happen-ing my parole agent hit the ground too, scrambling under his desk like a cockroach. So did the others. They were convinced Black militants had a contract out on all of them. Meanwhile, new organizations were popping up, feeding new conflict. Nate had gotten caught in the crossfire in 1977, a year after he got out, when he and Willie "Sundiata" Tate showed up at a San Francisco warehouse for a meeting of the Bay Area Food Sys-tem, part of a radical network of food cooperatives. We all knew

Willie as Sundi, and if you recall, he was one of the San Quentin Six who'd been acquitted the year before in that years-long legal witch hunt. Right after Nate and Sundi got to the warehouse, a Black former prisoner named Earl Satcher came out of nowhere and fired two shots into Sundi. Satcher was a rival who got out of Soledad and formed a new militant group called the Tribal Thumb, and they were making power plays.

Those two shots critically injured Sundi, but they didn't kill him. Satcher did die that day, and when police rolled up, they arrested Nate and two other comrades. Prosecutors later dropped the charges for lack of evidence, but when Nate passed the state bar exam, allowing him to practice law in California, those dismissed charges still held up his bar card due to questions of "moral turpitude." It was just one flavor of the bullshit that keeps formerly incarcerated people locked in an invisible prison for life. Allies helped Nate successfully fight that fight to practice law. But it took years.

As Nate and I walked and talked in the cold night air, his initial fear started making sense. The shit was off the hook, and it didn't bode well for our organizing. In fact, nobody in the movement had bothered to welcome me home. Suspicion, fear, and distrust had coated all of us like an oil slick. We were tainted by the traumas of life inside, and our notions of revolution proved out of sync with the realities of a world that had changed so fundamentally while we were in cages. Later I'd come to the conclusion that the whole notion that people in prison would or could be the vanguard of a movement was faulty, because it's impossible to see the landscape if you're up under a billion pounds of concrete and steel. It's like someone describing an elephant to you if you've never seen one. When you finally do, it looks absolutely different than what you imagined.

What Kind of Bird Can't Fly?

My conversation with Nate that evening helped me understand just one of the many reasons our movement got dialed down from a boil to a simmer. Others would soon make themselves known. We were entering the dark ages. And in that vacuum, the state would construct a prison industrial complex on steroids, with virtually no resistance. A mob mentality contributed, thanks to a new kind of legislating in California: the citizen-crafted ballot initiative. After voters passed Proposition 13 in 1978, a massive overhaul of California's property tax structure, making law at the ballot box caught on like wildfire. It was the backup any time elected lawmakers weren't prepared to go all in. Paul Gann was one of Prop 13's architects, and in 1981, while I was sweating my parole date and Nate was busy studying, Gann was working on an encore. The Citizens Committee to Stop Crime, which he chaired, got Proposition 8 onto the June 1982 ballot—and a majority of voters liked what they saw. The so-called "Victims' Bill of Rights" didn't just give victims and their families legal rights, it took away a bunch of ours, with sentencing enhancements, tougher bail practices, restrictions on plea bargaining, and more. It guaranteed more convictions and longer sentences. And direct democracy in the service of lock-'em-up fearmongering was just getting started.

Nate and I would join the tireless fight, each in our own way. But on this evening, as we headed west down Market Street, relieved to rekindle our brotherhood, we were still finding our land legs.

"You need to watch your back," he said quietly. Gentle, caring Nate. I couldn't even wrap my head around the thought of putting a bullet or a blade in him. I felt my tears forming.

"I wouldn't take you like that. I would never pick that up on you."

At least now I knew where he was coming from. We walked some more, to lighten the grief of our misunderstanding, and the conversation turned pragmatic. Nate had been out five years, so he could school me on managing parole. That address on Foothill Boulevard, he told me, I didn't actually have to live there, I just had to be there when the parole agent showed up. In those days, the man would generally call ahead, and if you couldn't get your ass back home in time, you just needed an excuse, like, "I was out jogging." I laughed so loud—part bellow, part cackle, part wheeze—that I turned a few heads down the block. I wasn't one to run if I wasn't being chased. Not long after, when a bunch of people came running past me outside Alma's place, I started running too. I could have sworn Godzilla had jumped up out of the bay and was chasing the public. It turned out to be the annual Bay to Breakers footrace.

I kept my apartment tidy as fuck, and Nate gave me some advice on that count too. Mess it up. Give the man something to do. Let him turn over the mattress, have a little fit, get in touch with his masculine side. I could feel myself grinning ear to ear. We traded phone numbers, and Nate flashed me that open smile that reminded me of home. Then I headed to Alma's, and Nate went home to study. That was Nate—singularly focused on his goal.

EVEN BEFORE NATE told me to watch my step, I was on edge. Prison had altered my body. When I busted out my first big-ass smile, in bed with a lover, my face hurt so bad I went to check it out in the bathroom mirror. Turns out, I was using muscles that had atrophied. For the rest of our fling, my lover called the way I held her at night "cuddling." I called it "making sure a motherfucker couldn't move when I was in bed with them." Every time she'd wiggle, I'd wake up, heart pounding. I trusted no one. My senses were heightened, and I seemed to flip into fight response at the speed of light. I guess my nervous system hadn't gotten the memo that I was no longer in the gladiator game.

I'd had plentiful fantasies about my first night at the club, and each involved a blowout good time. But with all those bodies moving in the dark, shadows lurching, my nerves were on fire. My former homies were deep into their drinks, celebrating my return, offering me any woman I wanted, even two, three, four, or five. They could make it happen. Instead, I spent the night with my back against the wall. A couple weeks later, some skateboarders flew past my apartment. When one blew a whistle, I hit the ground. To me that whistle meant gunfire on the yard. Ghosts kept pulling me back to the sounds, smells, and fears of the past eleven years: terror and the body's memory of terror. One night, when I was at Alma's place hanging with her and the kids, the power went out.

131

"Y'all stay right here," I said, assuming they were scared enough of the dark to do that. Then I headed to the downstairs hallway to search for the breaker box.

Alma's niece Anita was fourteen years old and already taller than I was. She was light on her feet, so I didn't hear her follow me. When I felt a tap on my shoulder, I spun around. The punch landed square on her face. An instant reflex, programmed in my physical body. Manufactured by those motherfuckers. That punch became a symbol for how much I lost, how elusive true freedom can be.

It scared the hell out of me. One flash of rage, I recognized, could flip my mental switch and throw me back to the primal choices of my life in cages. Kill or be killed. And just like that, I would be back behind bars.

What Kind of Bird Can't Fly

I'D GOTTEN A twenty-five-hundred-dollar student loan to study criminal justice at Cal State Hayward. It allowed me to purchase my first car, a run-down Pinto that spelled freedom a lot better than the bus did. Meanwhile, a counselor I met while I was in prison helped me line up financial aid, which I used for books and tuition. It also required me to work a campus job, and I took one with the landscaping crew.

On the day I'd come to view as a turning point, my shovel hit the dirt with a solid rhythm. The sun was blazing, and the earth and sweat were mixing on my chest and arms. I liked the physical workout of the job, and for a while I tried to put a good spin on it. But today, I was feeling like a lowly motherfucker on a chain gang, and it had more to do with my boss than with the nature of the work. The man was pushing the same buttons as one of my professors often did. Because he had credentials, a pat on the back from the world of privilege, he was making assumptions that he was smarter and more entitled than those of us doing his labor. There were older Black and Asian men on his crew who were infinitely wiser than he was in essential ways. They'd been gardening and landscaping for decades and could have told you which side of a tree the moss would grow on. But the boss man yelled at all of us. In his view, we were always messing up. He never thought to show me his blueprints so I could see for myself exactly what he wanted me to do—probably because he wrongly assumed I couldn't read them. On this blazing day, he came to check out our work and let us have it. The ditch wasn't where he wanted it. And when his raised voice reached my ears, just like that, it was on.

"You can get in the ditch your motherfucking self," I told him, so pissed off you could see the whites of my eyes clear around the iris.

What Kind of Bird Can't Fly?

I heard murmurs of approval and agreement from the rest of the crew. Then I threw the first punch. I put my muscle into it as if my life depended on it. And I just kept going. My higher brain went offline, and the primitive one was chanting, *survive. Survive.* My ears were full of cotton, my vision was tunneled. In time I heard muffled, far-off voices yelling for me to stop. When I finally walked away, I could see horror in their eyes.

I became *that* brother.

Nearly a decade would pass before I'd fully acknowledge what was driving my anger: deep, primal fear. Even today, I know I'm capable of tripping into mental spaces where it's hard for me to come back. So I preempt. I slow it all down, point myself toward resolution. It's a work in progress. A life's work. But at least today, I understand the extent of my injuries.

Chapter 10

BREATHING ROOM

Michael had steered me right when I was about to kill the guard who violated me. He showed me there was another way. And so, after I punched a punk on the 40 Foothill bus who was fitting to rob an old man, I called him to talk about my anger. As soon as that punch landed, I snapped back to reality and got off the bus. The sound of my closed fist on Anita's face I kept to myself. Hitting a child was lower than I imagined I would go. Pummeling a motherfucker who was doing people wrong was less of a stretch. But after I beat the shit out of my boss at Cal State Hayward, I was even more convinced that something in me needed fixing. So I dialed Michael again. I'd pissed away a job that was bringing me three dollars and sixty cents an hour, I told him, because I couldn't control my response to bullshit. Jobs weren't growing on trees for people like me. I was feeling fragile and scared, despite the spin I put on it about how the man deserved it. The line went quiet for a few long seconds.

"How about I put you to work here?" Michael said. "I'll pay you five."

When I managed a "thank you," my voice nearly cracked.

By hiring me on at the Prison Law Office, Michael gave me something more valuable than a steady paycheck. He brought me into an environment where people supported and nurtured me, a place where I could progress without being afraid of making mistakes, where I didn't have to hide my story. Michael gave me breathing room.

The downside of working at the Prison Law Office was the scenery. The repurposed hot dog stand was boarded up, and we were now working out of a rickety house on the same lot. It was the last residential house on the narrow street, meaning it was practically sitting on the San Quentin visitor parking lot. East Block loomed large. I was back in the orbit of my worst nightmare. But every day, Michael and the other attorneys reminded me of my own humanity. The house-turned-office was built in 1900, and like all the houses in that strange little community it had a great view of San Francisco Bay right out back. We used the lower level as a conference room. It had a dirt floor that we covered with a rug, and a renewable supply of cat shit from local strays that I got used to flinging out the door with a poop scooper. I hadn't been out a full year when I showed up, confused and distressed. I seemed to be pissed off all the time, I told Michael, and my hair-trigger reactions kept blindsiding me. Michael's wife, Bonnie, had just given birth to their first child, and they'd come straight from the hospital to the office. Michael was rocking his tiny daughter in his arms as we talked. He could see how agitated I was. So in the middle of our conversation, he did something remarkable: he handed me his newborn. I've added that to the list of lessons Michael taught me: it's hard to stay angry when you're holding a baby.

MICHAEL DID ME a favor by hiring me. He was also smart enough to know the Prison Law Office could use a formerly incarcerated brother like me with close ties on the inside. I had been a voice for justice on behalf of my fellow prisoners behind bars, and a source of weed too, which expanded my list of contacts. A lot of the men trusted me, and that served the PLO well. I had also left prison as a go-to for media on overcrowding and other conditions. So I wasn't too surprised when, not long after I started working for Michael, I got a call inviting me to appear on *The Merv Griffin Show*. National exposure. Of course I said yes. What came next would go down as a big mistake—and a valuable lesson.

Merv's people flew me to Los Angeles on a spring day in 1983. And suddenly, I was on stage. Not as a respected source on my own lived experience. More like a piece of red meat in a lion's cage. The panel was about that Victims' Bill of Rights voters had passed the year before, Proposition 8. And I was there as a punching bag, representing all evil in the world. I was facing off with a tender adversary, Marilyn Ettl, a grieving mother-turned-activist whose twenty-one-year-old son—a former high school football player—had been stabbed to death seven years earlier. Ettl had worked with George Nicholson, a former assistant attorney general and extreme right-wing tough-on-crimer, to persuade voters to pass the measure. It allowed families to attend parole hearings, which Marilyn Ettl had done the month before to successfully protest the release of her son's killer. Nicholson was on the panel too. They gutted me. I probably learned more with that ass kicking than I did in a semester of college. I felt humiliated, like I didn't handle myself right, like they were able to push my buttons and I wasn't in control. Not only that, I realized I'd done stuff that was irresponsible. I didn't assess who the audience was, I didn't know who all was coming, I didn't know they were setting me up. If I wanted to put my voice into the fight and win some hearts and minds, I needed to be more strategic. The next time I was invited to speak, I had my questions ready: Who else is gonna be on the panel? Who is gonna be in the audience? Future freedom fighters should keep that in mind. Do your homework.

The mood of the country was changing in ways I hadn't fully grasped. I had no animosity toward victims. I was fortunate no one in my close family had been murdered, but we'd been victims in plenty of other ways, as had my entire community. I'd seen men die horrific deaths behind prison walls, and I had personally been the victim of a brutal assault by a guard. I understood the scars of violence better with each passing day. But this false dichotomy that pitted victims with certain political views and class status against everyone who'd ever committed a crime—that shit caught me by surprise. How would denying the humanity of people in cages ease the pain of any victims? Punishing us more harshly wouldn't bring back a loved one, and it was becoming increasingly clear that it didn't lower the crime rate. Stripping us of dignity while we were serving time only drained us of hope, and that fed the flames of anger. Denying us the right to survive on the outside—no jobs, no housing, no voice—placed us in a purgatory where breaking the law often became the only remaining option. Many years would pass before we could nudge public sentiment in the direction of that logic, which brings me to a raw truth about ballot box legislating: You don't only need a majority of the public on your side, that public needs to be voting. For now, at least, we were losing on both counts.

I kept taking college classes for a while after Michael hired me. Thanks to my Merv Griffin ass kicking, I signed up for debate and public speaking. But I was already well aware that prison had offered me a truer education. I'd gone from a third-grade reading level through two years of college, leaving with an associate's degree. More important, I'd engaged in political, sociological, and philosophical conversations that were infinitely deeper and more stimulating than the ones I was having in the classroom. As a criminal justice major, I had found myself in the company of cops and prosecutors looking for upward mobility. I was there to dismantle the system altogether. Cal State Hayward didn't know what to do with me as a formerly incarcerated person, so right after I enrolled, they paired me up with another Black man who'd been in prison—on a dope charge in Japan. They gave me a pal. His parents were prominent San Francisco educators, and he taught me some early lessons about navigating the educational system. In the end, I quit before I'd earned enough credits for a bachelor's degree. I didn't finish. But I was finished. The Prison Law Office became my ticket back to the kind of learning I do best.

AT FIRST, I pulled weeds in the small yard and did other makework Michael found for me. But it wasn't long before I was plowing through stacks of prisoner mail, answering phone calls to record complaints, and interviewing men who were involved in our lawsuits. As a paralegal, I was fighting for an end to brutal prison conditions, conditions I had lived firsthand. In the four decades since, I have not had a job that wasn't about changing the circumstances that human beings experience in cages and coming out of cages.

In the fall of 1983, the Prison Law Office scored a major victory when we won that double-celling lawsuit. Marin County Superior Court Judge Beverly B. Savitt came to San Quentin twice to check out the forty-eight-square-foot living quarters for herself. Her final ruling: cruel and unusual punishment. Savitt also found that the heating, lighting, plumbing, ventilation, and sanitation were decrepit as shit. By then, most of San Quentin's three thousand prisoners had been on lockdown almost continuously since June of 1982, when a riot injured seven guards and sixty prisoners. She gave the state forty-five days to come up with a plan laying out fixes. A federal court order had already banned double-celling for longer than thirty days in max-security sections of certain prisons across California, San Quentin included. We were elated, celebrating big. It was the legal avenue at work. But a state appeals court later reversed Savitt's ruling. By then, the tough-on-crime free-for-all was on, and for lawmakers, prosecutors, and even judges, anything that could be viewed as leniency for monsters behind bars was political suicide.

Instead of compelling the state to shutter the fortress of torture that was San Quentin, lawmakers just shoveled more money into the prison industrial complex. That Determinate Sentencing Act that Jerry Brown signed into law explicitly stated that "punishment" was the purpose of incarceration. Still, it didn't *exclude* rehabilitation, and Brown was planning new prisons that would have expanded programming for people locked inside. Then, in November 1982, Republican George Deukmejian, the state's tough-on-crime attorney general, won the governor's race, and any surviving notions of helping people in cages prepare for productive life on the outside were crushed like a cockroach under a combat boot. Punishment in the form of "incapacitation" was the only goal left standing. The new Joint Legislative Committee on Prison Construction and Operations had just been set up, with the authority to bypass competitive bidding requirements. It was a free-for-all.

I BELIEVED IN the legal avenue. I still do. But I was starting to get a feel for the limitations of litigation as a sole means of change. The more I talked with prisoners in my role as a paralegal, the more I became aware of the difference between having a right and having access to a right. So many men at San Quentin didn't have a formal education. They may have had the *right* to go to the law library, do research, file their own legal petitions. But they didn't know how. That meant they couldn't *access* their right. Soon, Nate and I would have a run-in with the police that got me thinking about another hole in the cloth: people in power break the law all the time—and mostly get away with it.

We were walking down Market Street again, catching up at the end of Nate's day at law school, when an SFPD black-and-white rolled up on us. It was just like when we were kids on the wrong side of the freeway bridge, except the stakes were higher. Two officers got out, threw us up against a wall, and started to search us. Nate's mind was full of case law he'd been studying, and I'd been schooling myself too. So while these two cops felt us up and down, me and Nate were having a cogent conversation about our search rights, and we knew a lot more than the fools who were reaching in our pockets, squeezing our balls, and lobbing insults our way. I don't know if cops did it to everyone, but they had a habit of messing with the genitals of Black men. With our faces pressed against the brick, Nate

141

and I chattered away about Terry vs. Ohio, a case where the US Supreme Court had ruled that officers can search without probable cause, but only if they reasonably conclude a crime's about to be committed *and* they have reason to fear for their lives or the lives of others because the suspect might be armed. No and no, we pointed out to the cops. Even if they *could* have answered yes, the ruling made it clear they could only search our pockets if, during a pat down, they encountered an object that felt like a weapon. No again. "You're violating our shit," I told my date.

He twisted my arm a little tighter. "If you two don't shut up, we're taking you in."

They were pissed, possibly a little humiliated, and definitely tired of listening to us. They let us go. Nate would go on to become a lawyer who helped people in jail understand their own rights. But the experience that day disabused me of any notion of pursuing the law as my own profession. Alma lived in the heart of what was still a mostly Black neighborhood, and I was watching cops violate people's rights practically every day. Over the next four decades, I'd make good use of the law. At LSPC, we'd score key victories through litigation. But I'd achieve my proudest victories by grassroots organizing in the service of policy change. By movement building. Just as I'd done as a leader of the MAC, I stayed loyal to the least powerful among us. And little by little, I learned to change hearts and minds through oratory that came straight from the gut and straight from the heart.

The revolution that fed my mind and soul when I was inside, that prompted me to question the very basis, nature, and brutality of prisons, couldn't survive the chaos Nate had described to me, or the avalanche of dehumanizing laws that were lengthening sentences and draining the hope out of men and women

behind bars. I'd keep the struggle alive through the dark decades to come. For now, though, the breathing room Michael
had granted me was about to turn suffocating.

I HAD REACCUSTOMED myself to the smells of life on the outside. Perfume and flowers, barbecue, and gasoline. Smells I'd
craved for years but was already starting to take for granted.
Until I walked back through the gates of San Quentin. The
warden had refused to let me in as a representative of the
Prison Law Office while I was still on parole. Michael sued
the state on my behalf, based on my stellar record at the tail
end of my prison time, and we won at the district court level.
But a state appeals court reversed that, saying the access we
wanted, the same kind of confidential communication lawyers
got, was too risky. "As commonly known," one of the judges
wrote, "prison inmates with the best of such records often fail   143
on parole." I got a kick out of that. It was a clue that punishing
caged men at the expense of our humanity, traumatizing us to
the point where we came out and punched kids in the face on
instinct, was a failed experiment. But for now, logic was off
the table.

I didn't fail on parole, despite the judge's prediction. My low-
est moment came when a cop stopped and searched me while I
was driving with a fine-looking woman and her mother in the
car. But I cleared all my piss tests. And then, on October 24, 1984,
three years and two days after I walked out of San Quentin, the
state formally released its grip on my nuts. My business was no
longer any of theirs. Getting me into San Quentin as a paralegal
still took some mediation with the warden. But we got it done.
For the next four years, I spent half my week in the office and half
back inside the worst place on earth.

On my first visit, I emptied my pockets and cleared the metal detector, then walked along the yellow line to the red brick entryway. When I passed through the sally port, my muscle memory kicked in, and the sweat started beading on my forehead. I was coming to see a man who'd been stuck for months in an isolation cell. As I sat down in the segregated visiting room on the other side of a steel mesh screen, the stench flooded over me. Human waste and human sweat. Acid and fear. I'd lived immersed in it and learned to screen it out. But now, it hit me hard. *This* is what it must have smelled like to be on the bottom of the slave ship.

Lying in bed that night, I considered the constraints of our power. The legal cases the Prison Law Office fought involved constitutional violations that sometimes led to better conditions inside, but never did anything to bring human beings out of cages. Meanwhile, as I answered letters from prisoners, I was often writing, "No, we cannot assist." I cared about who I was saying no to. A new set of walls seemed to be closing in on me. To lighten my growing anxiety, I tried like hell to actively practice freedom when I wasn't on the clock.

After the beat-up Pinto stopped running, I bought a brand-new gold Turismo, a hatchback coupe with a muscle car vibe that played a part in my impending breakup with Alma. She cosigned for it, trusted her credit on me. She'd learn what a mistake that was when I defaulted on the loan. When I was late coming home or didn't come home at all, Alma would fly at me with accusations. She was convinced I was having an affair. And I was. With freedom gasoline, going any and every fucking place. She'd lived her wild years, had her club life, gone to all the concerts. I'd missed all that. So I drove. I spent days just bumping around. Sometimes I traveled at night. I drove down to Bakersfield late one Friday, just to be in Bakersfield. I didn't have a clue what Bakersfield looked like. I went because a brother in another cell who I knew in prison had talked about it. That's what we did in cages before there was TV, told each other stories about home. I drove to Los Angeles and cruised up and down the coast just to breathe the air and hear the waves. On my way to work at the Prison Law Office, I'd turn down random side streets just to check them out. Driving was control, a way of reclaiming lost geography. But my restlessness drove a wedge between me and Alma, and by 1987, we had called it quits.

The new bachelor pad I found for myself was in San Rafael, where the Prison Law Office was now located. I was hanging out with a wealthy hard-partying Marin County crowd, and at the center of it was a new white girlfriend with a rich daddy. In prison, my social analysis had been all about race. That made sense, because most everyone had come from poor back- grounds, especially the brothers. This new crowd planted the seeds for my class analysis. I was shocked when I first found out my girlfriend was feeding her dog the same kind of discount ground beef my moms used to cook for us kids. I was tasting the easy life. She gave me access to fine things: her father's min-imansion, designer jeans for my daughter, keys to the Mercedes Benz—and money for the drugs I knew where to find. At first I held back on the hard stuff. Just a little taste here and there. Until, one day, my past came crashing into my present, and all I wanted was relief.

THAT MORNING, I arrived at San Quentin's East Block to meet with a couple of men on Death Row. By happenstance, all the guards in the visiting room were women. Same with the visi-tors. It made for a visual dividing line between the free and the unfree. And suddenly it dawned on me: every man in the room was getting ready to die—except for me. As the first formerly incarcerated person to work for the Prison Law Office, my relationship to the law and to these prison visits that made up half my work week was singular. The other advocates could go home at night and shut that shit off. I couldn't. I personally knew a lot of men I was helping from my days locked inside. I had never spent time probing what they had or hadn't done to get there. To me, they'd never been monsters, and they still weren't. They were old neighbors. On this day, one brother leaned in across the table and asked me a question that sent my heart into my throat.

"You think they're gonna start killing us again?"

I could see from the way he looked at me how desperately he wanted me to say no. It had been six years since California voters brought the death penalty back. But Governor Jerry Brown had thrown a clog in the pipe by naming Rose Bird as chief justice of the state supreme court. She'd been blocking executions ever since, knocking them down one at a time. But the voting public was in no mood to play nice with human beings in prison anymore. In November 1986, nearly a year before my visit, voters had recalled Bird, leaving Governor Deukmejian to replace her as head of the high court with his own tough-on-crime guy. I didn't just *think* the state was gonna start executing death row prisoners again. I knew it.

I looked that man in the eyes for a long while across the visiting table, and as I did, I saw my own reflection. "Probably they will," I said, honest but hedging. Whatever was coming, I wanted him to know I'd be standing with him.

Five years later, in April 1992, Robert Alton Harris became the first man killed by the state of California in a quarter of a century. I was there, outside the San Quentin prison gates, help-

146

ing to emcee the protest. I was there as the clock ticked down to midnight, as the condemned man got a stay, and then a second and third and fourth. I was there when the cyanide dropped into the vat of acid under his chair. By the time the warden declared inmate B-66883 dead, the sun had come up. It was a long fucking night. Harris was a white dude who'd killed two teenage boys and used their car to rob a bank. I wasn't a personal fan. But death sentences fall hardest on Black and brown men. Since then, I've stood outside the San Quentin gates to protest every execution but two, one when I was out of town, the other when I was too sick to make it.

Telling a man who could have been me that he was almost surely going to be murdered by the state turned out to be my tipping point. I left East Block that day with a sense of dread. As I retraced my steps through the sally port and out into the open air of what was supposed to be my freedom, I was sure of one thing only: this work wasn't healthy for me. My apartment had turned into a party scene, with all kinds of people hanging out on a regular basis, getting high and doing every other thing. I was paying the rent and all the bills, I told myself, why not join the party? It was a "fuck it" moment, one that marked the end of my recreational drug use and the beginning of my addiction to crack cocaine. Getting high helps numb the moral implications of our actions, inactions, and reactions. I'd learned that young. It's a temporary fix. But after that visit to East Block, I was in need of some serious numbing.

LIFE DIDN'T FALL apart all at once. As the prison rights movement sank into silence, I sank too. And then, suddenly, I was in deep. Addiction constricted my geography, curtailed the distance of my drives. It made me strategic. I could make it from

East Palo Alto to just north of Santa Rosa before I needed to get high again. And I knew just where to stop, at the tiny house of a brother turned fellow addict I knew from prison days. Soon addiction would become as confining and impeding as the cages of San Quentin. In the long arc of my life, it marked a short chapter. But it was a formative one.

I had enough respect for the Prison Law Office to quit my job—a heartbeat before I was surely gonna be fired. Michael had left in 1984 to start a private practice, so he could have more direct impact on individual lives and actually get some people out of prison. He was doing criminal defense work and appeals. I'd stayed on when Don Spector was promoted to executive director. And we had a good run. But as my addiction took hold, I stopped showing up reliably—always with an addict's excuse, about the asshole who double-parked and hemmed my car in, the traffic jam that undermined my best intentions, the sick family member, and so on. Many of the PLO attorneys had become good friends. Lasting friends. Some had a strong hunch about what was going on. But Margaret Littlefield wasn't one of them. As an attorney, she was fighting for justice inside prisons like the rest of us, but she'd never had to contend with a full-blown lying-ass addict in her inner circle. By mid-1989, I had walked away from my apartment with a bag of clothes and nothing more. Margaret let me move in with her and her teenage daughter while I figured out what came next. Her family wasn't rich-rich like my now ex-girlfriend's, but they had deep Marin County roots and the good fortune to own a fairytale cottage in upscale Belvedere, on the Tiburon peninsula. It had a short white picket fence, a mess of roses out front, and a lagoon out back where I floated on an inflatable raft day after day, drinking beer. I wasn't doing shit to help around the house, and after I brought some stranger inside late at night, Margaret asked me to leave. I was tired anyway. Speaking a language of educated whites required constant self-censorship. Besides, you can cross a line in an addiction where you stop giving a fuck if people know or not. I was standing on that line, leaning over it. I knew I was about to cross it. But I wasn't about to let Margaret and her kin, or Michael, or any of my other Prison Law Office family witness that. They'd been too good to me. They loved me. Plus, I didn't want to kill my credibility. So I went back to my ghetto. Looking back, there's one small thing I'm proud of from that time: I never did steal from Margaret and them. It wasn't like I didn't get to stealing. I just didn't steal from them.

Chapter 11

CLASS ANALYSIS

W hen I showed up on the streets of my childhood, mother-fuckers had no problem calling me out for what I was: "Man, you a crack addict!" And not only that, but "Shit, I'm not sharing with you the way these other people have been sharing with y'all. I know where you coming from, dawg." Hanging out with white addicts from Marin County and Black addicts in East Palo Alto, I quickly realized, was day and night. Even the things they considered when they were doing harm to themselves and to their families were different. Them: "I stole my mother's checkbook." Us: "I robbed three motherfuckers down the block." Them: "My mom isn't pressing charges, and she got me into a private-pay rehab." Us: "We got people out lookin' to kill us, and the law lookin' to lock us up for life." All of it made perfect fodder for my newly evolving class analysis, and I was the kind of brother who kept talking about oppression and revolution even when I was high. That made me one annoying addict, even to my so-called friends.

I hadn't known such a thing was possible, but East Palo Alto and my hemmed-in triangle of Belle Haven in Menlo Park felt like even more of an invisible cage than they did when I was growing up. And I felt some responsibility for that: As oppressed as we were, as deprived of honest options, as driven, almost herded into the prison pipeline, my generation had taken drug sales from a backroom business to an on-the-street industry. Gangs that formed on the inside had spilled outside the walls to get in on the narcotics trade. And now, this small, segregated corner of one of the richest counties in the motherfucking state was popping off with street corner drug sales and gang violence. Cheap, plentiful crack was the star of the show. My mother and the Hill Avenue house she was barely holding on to were right in the middle of an open-air drug market. "Hill Street Blues" was graffitied on the fence across the street, marking it as gang territory. There was hardly ever an open bed at her house, what with kids from the extended family who needed feeding and loving and the open flow of neighborhood addicts coming and going to see my brothers. So I couch surfed. On my worst nights, I slept in the park or in abandoned cars. By now my father was dead and buried. At least he didn't have to see me this way. That left my mother, our matriarch, an enabler through and through. She loved us, and telling us all to get the fuck out would have hurt her more than it hurt us. I visited often, telling myself I was stopping by to check in on moms when what I was really doing was looking for a homie to knock on the door who was willing to slip into the garage with me and share a free high camouflaged as friendship.

Up until now, everything I'd done in relationship to drugs I'd done sneakily. Crack cocaine didn't allow me the space to

152

sneak. The streets of my ghetto had turned into *Night of the Living Dead*. Dozens of us standing around, high on crack, craving more. The police didn't know what to do. So on plenty of nights, when 11:00 p.m. or so rolled around, they'd bring the cars in three deep and herd us like cattle, yelling through their megaphones, "Disperse, disperse."

We were coming to the end of a terrible decade. What was left of the Black liberation movement had been crushed by addiction. Infighting between Huey P. Newton and the remnants of the Black Panther Party he had cofounded added insult to the injuries and paranoia the FBI had already inflicted. By the time I walked out of San Quentin, the party was more or less dead. Still, the legend whose apartment I'd craned my neck to spot from the Alameda County jail back in 1971 had kept learning and growing. He'd earned a Ph.D. in social philosophy from the University of California at Santa Cruz in 1980. But crack cocaine   153
didn't even spare the most intellectual among us. Huey became an addict too. In August 1989, as I was communing with my fellow zombies back home, he was shot to death near a West Oakland crack house.

Meanwhile, the federal government's war against Black and brown communities, commonly called the War on Drugs, was raging. The Anti-Drug Abuse Act of 1986 set mandatory minimum sentences for cocaine possession and distribution. When it came to selling the shit, though, for reasons called racism, racism, and racism, the law treated crack and powder cocaine like they were as different as arsenic and sugar. Distribution of just five little grams of crack would guarantee you a minimum five-year federal prison sentence. Distributing five hundred grams of powder cocaine would get you the same. It was a hundred-to-one disparity. The 1986 law also opened the tap for federal dollars to come flowing into state and local law enforcement agencies.

The state's laws and policies were just as bad or worse. Over the course of the 1980s, California's prison population nearly quadrupled—a rate twice the national average. The state had also dreamed up new ways to denigrate its captives: in 1989, Pelican Bay State Prison opened as a "supermax" facility, to house prisoners in solitary confinement indefinitely without access to kind human touch or a drop of sunlight. Meanwhile, sentences just kept getting longer. By 1990, one in three Black men in California between the ages of twenty and twenty-nine were either locked up or on probation or parole. And thanks to crack cocaine, parole revocations had doubled, sending a stream of men back to prison for the crime of addiction. You can guess where taxpayer dollars were flowing. The state borrowed $3 *billion* in the 1980s alone to build new prisons. It felt like our system couldn't get more dysfunctional. But it could and would. On the streets of my ghetto, we were feeling the pain. Law enforcement in San Mateo County arrested nearly three times as many Black people in 1989 than they had in 1980. And I, Dorsey Emmett Nunn, who'd made a promise to return to my community as an asset and not a liability, was about to become a part of that statistic.

THE BEEF THAT landed me in the San Mateo County jail went down on December 12, 1989. It was another unplanned act of stupidity that involved a liquor store. I was thirty-eight years old, too old, and me and my nephew were high as kites. Like the pool hall, the liquor store on East Palo Alto's University Avenue was our go-to, a place to hang out and act like we owned the whole fucked-up town. Black community leaders had been pushing an alternative vision for the unincorporated part of our ghetto ever since I was a teenager. And in 1983, they won the fight for cityhood—by a fifteen-vote margin. With incorporation, East Palo Alto realized its dream of self-governance, but it was a far cry from the ascendant Black cultural hub of Nairobi these dedicated brothers and sisters had envisioned. The Nairobi shopping center was boarded up even before the squeaker of a vote. There hadn't been a bank in town since Wells Fargo pulled out in 1986. And neighboring cities had cannibalized the rest of the tax base: Palo Alto took the airport, Menlo Park the industrial area. The remaining kingdom we liked to think we ruled was two and a half square miles of poverty and pain.

I pulled my mother's car up to the liquor store, and my nephew and I got out to kick it on the sidewalk with other cast members from *Night of the Living Dead*. A little while later, the owner came out yelling and started banging on my hood. Looking back, he no doubt saw me closer to who I was that night than I had ever seen myself. He wanted us gone, and it seemed like there wasn't a cell in his body that felt a shadow of respect for any of us. The feeling was mutual. The man was poisoning our neighborhood with a steady supply of booze. I'd heard rumors he sold guns out the back door, though I never saw it myself. Still, he didn't want a bunch of addicts high on crack loitering out front. After he was done pounding my family vehicle, he showed us he was packing. He was an asshole. But that's no excuse for what came next. My nephew and I drove around the block twice, firing a gun at that liquor store. A drive-by shooting half a block from the police station does not constitute a crime of genius. I puttered along at thirty miles an hour trying to get my moms her car back, an OJ Simpson–style low-speed chase before OJ made the move famous. And just like that, I was back behind bars.

WHEN RICH WHITE people get arrested, they talk about the shame of it. Like they're the only ones who can feel shame. I guess it comes from having an assignment of human status. But I absolutely felt ashamed. Embarrassed, humiliated, and afraid too. So many people, from Kathy and Shirl to Michael and Margaret and my other friends from the Prison Law Office had believed in me. Denise too. And here I was, contemplating a life in prison—the one place I swore I would never go again. I had so much to lose, and this time I knew it. Like every other man in the crowded preadjudication cell, I was too poor to post bail, and I couldn't bring myself to pick up the phone and call the people who could help me. So for a couple of months, there I sat, pondering my errors.

At the San Mateo County jail, drugs seemed to dominate conversation. Due to that common interest, every time a new brother shuffled in dressed in orange, he was almost sure to see someone he recognized. The two of them would then spend ten minutes reminiscing about the last time they used crack together as if they'd been on the red carpet at the Oscars. I could see our community was deeply fucked. The "Just Say No" public service propaganda playing on TV seemed geared to stopping the spread to other communities. As for ours, with prices at record lows, we were collateral damage. Maybe intentional damage.

By late January 1990, I couldn't take the loneliness, so I went to the pay phone and called Margaret collect. The class and race differences I'd been pondering had helped get me into this position. But for a poor Black brother living in crack central, I turned out to be one fortunate motherfucker. Because the privilege of my white friends and allies was about to work in my favor. Like lightning, Margaret got her hands on some bail funds, picked me up, and drove me to her little house of roses and harmony on the Belvedere lagoon. Night and day. This time, my appreciation knew no bounds. I wasn't clean. Not yet. But I was exercising as much self-control as an addict can. I put my muscle into earning back the trust I'd lost. I even built a fine-looking deck for Margaret's mother, Peggy. Margaret hooked me up with a job at her cousin's construction company. His mom, who I knew as Aunt Mary, would stop by the house nearly every day on her walks and we'd sit and talk, sometimes for hours. Margaret and her sister Tricia, who'd also worked at the Prison Law Office, let me use their uncle's beater just about every day to drive to the Elephant Rock Pier to fish. Peggy's English Springer Spaniel always came along. All of it got me pondering my own childhood. The Littlefield family absolutely knew how to shred each other with sarcasm, but physical violence was unthinkable. We Nunns were so accustomed to the extension cord in my father's hands, we barely considered it a beating. In the safety of the Littlefields' generosity, I dared to imagine a future I wanted for myself, for my children and my community: A home I owned in a neighborhood where gunshots weren't a nightly occurrence, and a chance to make a difference. I wanted to not just *get* a job but eventually to *give* jobs. To throw myself into work that was guided by the overarching goal of justice, not money. Looking back, I'm proud to say I exceeded my ambitions.

My Prison Law Office friends mirrored the same values I'd applied to my comrades in cages, and over time to my own father: To them, I was not my addiction or the sum of my worst mistakes. I was a man who had made a valuable contribution to the movement for prisoner rights and could continue to do so.

157

A man with a sense of humor capable of diffusing the darkest kind of tension. A man who had work to do to become my better self. In late March, Margaret handed me a flyer for an April Fools' Day fundraiser. The title: "Keep This Fool Out of Prison." The goal was to raise the bail money she had borrowed to broker my freedom. A whole bunch of people pitched in. Ellen Barry, a young lawyer who'd founded Legal Services for Prisoners with Children in the late 1970s to focus on the plight of women behind bars, offered up the fundraiser's venue, the Oakland blues club she and her husband co-owned with another friend. A couple of years earlier, while I was still capable of hiding my addiction, Ellen had asked me to serve on the LSPC board. I was honored to do it. Now she made it clear she was willing to keep me on as I navigated an uncertain future. She had that much faith in me. Still, it wasn't all roses and bubble gum. Not long after I got to Belvedere, these friends sat me down for an intervention. Margaret's opener: "If you don't snap out of what you're going through, Dorsey, you will wind up back in the pen forever." I knew they were right. I hadn't yet been sentenced, but prison was the logical option. If a roomful of white people with advanced degrees hadn't shown up on my behalf, it would have been guaranteed.

MY LATE BROTHER Robert, who died of sickle cell anemia in 1969, had a daughter named Tina, whose mother later wound up in prison for defending herself against an abuser. Ever since then, my moms had been raising Tina as her own in that house of love and chaos. Lula Mae Nunn didn't have it in her to come to my sentencing. She'd been there, done that. But Tina came. She turned out to be the only Black person in the packed courtroom. I'd never disappointed so many people at the same time. A few

158

dozen allies had written letters to the court on my behalf. Most of them were white too, with advanced degrees. As were the three people who testified on my behalf: Michael Satris, Margaret Littlefield, and Vincent Schiraldi.

The radical movement for the liberation of prisoners—especially Black and brown prisoners—had taken a beating, no doubt. But there was still a committed core of allies speaking up on our behalf, among them the rare policy wonk and academic. When Vinny Schiraldi got up in court to lay out an alternative sentencing plan for me, he was Western regional director of the National Center on Institutions and Alternatives, a fancy way of saying "prison reform" without scaring the shit out of the establishment. He'd also been appointed in 1987 to California's Blue Ribbon Commission on Inmate Population Management. The twenty-five-member commission wasn't exactly a group of lefties. Correctional officials, judges, and district attorneys served on it too. But even *they* knew dysfunction when they saw it. Just months before my sentencing, the commission issued its final report to the legislature: The entire California criminal justice system, with its sole focus on punishment and rigid mandatory sentences, was "out of balance," they wrote. Instead of building more prisons, the state needed more prevention programs, drug treatment, and community options to help people as they came out of cages. The report offered up a slice of sanity. But legislators ignored it. After all, their constituents, at least those who voted, were foaming at the mouth with lock-'em-up revenge fantasies based on the notion that every one of us was the Night Stalker with darker skin. The worst was yet to come.

The year after my sentencing, Schiraldi went on to found the Center on Juvenile and Criminal Justice and then the Justice

159

Policy Institute, advocating for criminal justice reform. After decades of trying to change the system from the outside, he took a shot at doing it from the inside, as New York City's probation commissioner and later commissioner of the city's department of corrections. The man oversaw Rikers Island for seven months in 2021—and came away calling it a "reflection of this country's racist and destructive fixation on imprisonment" and "Exhibit A for why we need to end mass incarceration." That's how much work still needs to be done. Schiraldi is still an ally. In 1990, he was one of a smaller number of allies. Meanwhile, Black America was hurting something fierce. Right after my arrest, Marion Barry, the Black mayor of Washington, DC, was arrested too, on a crack cocaine charge.

The judge fit the law-and-order mold of the day, but my respectable cast of supporters seemed to sway him. Instead of a prison sentence, I was directed to report back to the county jail in August for a brief stay, with an estimated release date of March 1991. I'd been given another chance, thanks to privilege by association. And I wasn't gonna mess it up.

WHEN I STOPPED using dope, it wasn't an act of love, it was an act of anger. I was back in the San Mateo County jail, once again surrounded by Black faces in a mostly white county in a mostly white country. When I scanned the chow hall, there were my brothers Ronald and Pat, along with two nephews, a bunch of homies from the neighborhood I thought I liked, and some I knew I didn't. The county jail packed us into communal cells. Ours had eight bunk beds, and on most nights, more than sixteen men. The unofficial rule was like a racist game of musical chairs: if you were white, you slept on the piss-stained concrete floor. I guess my time eating well, sleeping in a soft

John Henry Nunn Sr. in his fine
Florsheim shoes, around the
time Dorsey was born.

Dorsey and his brother Pat get a rare visit
at San Quentin State Prison from their
parents during the 1970s.

Dorsey in the sixth grade at
Kavanaugh School in East
Palo Alto.

Vertical aspect shot of Dorsey
sitting in front of boxes looking
to the side, Fang family *San Francisco
Examiner* photograph archive negative
files, BANC PIC 2006.029—NEG, box
1837, sleeve 145908 08 166.
© *The Regents of the University of California, The
Bancroft Library, University of California, Berkeley.*

A photo of Dorsey at San Quentin mailed to Kathy Labriola in the mid-1970s. Their friendship served as a lifeline to Dorsey's humanity.

Courtesy of: Kathy Labriola

Note to Kathy on the backside of the photo.

Kathy,
a person who defined woman in new terms. a person that made friendship have a meaning that I had to appreciate. One of your smiles is worth waiting for and something that I look forward to. In our conversations I find growth, In your arrival I find happiness, In your embrace I find strength, In your presence I find hope and love and I don't think I could ask for more — Dorsey

Dorsey with Alma Dorn, learning to smile again soon after his release from San Quentin.

Dorsey and Michael Satris in 1984 on the back porch of the Prison Law Office, just outside the gates of San Quentin.

Courtesy of: Bonnie Jones

Dorsey Nunn, posed photo in front of San Quentin State Prison, Fang family *San Francisco Examiner* photograph archive negative files. BANC PIC 2006.029—NEG, box 2132, sleeve 1985-08-28 09 18.

Dorsey in the mid-1980s relaxing at the Littlefield's peaceful home in Belvedere.
Courtesy of: Margaret Littlefield

Nate Harrington, in the dark brown bell-bottoms, at a Prison Law Office gathering at the Littlefield house in Belvedere.
Courtesy of: Margaret Littlefield

The ceremonial altar at the March 2003 inaugural gathering of All of Us or None, set up to honor historical and intergenerational trauma, ancestors, and all those still behind bars.
Photo credit: Scott Braley

Elder Freeman places sticky dots to mark his policy priorities at the March 2003 inaugural gathering of All of Us or None, the grassroots movement of formerly incarcerated people demanding their full civil and human rights.
Photo credit: Scott Braley

Arthur "Tha" League expressing his brilliance at the March 2003 inaugural All of Us or None gathering in Oakland.
Photo credit: Scott Braley

Linda Evans and George Galvis, key cofounders of All of Us or None, confer at the March 2003 inaugural gathering in Oakland.
Photo credit: Scott Braley

Arthur "Tha" League (in hat) and Susan Burton (center) listen with growing frustration to lawmakers at a September 2003 Black Congressional Caucus legislative event. All of Us or None members were scheduled to speak but denied the opportunity.
Photo credit: Scott Braley

Dorsey and Vicki Smothers console "Big Judy" Hendrix as she speaks about losing her job due to her criminal history at a 2004 All of Us or None Peace & Justice Community Summit in East Palo Alto.
Photo credit: Scott Braley

Dorsey demonstrates with All of Us or None in March 2005 outside Oakland City Hall to demand that Mayor Jerry Brown "Ban the Box" on public employment applications.
Photo credit: Scott Braley

Dorsey speaking outside San Francisco City Hall in fall 2005 about the "Ban the Box" campaign to remove the question from public employment applications that asks about criminal history. The campaign marked All of Us or None's first policy victory.

Hundreds gather for the LSPC/AOUON annual Quest for Democracy day at the California State Capitol, a cornerstone of the mission to engage, educate, and empower formerly incarcerated people to participate in the democratic process.
Photo credit: Mark Fujiwara

Poster of Dorsey from the ACLU of Northern California 2008 "Every Vote Counts" campaign in collaboration with All of Us or None.
Courtesy of: The ACLU of Northern California

Poster of Sheila from the ACLU of Northern California 2008 "Every Vote Counts" campaign in collaboration with All of Us or None.
Courtesy of: The ACLU of Northern California

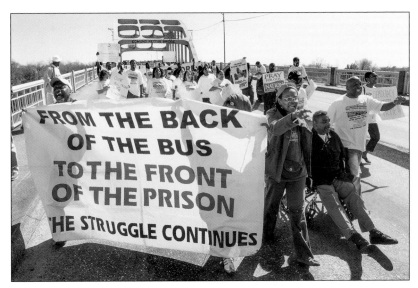

Members of the Formerly Incarcerated and Convicted People & Families Movement on the March 1, 2011, march across the Edmund Pettus Bridge in Alabama from Montgomery to Selma, reversing the direction of the 1965 "Bloody Sunday" march. The backwards march symbolized the work that remains in the struggle for Civil Rights.
Photo credit: © Mickey Welsh – USA TODAY NETWORK

Formerly incarcerated volunteers with LSPC and AOUON brave the rain to give bikes away to kids on behalf of their incarcerated parents. The annual Community Giveback in December 2022 was held outside the Freedom & Movement Center.
Photo credit: TaSin Sabir

bed to the sounds of a lapping lagoon, and soaking up the love of friends who truly cared had softened me. The other brothers hassled me for complaining about conditions—and even more so for not participating in the intimidation of whites. For obvious reasons, it didn't sit right with me. I was making Pruno again, earning a little jail money, trying to get my head back in the game of saving my ass from violent attack. One night, a brother I grew up with told me he had some weed. He even had rolling papers, which was rare. We'd gotten used to using pages torn from some other brother's Bible. Weed and wine go together like chocolate and peanut butter, so me and my former homie brokered a sharing arrangement. I was looking forward to the buzz. But the man harshed my mellow before we even got started.

"Man, we ain't gonna give none of this stuff to the white boys," he said while he rolled a skinny-ass joint.

161

"None of this stuff" meant none of his weed and none of my wine. Systemic racism was an oppressor, no doubt, but I'd learned from experience not to write off human beings for the color of their skin. And I wasn't about to let some motherfucker choose my friends or my enemies. I had a problem though: I'd gotten soft around the middle, and I'd never seen my cellmate lose a fight. If I challenged his views, he'd almost certainly beat the shit out of me. The only chance I stood of taking him was if he got drunk and I didn't. I handed him the Pruno. "This bag's for you, man," I said.

Deflecting him helped the anger drain right out of me. I guess I had learned a thing or two about controlling my rage, at least when I wasn't high on crack. I begged off and went to sleep. On Day Two, something told me I could live without the high of weed or wine. So I abstained again. Without booze and drugs as a common language, I recognized by Day Three that I didn't like half the brothers I'd been hanging out with. So I kept to myself.

BY EARLY FALL, I got good news, and it lined up nicely with Schiraldi's plan for me: if I agreed to enter a residential drug and alcohol rehabilitation program, my sentence would get cut short. I was taking it one day at a time, not thinking ahead. But on a fundamental level I knew sobriety was what I wanted. My dreams depended on it. And I sure as hell wanted out of jail. I got a day pass to do my intake at Project Ninety, the county's only drug rehabilitation program, founded in the city of San Mateo the year I got shipped to DVI. I got there around 11:00 a.m., just in time for "interviews," when prospective clients got a rundown of the program and people in charge sized us up. When it wrapped up an hour later, I walked out of the conference room, and standing there in front of me like a ghost was Al Haysbert. Al, who was King of Dope Sales on the inside. Steady, smooth-talking Al, who stayed out of politics in the interest of enterprise. Al, who kept me going on so many days with a warm buzz and left a beautiful vacuum for me to step into with my side hustle when he paroled. That day, I was no doubt the second-happiest man in San Quentin. Go, Big Dog, go! Be free. The world is mine!

Al had always been a velvet glove. It hid an iron fist, but Al's strategy mostly allowed him to avoid using it. He came soft and right to any business arrangement, never skimming off the product, even tossing in a bonus in the interest of peace and harmony. He stayed safe and rich that way for a long time. But once Al left San Quentin, he got too deep in the game. The brother had to go into hiding, and when he reemerged in 1988, he checked into Project Ninety. Now he was a counselor. When Al saw me, a big smile spread across his face, and he opened his arms and wrapped me in a tight embrace. Al Haysbert *hugged* me. I had no framework for this shit, and the first thing that crossed my mind was, "Is Al gay?" Not only was Al not gay, he told me, he wasn't using, and he was happy. My head turned into a cartoon bomb and exploded. As we walked toward his office, I stopped him in front of the bathrooms.

"Tell me, man, you're not using speed?"

"No."

"You're not smoking weed?"

"No."

"Heroin?"

"No."

"Crack?"

"No"

"You're not dropping pills?"

"No."

"You drinking?"

"No."

I ticked through every substance I could think of from our common history, just to be sure. When I was done, I took it in: Big Dog was clean and sober. It was news to me, but it had already been spreading from San Quentin to Soledad. On the inside, we always said recovery programs were for people who could no longer hustle. But Al was doing it. It became an inspiration to a lot of brothers inside. Cravings were pulling on the pit in my stomach, gnawing on the nerves in my teeth. I'd been clean for almost three months, but I won't lie. I was planning to find a homeboy, buy some dope, and take it back into the jail so I could pick up doing what I was used to doing.

Walking to the parking lot, I changed my mind. "If this Big Dog can get clean," I told myself, "I got a chance." I knew it was what I *wanted*, but once I saw Al, I realized I had a chance of prevailing in the endeavor.

My decision to get sober had nothing to do with moral judgment. To me, it's always been about bodily autonomy. The prison system robbed me of it, just like slavery had done to my ancestors. My body is mine alone, and what I choose to put in it is my own business.

I never used again.

MY THREE-MONTH STINT at Project Ninety passed in a flash. At the end, Al took all those questions I'd asked him that first day and turned them around on me. "I hope you didn't come in one snort too short, one puff of the crack pipe too short, one fix too short," he told me in his artful and deliberate way, like a man who takes his time drizzling syrup on pancakes. "I hope you got everything out there that you needed." Then he asked me how many years it took me to get dirty. The answer was quite a few. Well, he answered, it might take you that long to get clean. His advice: Stay longer. In time, he said, I'd learn to hear my cravings calling me in my own voice, by my own name. I'd learn to slow down my responses and make effective choices on my own behalf. That was the work. Al and I would wind up doing it together for the next two decades in an elite men's recovery circle. Members only. Incarceration history required. For now, Al knew that if I walked away, I'd probably fail. He pulled some strings and got me hired as a house manager. I stayed for nine more months.

The sober house I managed served six or seven men at any one time, each of us working to change in fundamental ways.

Class Analysis

Almost immediately I snuck out and bought a pea-green 1968 Ford Galaxy for twenty-five dollars. It had no back windows and no ignition switch, so I had to jump-start it every time I needed to go someplace. Having a car was a program no-no, but I was never one to abide by rules that didn't sit right with me, and sobriety didn't change that. Besides, I was able to do something in that shitty car I never had the capacity to do in my ex-girlfriend's Mercedes Benz: be a decent son, pick my mother up every other day, and take her to dialysis. With each month of sobriety, I felt a little more capable of repairing the damage I'd done, of making amends. And my daughter was high on my list.

I searched for my son, Anthony, on my first night of freedom because we'd been cut off from each other completely. The relationship we wound up building we built from scratch. Denise was a different story. She was my motivation for following prison rules, and at the top of my mind when I chose to pursue a formal education behind bars. I'd imagined slipping right back into a nuclear family where I could be her dad from morning until night. Unfortunately, I blew a massive hole in my relationship with Faydell as soon as I got out of San Quentin. Only a few days had passed since I tracked down Anthony when I asked Faydell to meet me outside my moms' house to talk. I laid out my little vision for her. She told me she already had a man in her life. I told her to drop the clown. She held firm on her boundaries and made it clear I couldn't barge in and call the shots about Denise. My anger got the best of me. I called her a bitch and told her I'd sue her for full custody. I wanted her to return to me everything I'd ever given her, including the seeds I'd planted in her body. I was off the hook and absolutely wrong. That night, Faydell closed the door on our relationship for good, though she did allow me to maintain a relationship with my daughter.

We did all right, until my addiction betrayed her and everyone else I loved. Denise had already seen her daddy in a way no child should, shackled in a concrete and steel fortress. I never wanted her to see me high, and she never did. I didn't want her to see the way I was handling my relationships with women either. They were dysfunctional, and I knew it. The only thing I felt I *could* do, other than give her money now and then, was tell her I loved her and tell her the truth. So when she asked me, "Daddy, how come I can't see you?" I said, "Because I don't want you to see me like *this*." It wasn't good enough. I had let her down, injured her deeply. So when I got clean, I had some repairing to do.

On August 20, 1991, my first sobriety birthday, Denise agreed to see me. Everybody around me thought I was struck wonderful, all of that and a bag of chips. Not Denise. We met at Heidi's Pies, a twenty-four-hour family diner on San Mateo's main drag about a mile from Project Ninety's headquarters. People smoked in restaurants back then, and I was a smoker. It's almost a requirement when you first get sober, just like the coffee at NA meetings. Denise was twenty-one years old, a young adult and older soul. She and her mother and I all shared a trait. None of us care for ultimatums, but none of us are beyond declaring some of our own. As I brought a cigarette to my lips, my daughter stared straight at me and laid down the law.

"Daddy," she said. "If you fire that up, I'm gonna have to move, because I don't smoke."

I put it down. "I think that we wasted too much time already," I said, meeting her determination with my own. I never smoked again. Denise became my rock, a beacon of right relationship. I worked my ass off to never let her down again, and I wound up walking her down the aisle, just like she'd made me promise back when I was playing Disneyland with her behind bars. She lived long enough to tell me not only that she loved me, but that she liked me. That meant the world to me.

I spent the next four months working my program and shuttling my moms to her lifesaving care. That brought me to the Hill Avenue house at least three times a week. Ronald was back, and the drug activity was more off the hook than ever. Let's just say the setting posed its challenges. One of the slogans of recovery goes like this: If you hang around the barbershop long enough, you're bound to get a haircut. Meaning, don't go kicking it in your old drug haunts, because you will slip. But suppose the barbershop is your whole neighborhood? Your entire community? Your closest family?

One afternoon, after I got my mom settled, I went out front to sit on the rounded curb under a towering pine tree. That tree was so sick with rot it would later fall on the roof. The lawn I'd planted was trampled to dust, incapable of supporting growth. Despite the love inside the house, I could see I needed to get away, at least for a while. My stint as a sober house manager was coming to a close when Al popped the question: How about we move in together? By January 1992, we had us a bachelor pad just east of Project Ninety's main office. The rented two-bedroom condo in Foster City was a much sweeter setup than side-by-side cells in San Quentin. Al and I weren't getting loaded. We weren't fighting. And we weren't competing for customers. The cherry on the cake was that we each got our own bathroom. Meanwhile, I had landed my dream job. The month before—on the day I turned forty—Ellen Barry had called me up and asked me to work as a paralegal at Legal Services for Prisoners with Children, the nonprofit I would one day come to lead.

Chapter 12

RUNNING SHOES

first met Ellen when she stopped by the Prison Law Office to talk about our collective struggle. She'd created Legal Services for Prisoners with Children in 1978, when she was fresh out of law school. The organization didn't exclude men, who have children too. But in the early days, it absolutely centered women. Ellen's work lit a fire in me from the start. I raised my hand to volunteer for her as she built the National Network for Women in Prison. Every chapter had to have at least two formerly incarcerated people in leadership. That shit was extraordinary back then, and it impressed me. Still, it was only when I got into deep conversation with Ellen on live radio in 1988, as I was sinking into my addiction, that I got close to understanding the nature of the battles she was fighting.

The injustice system controlled the kind of information San Quentin prisoners could access, so we at the Prison Law Office turned to local radio to get them educated. I was the one who made the rounds to KPOO 89.5 FM, KMEL 106.1 FM, and

KPFA 89.3 FM to get the word out. About once or twice a month, Cheyenne Bell at KPOO would even let me host her popular interview show in her place. Sister Chey was an attorney, civil rights warrior for people behind bars, and leader in the fight to secure a new trial for Geronimo Ji-Jaga Pratt. She went on to run community programs for San Francisco's Juvenile Hall, and in that role broke ground by bringing in the Center for Young Women's Development (CYWD) to deliver services to system-involved girls and young women. CYWD's mission was to restore hope and dignity to young women who were addicted, trafficked, abused, or often all of the above. As they healed, they stepped right into CYWD jobs and became organizers. The whole staff walked it like they talked it. I was the first hire at the Prison Law Office who'd lived the conditions we were trying to correct, and I know it made a difference in the success of our outreach. Ellen at LSPC had partnered with people in and out of prison from the start, and I would take that ball and run with it. Who better to lead the resistance than those who've lived the struggle? But on the day I dragged my worn-out ass to KPOO's tan brick building on San Francisco's Divisadero Street to interview Ellen in 1988, organizing that movement was a long ways away. That day, a big part of my brain was plotting my next high.

As Ellen and I got into it that day, I learned that even though their incarceration rate was taking off like a bottle rocket, women remained more or less invisible, as did their stories. Men like me who'd been to Gladiator School and survived San Quentin in the 1970s tended to assume the women had it easier, but we didn't know the half of it. As Ellen talked about forced sterilizations, pregnant women denied medical care and forced to give birth in full restraints, mothers who were banned from holding their own babies and denied visits as their kids grew up, my eyes got wide. It was a new world of pain, a new language. To me, anyway. When Ellen lamented the lack of OB/GYN care that day, I thought she was talking about a prison gang. For real. We'd laugh about that for years to come.

As soon as I got my ass out of Sister Chey's chair and left the station, I went and got high just like I'd planned. But I couldn't stop thinking about what Ellen had shared with me and all I still needed to learn. Yes, I was an active addict, but I was nevertheless humbled. Those two things are not mutually exclusive. Two days later, I came to a conclusion: "Dorsey, you been an asshole." All those one-way conversations I'd had since I got out of the pen were replaying in my head. Women would be telling me about what they endured in cages, and I'd be nodding, saying, "uh-huh." But I was a dog fixed on a bone, just trying to come up with the next smooth line that would get me closer to peeling off the sister's clothes. The truth hit: I was not such an expert on prison life after all, and I definitely wasn't the paragon of feminism I'd made myself out to be to Kathy Labriola. Thanks to Ellen, I'd soon get a chance to further my education.

I found out later that Ellen knew I was a full-blown addict the day I interviewed her on KPOO. She also knew it didn't define me. She'd grown up in a family of ten kids, and almost every one of her siblings experienced addiction and fought like hell to achieve recovery. She waited in my corner while I worked the program at Project Ninety. And when she heard I was clean, her response wasn't doubt about how long it might last, it was respect. When she called me on my birthday on December 5, 1991, to offer me the job, I jumped on it like a wild dog surviving on carrots and celery. I would have worked for her for free and slept on the office floor for the opportunity, but she offered me a good salary. Recovery teaches you not to be restless, to take small steps. But all I'd been doing to be an asset to my community was making the coffee at NA meetings. I was ready, and LSPC became the vehicle I was searching for to exercise my political beliefs. The organization had already successfully sued to create programs in California where women prisoners could bond with their newborn babies and breast-feed, where children could live *with* their mothers in special facilities. It was also shining light on the fact that incarcerated women were losing their kids to the child welfare system. It happened fast, and often for good. Unlike men, most incarcerated women couldn't rely on the other parent to care for the kids on the outside. Worse than that, I'd learn, many women serving life sentences had landed in prison for defending themselves against violent abusers—who *were* the fathers of their kids. I'd come from a prison that was male dominated to a job at the Prison Law Office that was male dominated to one now led by and dedicated to women. They would teach me more than I could have imagined.

The LSPC staff was small, and from day one, I was valued as a key part of the team. Lawyers weren't necessarily the bosses of nonlawyers, partly because the team was collaborative, and because litigation was one of many tools. We all spent time offering direct services to women prisoners, helping them hold on to custody of their kids and more. LSPC also understood how important it was to educate the larger community about the impact of incarceration—on *all* prisoners, and on their families too. Almost overnight, I became that community spokesperson. My Merv Griffin humiliation was a decade behind me. It was some foul-smelling fertilizer, but fertilizer nonetheless, and I grew from it. I knew who I was

172

engaging with. I was intentional about my audience. And I made a conscious commitment to present cogent arguments in spaces where people didn't want to hear me, where I knew they disagreed with me. Because they had a flaw, a weakness. And it was bias. I was Black *and* formerly incarcerated, and their expectations were as low as a piece of shit paper stuck to a shoe. Just by showing up and making my points with respect and coherence, I was taking them by surprise. If I got through to two or three people at any one event, I figured I was two or three people ahead of where I'd been. It was exhausting and necessary work. Because just when we thought the tough-on-crime talk and false dichotomy of victim versus perpetrator that sprang up on us in the 1980s couldn't get any more hysterical, the 1990s came along and disabused us of that notion.

BY THE FALL of 1992, as the presidential campaign that put Bill Clinton in office was coming to a close, it was nearly impossible to find a politician in the country who wasn't singing the lock-'em-up song. Crime rates were down. But the US Department of Justice had officially declared that building more prisons to put away more people was the only way to keep that trend going. By 1994, California was one of more than half a dozen states that had passed so-called "three strikes" laws to come down hard on people with multiple convictions, and many more would follow. But our law had the distinction of being by far the most extreme. The crimes didn't all have to be violent. In fact, none of them did. If you had a single "violent *or* serious" felony in your past, then any felony conviction at all (and there were five hundred to choose from) would automatically double your sentence. Any felony conviction when you had two prior "violent or serious" felonies would strike you out: twenty-five to life.

California's law also stood out for counting felonies committed by juveniles as young as sixteen. And prosecutors could apply it to wobblers—crimes they could charge as misdemeanors or felonies. You could steal a pair of shoes for your kids or get caught with a vial of crack because you were addicted just like everyone else in your neighborhood and you'd get sent away for life—even if you hadn't landed so much as a jaywalking ticket in decades. Meanwhile, the law said anyone with a strike was ineligible for probation or for diversion to drug treatment, and it scaled back the good time credit people sentenced under the law could earn. It did so many fucked-up things it was hard to keep track of them all. But we'd quickly see the effects in our communities as the largest prison construction boom in the history of the world went into overdrive. In the 1980s, California built eight new prisons. In the 1990s, twenty more came online, springing up like tumors across the state's rural landscape. The mood for vengeance meant every legal and policy victory Michael Satris and other allies had managed to score on our behalf in the 1960s and 1970s was in jeopardy. I always say the 1990s marked the era when soldiers in the prisoner rights movement took off our combat boots and put on our running shoes. In 1994 alone I wore out a whole lot of those shoes and put tens of thousands of miles on my shitty car as I drove up and down the state, sleeping on couches and floors, to debate people who thought I should never have come out of a cage.

The seed for the Three Strikes and You're Out law was planted in July of 1992, when Kimber Reynolds, an eighteen-year-old woman from Fresno, was shot and killed by a man on parole during a robbery that went south. Her father, Mike Reynolds, was understandably enraged. Less understandably, he was out to destroy pretty much anyone who had ever violated a criminal law. The toxic public sentiment made him some quick allies, and by spring of 1993, Republican sponsors in Sacramento introduced Reynolds' three strikes law for the first time. Democrats held it back. Reynolds was not an easy man to like. If he'd been the main face of the law, I'm not sure how things would have gone down. But in July 1993, twelve-year-old Polly Klaas was kidnapped in the night from her own Petaluma bedroom during a slumber party. Two months later, a dude with two prior kidnappings on his felony rap sheet admitted to strangling her to death, and the whole country went ape shit.

Most of the time, it was Polly's daddy, Marc Klaas, sitting on the opposite side of the panel discussion from yours truly. Sometimes Reynolds was there too. Going up against families in anguish was a dark assignment. But somebody had to introduce sanity into the conversation. We had allies in the fight. The American Friends Service Committee raised money to oppose the Three Strikes initiative. Naneen Karraker, director of the Criminal Justice Consortium, was speaking up loudly too. She'd supported me at my sentencing, and years later would donate her time to us as LSPC treasurer. None of us were apologists for the twisted motherfucker who had kidnapped and strangled Polly Klaas. Yes, my first solution to massive prison growth has and always will be to let more people out, even to let *most* people out. But I'm what you call a practical abolitionist. I've been inside, and I think some people need to stay there. I sure wouldn't want them living next to anyone I love. The thing is, we knew the Three Strikes law was not going to come down hardest on the small number of violent white serial sociopaths. When I sat across the table from victims' family members, I spoke to that larger picture: treating human beings like chattel slaves, depriving us of dignity, locking us in boxes for decades at a cost of billions of dollars a year was

175

not only throwing away promise, it was not only a human rights violation, it was guaranteed to create angry, hopeless captives by the hundreds of thousands while blowing apart poor communities of color. What folks who advocate for harsh punishment as a deterrent to crime don't recognize, I pointed out, is that punishment is not conducive to remorse. When your life is under threat, when you're being treated like a dog in an orchestrated dog fight, the mental bandwidth for reflection is lacking. For me, true remorse bloomed when I no longer hit the floor every time I heard a book drop or a whistle blow, when I was finally able to open my heart to family and community and contribute to their well-being. Life sentences can't get you there.

I knew in my bones what was coming. But there was no stopping the fever. By the third attempt to pass the law in Sacramento in the spring of 1994, even Democrats got on the bandwagon. With that, Three Strikes was on the California books. Still, Reynolds kept his Proposition 184 on the November ballot. Nearly three-fourths of voters embraced it, locking the legal changes into the state constitution so lawmakers couldn't turn around later and undo it.

Three Strikes wasn't our only battle in 1994. I had joined a Bay Area coalition that was also fighting another racist measure on the November ballot. Proposition 187 denied basic rights like health care and education to undocumented immigrants. A lot of activists framed it in the context of the civil rights movement. I viewed it as a South Africa–style move to create a kind of apartheid in our state, a caste of people so disenfranchised they could be exploited beyond measure. Sound familiar? To me, Propositions 184 and 187 were a two-headed dragon, and our Violence Prevention Coalition spoke out against both. Prop 187 stirred a lot more public outrage. That was the reality. It passed anyway, though it was later determined to be unconstitutional. We were losing big, but there were lessons in that bitter fruit. I'd seen the need to build alliances among the oppressed, whether they were poor immigrants, poor Black folks, or poor women.

The decade kept on taking, and by 1996, California lawmakers and Governor Pete Wilson rolled back the Inmate or Prisoner Bill of Rights, those two hard-won statutes from the late 1960s and early 1970s that restored some humanity to those of us in cages. It sure hadn't felt like a honeymoon when I was locked up, but in some ways, it turned out to be a golden age for prisoner rights. I argued to maintain those rights on televised panels and at community gatherings, facing off with Republican lawmakers and the ever-present family members of victims. It didn't help. They'd be scaled back to what the Constitution guaranteed. Everything beyond that would become a privilege prison officials could withhold for broad and vague "penological" reasons. Meaning, whenever they wanted to. Soon weights were banned on prison yards. So was wearing articles of your own clothing. Military haircuts became mandatory. More books appeared on the banned list, and others disappeared from prison law libraries. But it was the rollback of the right to visiting, the increased use of forced isolation from loved ones as punishment, that I believe had the most profound impact of all. The legal right to prison visits was relatively new when I was at San Quentin. I know from experience that they don't just help prisoners hold on to their humanity, they strengthen families, and those bonds make for healthy communities.

177

Public opinion wasn't running in our favor, but we kept on putting ourselves out there, hoping the basic fact of our humanity would win hearts and minds. Meanwhile, we prepped for a major legal battle to secure adequate medical care for women prisoners, who were being treated worse than dogs at the pound. I'd learn deep lessons from the hundreds of women I interviewed at the Central California Women's Facility (CCWF) in Chowchilla and the California Institution for Women (CIW) in Chino. Especially from Charisse Shumate, known to her friends as "Happy."

CCWF WAS THE biggest women's prison in the world. On the day in May 1995 when I visited with Ellen and Karen Shain, our brilliant soon-to-be administrative director from LSPC, the place was on lockdown. We waited for hours along with parents, kids, and crying babies. There were rarely many men in that visiting room. In the end, two prisoners came out: Charisse Shumate and her friend Marcia Bunney, a comrade in the fight for dignity. LSPC had filed a lawsuit the month before as part of a coalition with other legal organizations, demanding improvements to medical care for women prisoners. We relied on larger law firms as pro bono partners because our budget was so small. But we were the ones who did all the work with the plaintiffs, and to us, they were our equals. That right there was a lesson for me. Most of the litigation I followed treated incarcerated men like logs thrown on a fire. Named plaintiffs were vehicles to constitutional claims, and that's about it. At LSPC, we let nothing happen in the case without their buy-in. It was *their* case. We already knew the women weren't getting routine mammograms or pap smears that would have caught cancers early enough to treat them. We knew women in agonizing pain from advanced disease were getting nothing stronger than Tylenol. Guards openly talked about the private medical information of prisoners, as punishment or just for kicks. In other cases, women went years before prison medical staff got around to telling them their medical files listed chronic, life-threatening diseases like hepatitis C. Charisse "Happy" Shumate was living with sickle cell anemia, the disease that killed my brother Robert in 1969, the same one my daughter, Denise, was carrying inside her. And she had a horror story of her own.

Happy always said, "It's not a me thing, it's a 'we' thing," and that first day we met her she said it to us. She was fierce and charming and selfless—and in near constant pain. But she used that pain to power her advocacy on behalf of other women. We knew right away we had our lead plaintiff. Charisse would also become my guide to a disease I'd been afraid to know too much about. It's inherited, just like the color of your eyes, and mostly affects Black people. It makes the red blood cells sickle shaped and sticky. They get jammed up in the blood vessels, which is agony. And they can't carry enough oxygen through the body, which destroys organs over time. Treatment comes through blood transfusions and sedation, and on the rare occasions where the prison took Charisse to the hospital for a transfusion, they withheld the medications she needed afterward to counteract iron buildup. That killed her slowly too. Dehydration makes symptoms worse. Ice brings some pain relief, but COs withheld that from Charisse as punishment, even as temperatures soared past one hundred degrees. As she suffered, guards often called bullshit on her. When she did get care, it was always delayed and always inadequate. In the years after we filed suit, Charisse would go blind in one eye because of medical neglect. Still, if we expected a sister who looked beaten down or embittered that day in May 1995, we had something else coming. She sat up straight and told us she understood the risks of putting her name out front. She knew the load would

179

be heavy, and it was. Retaliation against her only got worse as the lawsuit progressed. But by the way she walked out, with her head up and shoulders back, I knew she was strong enough to bear the burden. I came to love her as a leader and a person. She allowed me to see how women in prison exercised their own love—by protecting one another from violence and injustice. Charisse felt in every sickle-shaped red blood cell in her body that she was responsible for her comrades, and that was beautiful and educational for me. I would keep her in mind as we worked to unite prisoners in men's and women's prisons toward a common goal, and connect them with our foot soldiers on the outside.

Lawsuits are not only fought in courtrooms, they're also fought in the public eye. Charisse and Marsha Bunney and others were already organized inside. When they asked us to form an outside group to work in tandem with them, we jumped at the chance. We called it the California Coalition for Women Prisoners, and I helped convene the first meeting. The litigation would prove bitter and complex. But now we had allies on the outside who picketed and protested outside CCWF and CIW to demand better conditions and more releases. That got the attention of the media and prison officials and lifted the spirits of those locked inside. The California Coalition for Women Prisoners is still based out of our LSPC offices under our fiscal sponsorship. It's going strong more than a quarter century after its founding. So is *The Fire Inside*, the quarterly newsletter CCWP rolled out in 1996, filled with poems and essays of women, transgender, and gender-nonconforming people. The *Shumate* case settled in our favor in 1997. The agreement laid out dozens of changes the prison system had to put in place for women's healthcare. Compliance was a struggle. It involved four years of constant monitoring. So we'd keep on fighting. But we had lifted up the voices of so many women and built strong and lasting support for them. They were no longer invisible. I was involved each step of the way, and it reaffirmed my commitment to movement building that crosses barriers—of gender, sexuality, race, and class.

Happy knew she would suffer for her advocacy. So did we. But it was painful to witness. I went to visit her in a Madera hospital at the ass end of her struggle. She was weak, shackled to the bed, and naked; she'd kicked off her blanket while writhing in pain. That vision stayed with me. It inspired me to keep working on behalf of all ill and dying prisoners. As she got closer to death, we helped petition the parole board for her compassionate release. The board recommended clemency, which required the governor's signature. But Governor Gray Davis, who'd taken over for Pete Wilson, was a tough-on-crimer too. The document sat on his desk unsigned for weeks, and on August 4, 2001, Charisse Shumate died. She never saw freedom. Like so many women, she'd been locked up for acting in self-defense against an abusive boyfriend. He pulled his gun on her during a vicious fight; she used it on him. Beginning in the 1990s, we at LSPC took on that issue too, helping women in similar circumstances win their freedom through the courts.

The vengeance ideology of the 1990s interfered with our vision. But it was still a fertile time. From the moment I joined LSPC, Ellen cultivated my intellectual growth, research, and writing. She urged me to ask big questions about social change and gave me the space to explore the answers. My dream at San Quentin—and promise to Kalima—was to come out and help rebuild my own community. So I wrote a paper laying out what recovery should look like back home, what my own sister, brothers, friends, and other fellow addicts needed to find meaning outside of their next high. Then I got to work putting theory into practice. And I didn't need Republican lawmakers or Kimber Reynolds's daddy on my side to do it: there were plenty of people California was spitting out of its swollen prisons who would roll up their sleeves to help.

Chapter 13

FREE AT LAST

On a bone-chilling afternoon in January 1993, a group of us recovering addicts met up at a community space on East Palo Alto's Bay Road, near a row of junkyards piled with beat-up rides and a hazardous waste management facility that had been spewing toxins into our ground since 1964. We were there to brainstorm positive change, and this weed-choked part of town with its poisoned soil felt like a fitting metaphor for our community: neglected and in need of some serious loving. David Lewis had organized the meetup. A towering man with a Fu Manchu mustache and a bad eye from a violent attack inside San Quentin, he'd come by my moms' place to meet me after he paroled. He knew the Nunn name and wanted to introduce himself. David had heard about Al Haysbert from the whisper vine in prison and gotten clean himself. We'd been spending time with him ever since he invited me and Al into the Circle of Recovery, a sobriety group for men who'd survived years in cages. Sitting in that circle, it went without saying that we'd seen other men shanked, maybe had to push that home-made blade ourselves. No judgment. It was the safest space I'd known since I walked out of San Quentin, a place where we could openly laugh and cry and grieve and admit to the damage. Listening and sharing with those brothers every week for years helped me wrestle with that anger that could put me in fight mode with the flip of a switch, those instincts bred into me while I lived in cages. So have the thousands of other Narcotics Anonymous meetings I've attended.

On the day we filed into the borrowed meeting room on Bay Road, we'd come to discuss a different kind of sobriety program, one rooted in our own community. Project Ninety was fourteen miles to the north, and the one rehab program right down the road in East Palo Alto that was taking advantage of basement-level rents preferred to accept private, paying white clients while the rest of us got locked up. That's why my homies always looked healthier on the inside than they did on the streets. The shit had to end.

David Lewis had already recruited Priya Haji to the cause. A Stanford University senior, she was full of energy and had contacts in the world of grantmaking. She'd wind up with a powerful national reputation as a "social entrepreneur." But her first success was teaming up with us, and on the day of our first gathering, she was all in. David and Priya already had an idea for a name that we all found fitting: Free at Last. Vicki Smothers was with us that day too. She'd dedicate the next three decades to the organization as vice president of the board of directors. Other than Priya, we had all been incarcerated, conditioned by the prison system and every other system we'd encountered to believe we were unworthy. Shit, my own vocational counselor at San Quentin told me I *might* make a good janitor one day.

Meanwhile, our ghetto east of the Bayshore Freeway had closed out 1992 with some twisted achievements. At 2.3 square miles with a population shy of twenty-four thousand, the little city of East Palo Alto was making headlines coast to coast as the "murder capital of the nation." The per capita murder rate was six times higher than New York City's, more than double Detroit or Washington, DC's, and nearly triple that of Compton, home of the Crips and Bloods. You know you're in trouble when you're leaving the OGs of street violence in the dust. Most of it came from turf wars over dope sales controlled by rival gangs that had consolidated power behind bars. Deals gone bad also took a toll, killing some of the out-of-towners who were flooding into town to do their crack shopping. Our own elementary schools were holding fundraisers to bury kids caught in the crossfire. And there were other "firsts." East Palo Alto topped the region for residents on welfare and on felony parole, since so many of us had been churned through the prison system and spat back out with no access to a livelihood. Violence wasn't the only public health crisis. East Palo Alto had the highest HIV rate west of Chicago. That hit home. My brother Pat was sick with AIDS, my brother David was HIV positive, and Ronald and I would later learn we'd contracted hepatitis C. With all the surviving Nunn brothers sickened from sharing needles, we were just shy of a straight flush. And we had plenty of company. The Belle Haven neighborhood just to our north mirrored the same conditions, and the Hill Avenue house was a hot spot. (Since Belle Haven wasn't its own city, the rich side of Menlo Park diluted the numbers.) Punishment clearly wasn't working for our community unless the goal was to kill us all off. We knew we needed a nonpolice solution. And who better than us to come up with one?

Most of us who'd gotten together on this January day amid the wafting smells of motor oil and Bay brine had contributed to the damage. David Lewis started slinging heroin on these streets at age fifteen and kept on doing it for decades as he cycled in and out of prison. We were ready to take responsibility. The day grew dark, and when the community space closed, we headed to Priya's house to continue the conversation. We knew we didn't want another standard twelve-step program. Instead, we dreamed of something that would help stop the cycle of incarceration and multigenerational addiction, incorporate access to care for HIV and AIDS, and feed and house our community members until they were ready to reunite with family. We pledged to treat our brothers and sisters, nephews, aunties, neighbors, and friends with dignity and acceptance. We knew we were full of brilliance. If we learned together to love ourselves, to heal ourselves, we could reclaim that brilliance collectively.

AS THE FIRST of the Nunn siblings to get clean, I was catapulted into a family leadership position whether I was ready or not. Through sober eyes, I took in the shit show as my brothers and their friends and occasionally my little sister, Gloria, turned the Hill Avenue home into a full-blown crack house. I was still driving my moms to dialysis three times a week, but her health was failing fast. One day I realized I couldn't leave her there, so I moved her in with me and Al. On some nights we'd talk for hours, about the early days in the church she cofounded, about her own regrets as a woman, a mother, and a Christian. I tried to make up for the hole I'd left in her heart when I asked her to put her hand on the Bible and lie for me. She slept in my bed with me. I kept her fed and warm, and I tried to keep her safe.

But I was out of my depth. Even though my son had made me a grandfather at age thirty-one, I'd barely mastered the art of changing a baby's diaper. Being the sole caregiver for a dying parent was another level of real. One day, while I was at work at LSPC, my mother fell out of bed. I found a nursing home for Lula Mae Nunn. And that's where she died on August 27, 1992.

Pat was at Project Ninety at the time; he'd finally agreed to give it a go. But when our moms died, he went AWOL. Being sick and weak made him a target on the streets, so when I found him living in a storage shed, I brought him to the Hill Avenue house. At least it had a bathroom. I wanted to find a rehab program close to home that would welcome him, even with full-blown AIDS, a program that could teach him to love himself and allow him to die with dignity and a clear head. It didn't exist. Pat's circumstance helped steer my vision for Free at Last. It became a testament of my love for all my addicted siblings, and for my entire beautiful, battered community.

187

At LSPC, I spent my workdays reading and answering all the prisoner mail, hustling around the state to panel discussions and debates, helping to advocate for women inside, and developing a theory of what community recovery should and could look like. Meanwhile, for nearly two years, I met biweekly with the other Free at Last cofounders to fine-tune our vision, formulate our bylaws, and painstakingly design each aspect of the program, from the services we'd partner with to the housing we'd provide. We knew we wanted participants to understand their circumstances in political terms, just like I'd learned to do on the prison yard at DVI and at San Quentin. Poor Black and brown communities, with shit education, sky-high unemployment, and soaring incarceration rates disadvantaged us before we were out of diapers. And the thirst to lock us all up was reaching a peak. I knew from experience that understanding that context helped replace self-loathing with self-determination and self-respect. As founding board members, we were determined that Free at Last serve as a declaration of how all human beings should be treated and valued. We pledged to save our community one addict at a time, one house at a time, one block at a time. Getting the word out was easy. Most of us were already attending every criminal trial and funeral in town. It was a busy year-round schedule. With some guidance from Priya, I also learned to reel in the green. It wasn't long before we were celebrating my first catch: twenty-five thousand dollars from the San Francisco Foundation. As I made my rounds to speak out against Three Strikes and the repeal of the Prisoner Bill of Rights, I made a point of telling the family members of victims of violence what I was up to. Punishment was not the only answer. My community was in the crosshairs of tremendous violence, *caused* in part by all that blanket incarceration. "I'm concerned about these problems too," I'd say. "And I'm helping to create programs out there on the streets that will reduce violence."

Pat didn't live to see us open our doors. He was dying before our eyes, and the only coping skill he had was self-medication. It wasn't serving him. Addiction is a survival tool, but it stunts emotional maturity, and catching up takes time. It's hard fucking work. Al had run with my older brothers before I'd even met him, and as a counselor at Project Ninety we hoped he could bring Pat back into the fold. He was skinny as a fishing rod, and we'd bring him over to our place and prod him to eat. Most of all, we let him know he was loved, whether he got clean or not. He spent his final weeks in a convalescent home for penniless rejects. We could hear dying men all around him moaning and screaming in pain. There was fear in the air, and some of it was Pat's. The God he'd grown up with was a punishing God, and he had nothing to look forward to for living a life of addiction and crime other than the fires of eternal hell. When his spirit gave up in early November 1993, I made a pledge never to let another family member die this way.

We buried Pat the day after his funeral. It was a holiday, with just a couple of gravediggers on duty. So me, my little brother, David, and Pat's son, Tiny, helped them get the casket into the ground. There was no one else around. I hadn't planned it, but that's where I did David's intervention. Just like Pat, David had contracted HIV. But I knew that if he held on, if he got healthy and bought some time, he'd have a chance of surviving.

"Dave, this is not like sickle cell anemia," I told him. "There's too many white people that got this shit for it to be ignored. It's not gonna be incurable for long."

I wasn't attuned to the war gay men were waging to pressure the world of science to get off its ass and develop some effective medicine. But I was right about one thing: there was politics in medicine. By the time we buried Pat, HIV was the number one cause of death among Americans aged twenty-five to forty-four. Better treatments were coming.

With Moms and Pat now gone, my heart was cracking. I couldn't face losing another brother, especially David, my ally and best friend when we were small. By now, I was crying. Gravestones as far as the eye could see weren't helping.

"Man, look around," I said. "You gonna make me drag your ass out here by my fucking self? It's unfair. It's fucking unfair, homeboy."

The words reached Dave. He agreed to treatment, and we needed to move fast. Free at Last wasn't quite ready—we opened the drop-in center in January 1994 and got our recovery homes up and running later that year—so we took him to Project Ninety. Later that night, the staff would call me and tell me to come get him because he was so loaded. You're supposed to have at least a certain number of hours clean when you show up, so you don't prance in on a cloud and make everybody else dream of using. It was a rough start, but Dave went back. On his one-year sobriety birthday, I asked him what he wanted. He chose Disneyland, for the Fourth of July parade. I took the whole family.

My sister Gloria got sober next, at Free at Last's outpatient program. Once she got clean, she got a job too, as the Free at Last childcare specialist. She was later hired as a mentor and shared her love until she moved to the Central Valley. These days she sings in a church choir.

FREE AT LAST would eventually expand beyond the city borders, serving people in our residential drug treatment program and another program geared specifically for those coming out of incarceration. But building something so novel from scratch was a slow process. David Lewis and Priya Haji were the youngest among us, so we made him chairman of the board and her executive director. (Both would die tragically, and far too young.) As formerly incarcerated people, we had our own language and our own way of doing outreach. Those of us who'd lived in cages and gotten clean led by example. We showed up in nice cars, wearing nice clothes. We wanted the younger generation to see that we had places to live and legal ways to survive. That we were healthy. And we fished for other older addicts we knew, people who'd been out on the streets with us when we were coming up. People like my own siblings. As they got clean, their example trickled down too. I practiced the kind of organizing I'd learned inside San Quentin, talking to men one by one while I was selling weed and serving on the Men's Advisory Council. The violence that had put East Palo Alto on the national map was one of the issues we set out to address, but not by locking up the whole community. We knew exactly which drug dealers to go to, and we laid out the logic. All this killing was bad for business. There had to be a better way for the dope world to address conflict. Some of them heard us. In 1996 I was recognized for my efforts when I was selected as a Community Fellow of the California Wellness Foundation's Violence Prevention Initiative. It came with fifty thousand bucks. Sometimes, in academic circles, people ask, "What is your theory of change?" I did have some theories, spelled out in my LSPC research paper. But when you're living it, sometimes the change comes before the theory. Sometimes, it outpaces theory. The real question should be, what is your motherfucking practice? Me and David Lewis and Vicki Smothers and the other core team at Free at Last could sleep at night when it came to practice. While the mainstream voting public and nearly every elected official poured billions of dollars into locking up poor Black and brown communities, we were taking in our homies, cleaning them up, feeding them, and housing them so they could heal and return to their families in productive ways. We were showing our love, and the statistics proved it was working. We not only helped reduce violence, we reduced homelessness, so my own brothers and hundreds of other men and women didn't have to sleep in cars and storage sheds. It was a template for building a grassroots army, and when we formerly incarcerated people later united as All of Us or None, we'd have eager members in East Palo Alto prepared to form a chapter of their own.

I WAS WORKING hard for my community, and for the most part my family was part of that equation. By the time my sister Gloria was in outpatient treatment, my brother David was doing what I had done, stretching out his stay at Project Ninety long enough to make it stick. As for Ronald, when he wasn't squatting at the Hill Avenue house, he was bouncing from jail to the streets. I bought him a van, so he wouldn't freeze to death, only to find it parked at his dealer's house. At one point I showed up at the Hill Avenue house, and not a single relative was staying there; a bunch of other people were. My eldest sister, Joyce, and I had already busted our asses several times fixing up our trashed family home while my moms was there in response to city code violations. We'd replaced the busted windows, installed new floors, scraped out the blackened, rotting windowsills where the rain had gotten in. But it never lasted, and the truth is, all that sweat labor didn't get at the heart of the problem. David Lewis knew I was dedicated to healing the community, but one day, he turned to me and uttered some blunt, plain truth.

"You do all this fucking work. Why don't you come home and just shut down the motherfucking street where people are selling dope right in front of your momma's house?"

I knew he was right. Being an absentee landlord wasn't working. Besides, my little brother would be needing a place to stay, and ultimately a place to die. I kicked everyone out and threw everything except the family photos in the trash. There was a rotting sandwich under a mattress. That went in the garbage too. There was also a foreclosure notice in the mail. It was New Year's Eve, and I didn't have the money. So my niece Tina and I drove up to Ellen Barry's house in Oakland, and she gave us a loan. Thanks to Ellen, I was able to save the Nunn family's only asset. I moved back in and stayed for good. When David came out of rehab, his room was clean and waiting. Then, just like Al had, he went back to school and became a drug and alcohol counselor. My new roomie and I got tighter than we'd been when we were kids.

Finally, it was Ronald's turn.

I've always maintained good relations with addicts and dealers in my community. We come from the same circumstances, so there's no judgment. When I gave myself over to crack, some of them wouldn't sell to me. They'd tell me, "Dorsey, man, you too good for this shit." Or they'd share some product free of charge and then tell me to get the fuck out of their house. When we experienced our first relapse of a Free at Last staff member, it was dealers who walked in to tell us, "This motherfucker ain't on your side." Even they were conscious enough to recognize the positive nature of the work we were doing. We fired the brother right there on the good word of a dope dealer. To this day, I don't snitch. And I don't judge. I'm just there to help when they're ready for it. All of this came in handy at Ronald's intervention, in the fall of 2005. It came a dozen years after David's and also involved a funeral, this time of a childhood friend named Michael Tate. Tate was a root family name, just like Nunn. There was even a Tate Street in East Palo Alto. Michael was among the many who'd gotten clean at Free at Last. But he shared needles, just like most of us had. He died of AIDS.

Being an active addict isn't conducive to processing death and grief. Ronald freaked out every time someone close to him died, just like Pat had. So I had to hunt him down to drag his ass to Michael Tate's funeral. By the time we got to the church, the only place left to sit was the front row. If all your friends are

193

thugs, gangsters, and addicts, even recovering addicts, they're gonna leave that row nice and empty. As Ronald and I walked up the aisle, I could see he was already getting dope sick. So I motioned for one of the local dealers to meet me at the back of the church. "Man," I told him, "if you fix my brother, I'll pay you. And this'll be probably the last time you fix my brother—because I'm about to put him in a program."

Ronald didn't know it, but I'd been struck brilliant by an idea. All those familiar faces in the church pews were a map of Ronald's long life of misery. First, I pulled out David Lewis. Then I pulled out three other brothers of varying ages, and we all stood around Ronald in a circle. I told him I'd fix him, but I had something else to say.

"Ronald, look at us," I told him. "You done got loaded with four generations of people. So when do you stop using? What are you missing? What are you scared of?"

As his high wore off later that day, I brought him over to Free at Last. I should've sat him in a chair in the window. Like Al, Ronald was hope for the most hopeless addicts out there. When we got him to the men's residential program, I learned he'd started shooting heroin as a fourteen-year-old on Easter Sunday, 1958. He hadn't been clean more than thirty days at a stretch since, days he'd spent in jail. He was now in his early sixties. If Free at Last could help Ronald shake addiction, that in itself was all the proof we needed of our theory of change.

AS A MAN coming off an addiction, year after year I was recovering pieces of my humanity that had been buried under dope. And it was Ellen and my other women colleagues at LSPC who helped me reflect in a deep and genuine way on the damage I'd caused. Just by sharing their life stories, they helped me recognize how many people I'd hurt while I was chasing a high, how many kids I'd stepped over on the way to play sticky fingers and get loaded with their mothers. I also heard every one of my coworkers' broken hearts tales. *Damn*, I'd think to myself, *that is some doggish shit. I don't want to be like* that *motherfucker*.

For a while I was the only man on the payroll. I was so in tune, so much better educated about the bodies of women, that when some of the staff started going through the change, I bought each and every one a personal desk fan. I didn't know it at the time, but with all their wisdom and their ability to call me on my bullshit, the women of LSPC were preparing me for true love. They were preparing me for marriage. Thanks to them, I fell in love with the idea of being in love before I even had somebody to love. It became a socially acceptable state of mind. Then, one evening, I laid eyes on Sheila Hackett at an NA meeting in East Palo Alto.

Sheila wasn't that much taller than I was, but her quiet self-assurance gave her a special kind of stature. She had caramel skin and eyes like sparkling firecrackers that pulled me into her orbit and held me there like a rabbit in the crosshairs. I couldn't take my eyes off her. She was managing a sober living home for women and I knew right off she was good at it: tough yet tender, fair-minded, and straightforward in a "don't even think of pulling bullshit" kind of way. In the postmeeting mingle around the coffee pot, I asked for her phone number. It went into my front pocket and stayed there. I didn't call, and that was yet another sign of how I was maturing as a man. I had a serious girlfriend at the time. There were many years when that wouldn't have stopped me from calling or from cheating. But my sobriety, my homies in the Circle of Recovery, and the wall-to-wall women back at the office had bestowed some gifts on my disposition. I was able to slow down, to *not* respond to my cravings. I guess overcoming temptation takes practice, because I'd ask Sheila for her number three more times over the next four years before I finally dialed it. New Dorsey didn't want to cause pain. I'd like to think that's why I waited. But I could also see in Sheila's unspoken power that coming to her as a cheater was not the way to start something that had any chance of lasting. The fourth and final time I asked, she looked up at me with her shining eyes, raised her eyebrows, and asked, "Are you really ready?"

AS THE 1990s wore on, we tracked the toll on our communities like gamblers on a losing streak. By 1996, 43 percent of California prisoners locked up on a third strike were Black, even though we were just 7 percent of the state population. About a third of third-strike prisoners were Latino. Only a fourth were white. Meanwhile, prisons were packed—but not with the kinds of people who kidnap and strangle little girls. In 1980, the year before I got out, nearly two-thirds of the human beings in California prisoners were committed for violent offenses, a fourth for property crimes and only 7 percent for drug crimes. In 1995, those sent up for violent crimes were down to 42 percent of the state prison population, property crimes held steady, and those sentenced for drug crimes had climbed to one fourth. It was a wholesale assault on our communities with no evidence of any benefit to public safety.

One day in early 1997, we looked around and realized how much the number of organizations working in the trenches to challenge our ballooning prison system had grown. All those folks who had filled the courtroom at my sentencing were still speaking out on behalf of prisoners. Also raising their voices with new and cogent arguments were academic abolitionists, including two powerful Black women: former political prisoner Angela Davis, who had become a tenured professor in UC Santa Cruz's graduate program on the history of consciousness; and Ruthie Gilmore, an assistant professor at UC Berkeley who was breaking ground with her theory of carceral geography while working to cofound the California Prison Moratorium Project. New activists were also springing up to advocate on behalf of specific communities—transgender prisoners, people with HIV or AIDS, the Filipino community, Black and brown victims of police violence, sex workers, and so on. Sometimes it seemed like every overcriminalized community was waking up out of a deep freeze to stir in protest. Our collective connections to prisoners engaged in the struggle on the inside were also expanding year by year. The magnitude of the crisis had seeded a revival of the prisoner rights movement—just how vibrant, we were yet to realize. But we knew it was time to come to-   **197** gether, share strategies, and build alliances. For the most part, we at LSPC considered ourselves practical abolitionists. We absolutely wanted to block new prison construction, shut down existing shitholes, and work toward the large-scale release of people confined to cages. But we were also invested in improving conditions for those who remained inside, even though that invariably channeled dollars into the prison industry. The need to unite was so urgent these differences felt inconsequential at the time.

It was two LSPC interns who came up with the idea for a national conference: Gita Drury and Cassandra Shaylor, who'd set aside her pursuit of a legal career to pursue a Ph.D. in Angela Davis's program at UC Santa Cruz. Gita and Cassandra brought in the first batch of funding we needed to make the conference real, and came up with the title too: Critical Resistance. Then,

What Kind of Bird Can't Fly

Ellen blessed me once again when she tapped me to sit on the conference organizing committee. Of the more than two dozen of us, most were women. For nearly two years, we met weekly, breathing life into that collective vision. We even held a series of preconferences around the country to gather feedback and ideas from other community organizers and incarcerated people. We were holding on to the tail of the dragon. Still, we had no idea how much our creation would change the course of history.

Chapter 14

PREACHING TO THE CHOIR

I sat on a raised stage in the Pauley Ballroom at UC Berkeley with a stunned smile on my face. The crowd was huge, and every single person had shown up to deconstruct and demolish the economic machine that was locking up more brilliance than any other nation in the modern world. The setting was no accident. The oak-paneled ballroom with a thirty-foot ceiling and views of Sather Gate and the iconic campus clock tower made it clear we were on the inside for a change, situated in the heart of academia, where intellectual movements get made.

It was an early Friday afternoon in September 1998, and I was about to moderate the opening plenary of "Critical Resistance: Beyond the Prison Industrial Complex." Though we called it a conference, it was part revolution, part multicultural celebration, and part leftist study session. The plenary featured formerly incarcerated people and current prisoners who were speaking through proxies. We called it "Voices for Freedom," and our lived experience was arguably at the heart of this three-day happening. That also went for the men and women in the San Francisco County jail we'd be looping in by video conference for panel discussions the following day. But there was so much more on the schedule that our program covered seventeen pages in small print. Every one of the more than two hundred panels, skills workshops, roundtables, films, and live musical performances was geared to redefining the nation's thinking about people in cages and the system that was confining them. We knew people of color were wildly overrepresented in lockup. We knew women were the fastest-growing group of prisoners. And that juveniles now deemed "superpredators" were being cut off from any chance of life before they had even developed common sense. If you were down for a radical critique of the prison industry, you were welcome as ice cream on apple pie.

At first, we estimated that five hundred people would turn out. We doubled that to a thousand when we released the conference program. More than thirty-five hundred attended. Radical organizers, nonprofit leaders, lawyers, students, and academics came from every state in the US and eleven different countries, along with some formerly incarcerated people and family members of those still inside. We charged no registration fee, asking people to donate what they could. The big open tent only enhanced our sense of unity. Some of us had been sprinting in our running shoes throughout the nineties, as if our house was on fire. Because it was. They say power abhors a vacuum. In my view, the prison industrial complex exploded in the eighties and nineties *because* of the vacuum created when intellectuals abandoned the reform movement—and that started happening even before I got out. Now we could see the intellectuals coming back. We had professors and lecturers sitting on panels from UC San Diego, UC Santa Cruz, UC

200

Berkeley, Stanford University, and more. Some attendees were self-proclaimed progressives whose work wasn't dedicated to conceptualizing the role of punishment in our society—yet. But it would be soon. Because the conference was a game changer. In 1994, I'd helped unite defenders of the rights of undocumented immigrants with those of us fighting to stop blanket criminalization of Black and brown communities. The Critical Resistance conference took that kind of alliance building to the next level, bringing Latino, Filipino, LGBTQ, and Indigenous organizers into the fold along with labor leaders, civil rights attorneys, and even environmentalists.

On opening night, we packed into Wheeler Hall to share our collective outrage, energy, and commitment to change. There wasn't a free seat in the auditorium, and there were plenty of people standing. Singer-songwriter Faith Nolan, a lesbian Canadian sister of African and Indigenous descent, blew her mouth harp and belted out the blues in a gravelly call to action. *It's been a long time, it's been comin'. It's been a long time it's been here. / We got no jobs, no schools, no future. There ain't much happening here. / It's been a long time comin' . . . gonna be a long time here.* She was right: it had been a long time comin'. An era of setbacks that felt like endless Arctic winter. Then, Angela Davis brought the house down.

"We want to talk this weekend about radical strategies," she said to shouts and cheers and screams. "Radical strategies that help our brothers and sisters who are inside, that help to alleviate the misery and the pain and at the same time move toward the abolition of prisons as the only attempt to solve the major social issues of our times."

We were done with "reform." It was time to transform. Even those of us who weren't strict abolitionists agreed. We were there to take back the conversation.

Writer, activist, and scholar Mike Davis was the person who came up with the term *prison industrial complex*. He got up on stage holding a chunk of prison-gray concrete. As a white kid growing up in the 1950s, that mix of cement, sand, and gravel symbolized a different kind of growth: dams and highways and hospitals that for a lot of people meant unionized jobs with decent pay. Even Black folks landed some of those jobs, though my daddy sure wasn't one of them. Now, Davis told the crowd, that concrete told a different story, about claustrophobia and human oppression. Because across the state and especially in rural counties hungry for jobs, prison after prison was spoiling the horizon. To call them warehouses was generous. One prison administrator had described them to Davis as "human landfills."

The engine powering all this growth had made some people damned rich and left our communities more hollowed out than ever—*no jobs, no schools, no future.* That was what we were convened to discuss. It was a new analysis for a new circumstance. Every bit of our seventeen-page conference schedule came back to the connection between the punishment industry and the corporate economy. Until now, the term *prison industrial complex* was limited to academic circles and pointy heads who talked about Michel Foucault's panopticon. By the time we wrapped, *prison industrial complex* was on its way to becoming a part of the movement lexicon. It even had an acronym—PIC.

When it was my turn at the microphone that night, I called that multicolored crowd of all ages and sexual orientations sitting in front of me the "choir," because when we first started organizing, that's what some skeptics kept telling me we'd be preaching to.

202

"The first thing I need to say, choir, is that *somebody* needs to preach to the choir, because we all been singing a different song," I said to a shout or two of "Amen."

In the span of my own lifetime, our state prison population had broken the charts. And the trend was national. As I stood on that stage, the total number of human beings our country was holding in prisons and jails from coast to coast had topped 1.8 million. Women were still in the minority by far, but unjust drug laws had sent the rate soaring. Back in 1970, there were only five thousand women doing time in the nation's prisons. When we convened at UC Berkeley, that number had topped one hundred thousand.

"Choir," I said, "somebody need to preach."

For the next two days, we took over classrooms to hold dozens of brainstorming gatherings. There were practical sessions on how to become a prisoner rights activist. Participants pulled chairs into circles to deconstruct racism and the War on Drugs, police abuse, the school-to-prison pipeline, the plight of criminalized battered women, the powerful role of jailhouse lawyers, medical neglect, psychiatric abuse inside the walls, and more. Sexism, classism, racism, and heterosupremacy was front and center. And the talk wasn't just about tearing down prisons. It was about redirecting wealth. What *if*, we asked, all that money getting suctioned out of our communities went instead to housing, to education, to respect for human dignity at the front end of the equation? It had been a long time comin'. And it was well past time to band together.

JUST AS WE started piecing together plans for the Critical Resistance conference, I got myself invited to New Zealand to attend

203

ICOPA VIII—the eighth International Conference on Penal Abolition. It turned out the rest of the world had been talking about prison abolition for years—in Canada, the Netherlands, Poland, Costa Rica, and Spain. The Quakers had even held an ICOPA conference in Indiana. But the people attending had been mostly if not exclusively academics. My invitation to the February 1997 conference broke ground. I had already traveled to visit Mariona prison in El Salvador. Not long after, I'd fly to Havana to interview political fugitive Assata Shakur, a powerful sister who'd been granted political asylum in Cuba. She helped me understand how Fidel Castro's socialist experiment was handling domestic abuse, especially when women committed acts of violence in self-defense. Next came a trip to South Africa with Angela Davis. The exposure was expanding my analysis, helping me develop a deeper understanding of punishment and healing.

204

My visit to New Zealand, though, came with a glitch that pointed to my own naiveté after so many years in cages—and to the cluelessness of ICOPA organizers. They'd clearly never invited a formerly incarcerated person to pop on over to another continent before. I had a passport and thousands of dollars of cash in my money belt, and when I hopped on the plane, I was feeling happy and strong, even smug. Then I landed in Auckland.

"Your visa, sir?" the customs and immigration agent said, holding out her hand.

I assumed she was talking about a credit card, and I only had a MasterCard and Amex on me. In a small room away from the crowds, I answered questions on a form and scored seven out of ten. *Not bad*, I thought. A solid C. But the ones I got wrong did me in: Have you spent up to five years in prison? Up to ten?

Have you been to prison during the past twenty years? Turns out I'd neglected to apply to enter the country. That kind of visa. If I *had* applied, I might not have been accepted. Luckily I'd thought to stuff a conference brochure into my bag. There was a fax number in tiny print at the bottom. I faxed the conference organizer. Hours later I was told I could go. I crept out of the airport paranoid as a motherfucker. Suddenly I felt a personal affinity for undocumented folks back home. I wouldn't learn until the conference opened a few days later that the country's former prime minister—the conference keynote speaker—had secured me one-time permission to enter.

An international gathering of people talking about the need to get rid of prisons was enough to blow a brother's mind. But my deepest education came on our visit to Mt. Eden Prison. It helped me recognize our practices in the US were not inevitable or unchangeable. I was standing on the gun rail as our guide explained how the Mt. Eden establishment responded to prisoners who got violent. They used high-powered water hoses. Nonlethal weapons. I thought back to all those dead bodies I'd seen at DVI and San Quentin. Guards firing real bullets at real men. Guards orchestrating deadly race wars and sitting back to watch the show. The reality hit me hard, and I felt the tears. In New Zealand, they valued the life of the incarcerated more than we did. Punishment is political. I'd known it. Now I felt it.

Despite the gentler treatment from the gun rails, the oppression of dark-skinned and Indigenous people was and is a fact of life in New Zealand, and oppression makes for natural allies. I made some Maori friends on that trip, and that's how I first learned about restorative justice. New Zealand was so far ahead of us that the mainstream criminal justice system had already started embracing those old Maori traditions, employing community problem-solving to repair harm. It was fodder for dialogue when our own conference exploded like a bomb of righteous energy the following year.

By the time it wrapped up, the Critical Resistance conference had already spun off a couple of new organizations. The most central among them was the abolitionist group by the same name, cofounded by Angela Davis, Ruthie Gilmore, and others. LSPC served as the group's fiscal sponsor until it became its own nonprofit. Meanwhile, all our new alliances were bearing fruit. A couple of years after the conference, we teamed with environmentalists in an effort to halt construction of Kern Valley State Prison, known as Delano II. In 2001 a judge agreed—at least temporarily. I wanted that project killed because building more concrete human landfills violated our civil rights and degraded our humanity. I also thought it was an outrage that California would put a prison in the Central Valley birthplace of farmworkers union founder Cesar Chavez. That was shitting on a hero's holy ground. My arguments didn't persuade the judge. What did was the prospect of the Tipton kangaroo rat going extinct and the watershed running dry. I'd lived in some rat-infested places, and I didn't care much for them, even the kangaroo variety. But I learned a lot—about biology and hydrology, but mostly about strategy.

By now my analysis of what needed changing had deepened beyond working to improve conditions of confinement, which is where it started when Michael Satris walked into San Quentin to demonstrate an alternative to rage and violence. To be clear: I will *always* work to improve the lives of human beings in cages and coming out of cages. But by the time our Critical Resistance

206

conference wrapped up, I knew we had to speak forcefully, un-apologetically, and in unison about the systemic racism and profiteering at the heart of our nation's criminal justice system and push to dismantle it. We called it by a familiar name: slavery. The parallels had been on my mind ever since the very first guard ordered me to do that denigrating dance: *Squat, cough, lift up your nuts. Let me look behind your ear.* Now the concept had crystalized. The US prison system grew out of the abolition of slavery and was powered by the same marriage of racism and profiteering. Both sucked up our labor while brutalizing us psychologically and physically. What I didn't know back when I was hollering to the choir and getting high off our collective commitment was that a quarter of a century later, as I eased into my seventies, I'd be working my ass off to remove the vestiges of slavery from the California and US Constitutions, to prohibit the practice by making it illegal, not just invisible.

207

THE CRITICAL RESISTANCE conference marked a cultural moment for the prison abolition movement. I was proud of the work I did to help make it happen. But I wasn't satisfied. In the aftermath, I worked through those feelings with a brilliant new comrade who swore as much as I did. At twenty-two years old, George Galvis was already an activist, plugged in with Barrios Unidos, doing deep work with youth to heal rifts on the streets and behind bars that lead to too much dying. He'd done his time as a juvenile and was getting his degree at UC Berkeley in ethnic studies. He'd go on to earn a master's in urban planning. I was a generation older than George, and in late-night talks he confided in me about the shame he'd been taught to feel about his past. His record was sealed. He could have buried it, gone on to be a university academic and made himself some real money. But later, he thanked me for the fact that he hadn't. I helped him understand that he didn't have to apologize for who he was. His lived experience was a strength. The truth is, there weren't that many directly impacted people like me and George in the organizing mix at Critical Resistance, so we gravitated to each other and made bonds that haven't broken. He was having some of the same imposter syndrome I've experienced my whole life and have become so expert at covering with laughter and rough language. I know it's a trap. As men of color who've been formerly incarcerated, we carry the stigma of being perceived as predatory, dangerous. We're made to feel like it's *our* job to help others feel safe around us. In doing so, we compromise ourselves. I decided on the prison yard back in San Quentin not to play that game. I *can* code-switch, but I do it on my own terms. It's kept me true to myself and to my mission on behalf of others similarly situated, even if it's cost me. I modeled that for George from the moment we met, and because of that, he's told me, he learned to be unbroken, uncompromising, and unapologetic. My loud voice and George's loud voice found a lasting brotherhood. Because as George says, sometimes making people uncomfortable is a good and necessary thing. More than two decades later, I can be in a room where he's cussing up a storm and everyone says, "Man, Dorsey, George been around you too long."

As George and I got to deconstructing the conference, we recognized that even antioppression efforts can reproduce systems of oppression. Yes, the event had tried hard to center the voices of the formerly incarcerated, but we'd been in the minority, and when it came to the movement building that followed, we were mostly relegated to secondary roles. At my sentencing back in 1991, I had been beyond grateful to have Vincent Schiraldi, Margaret, and Michael in my corner speaking for me—and I still held those relationships close. But even with our allies, it always seemed that those of us who had survived the prison system were being spoken *of*, spoken *for*. As the next few years went by, not much changed. A lot of folks with academic credentials and class privilege still seemed comfortable standing in the spotlight, talking about us. That's when George and I concluded that it didn't have to be that way. And the only people who could change that status quo were us. One by one, then in small groups, we'd come together to have that conversation. Then we'd make our move. I didn't know it yet, but a core group of women newly released from federal prison would be critical to the effort.

Chapter 15

ALL OF US OR NONE

As members of All of Us or None, we pledge:

• To demand the right to speak in our own voices • To treat each other with respect and not allow differences to divide us • To accept responsibility for any acts that may have caused harm to our families, our communities or ourselves • To fight all forms of discrimination • To help build the economic stability of formerly-incarcerated people • To claim and take care of our own children and our families • To support community struggles to stop using prisons as the answer to social problems • To play an active role in making our communities safe for everyone

—From our founding document

A couple of years after the Critical Resistance conference, a crack appeared in the ice of our Arctic winter when we experienced our first ballot victory. Proposition 36 called for probation and drug treatment instead of jail or prison for people convicted of possessing, using, or transporting drugs. All those sentencing enhancements, the militarization of policing, and the impact of the Three Strikes law had finally brought us into a space where people other than us soldiers found endless punishment to be unacceptable. In the November 2000 election, 61 percent of California voters pushed it over the victory line. It was clear that punishing addiction wasn't working. That same year, only a fourth of prisoners committed to California's prisons were there for acts of violence, while 39 percent had been sentenced for drug crimes. Proposition 36 was our first attempt to slow that shit down, and it was personal: My son, Anthony—who we now called Sockie—was no stranger to county jail. Drugs had landed him there. My work on Prop 36 came just in time to spare him the prison experience, just like I'd promised myself I would when I tracked him down on that winter evening in 1981. The measure's passage also marked our first successful effort to chip away at Three Strikes, however modest, because it applied to *some* people who otherwise would have gone away for life.

Meanwhile, a trickle of people was starting to come home, including some high-powered women I had the pleasure of meeting at the Federal Correctional Institute (FCI) in Dublin, California. Donna Willmott and Ida McCray—both political fugitives before they did time—were first to come out, joining us at the Critical Resistance conference in 1998. I was enjoying the company of these women, and as we talked, we realized it was time to broaden our focus beyond the shit show inside prisons to what formerly incarcerated people faced when they came out.

Around the same time, I also started meeting with another group of radicalized former prisoners. Geronimo Ji-Jaga Pratt had won his release in 1997, when a judge agreed that prosecutors withheld evidence at his trial that would have proved him innocent. Of the San Quentin six, David Johnson was recently out while Sundi Tate and Luis Talamantez had hit the streets decades earlier. So had Tha. All of these men had impacted me deeply when I was inside, and along with a brother named Robert Moody, they invited me to riff with them about community needs. We got together a couple times a month at a downtown Oakland office Robert Moody leased to teach job skills. We called ourselves "Timers" and had matching T-shirts made with the symbol of an hourglass. We brainstormed about how to reach brothers and sisters inside jail to let them know we weren't poverty pimps, we were for real and here to help. We puzzled through what to do to help our elders. And when we could, we doled out material help to homies in need. Sometimes all it took to help a formerly incarcerated brother keep his family together was enough money to pay the PG&E bill and buy his woman a load of groceries. It was Geronimo who posed a big question one day as we were leaving a meeting: As formerly incarcerated people, why weren't we better organized? It was another seed planted.

213

At the end of 2001, nearly a decade after Ellen Barry hired me right out of rehab, she sprinkled more fairy dust on me. It was time for her to step back from the organization, and true to the collaborative nature of LSPC, she promoted me to director of programs and Karen Shain to administrative director. We'd run the place together as codirectors for nearly ten years until I took the reins on my own. I'd already become one of LSPC's most prominent public faces, speaking at marches and rallies. But they were always other people's marches and rallies—antiwar, women's rights, or immigrant rights events where I'd get five minutes at the mic. As formerly incarcerated people, we decided we were done with that. Our first solo event took place in San

Francisco's Dolores Park in 2001. For the first time we were the headliners, not the backup singers. Ida McCray, Angela Davis, and Frank "Big Black" Smith, a leader of the 1971 prisoner Attica Prison uprising, spoke. So did I—about our trampled civil and human rights on the outside, after we'd supposedly done our time and paid our dues. Up at the mic, I imagined what it might take for us to have the ability to be employed, to be housed. And I asked the question, "Don't we have, not the privilege, but the *right* to be considered human beings?" The park gathering wasn't big, but it was ours. And it felt right. We were at a fork in the road.

The next powerhouse to come out of FCI Dublin was Linda Evans, Ida's longtime cellmate. She and her now life partner, filmmaker Eve Goldberg, had participated in the Critical Resistance conference organizing, even though Linda—a former Weather Underground member doing time as a political prisoner—was still locked up. They authored "The Prison Industrial Complex and the Global Economy," a pamphlet we distributed in each registration packet. Linda had been organizing inside for years to help women prisoners with HIV and AIDS. She'd also managed to finish up a master's degree. After President Clinton commuted her sentence on his last day of office in January 2001, she moved to Los Angeles—and hated it. But luck or fate soon smiled on all of us. While Linda was searching for jobs on a radical listserv, one popped up that had her name all over it. The Center for Third World Organizing in Oakland was looking to hire someone who'd done prison time *and* had a postgraduate degree to head up a project organizing formerly incarcerated people. The hitch: the candidate would have to use the already-created project proposal to land a highly competitive Soros Fellowship from the Open Society

Foundation. For someone who just walked off sixteen years, it was a high bar to jump as job interviews go. But Linda flew to New York, nervous as hell, and sealed the deal in a boutique hotel. She felt out of her element, but just like that, she had a dream job and some funding. Her marching orders in late 2001 once she got to Oakland: "to increase civic participation of former prisoners, launch a public education campaign highlighting the social, political, and economic obstacles faced by former prisoners and engage in policy advocacy on behalf of them." The timing couldn't have been better. "Them" was us, and we were itching to increase our civic participation. It didn't take long before Linda picked up the phone and called. Soon she was spending just about all her time at the cramped LSPC offices on San Francisco's Market Street.

The capper on our righteous band of agitators was a fierce warrior for justice with softness in her eyes and steel in her soul. She was a damned good planner too. Hamdiya Cooks-Abdullah, whose cell was downstairs from Linda and Ida's at FCI Dublin, walked out in mid-2002 after serving a twenty-year sentence. For much of that, she supported Muslim women, most of them Black sisters, in the fight for access to headgear and the rights to prayer and religious celebration. She stood shoulder to shoulder with Native American women demanding a sweat lodge and headed up the Black Culture Workshop too. I'd met them all briefly in the late 1990s when Hamdiya and Linda organized a resource fair and invited LSPC to come hand out literature. That's when Hamdiya walked right up to me and, wasting no time on small talk, looked me in the eye.

"When I get out, I want to come work for you—as a paralegal," she said. I'm not a tall man, and Hamdiya and I stood pretty much face to face. I smiled at her. "I'm serious," she

215

added, quiet but firm. And she was. Hamdiya would stand with me at every turn and trial for the next two decades—through our struggle for self-determination, as I grew into my leadership, and as we labored together to build a national movement. I always will stand in awe of the degree to which she and these other women fresh out of prison took chances for the cause, when they were *still on parole*. I was used to working ninety-hour weeks, sleeping on other people's couches and floors while fighting for freedom. It felt good to have these comrades by my side who were willing to do the same.

The five of us who'd lived in cages met up a lot to talk, formally and informally. We shared our experiences with all those barriers that kept slamming down on us because of our felony convictions, even though we'd done our time. We didn't want to be viewed as other people's clients anymore, as other people's causes. We didn't want "services," didn't want to be seen as victims, people on the take, or a cause for charity. And we sure as hell didn't want to be stage props while people with more letters after their names fought on our behalf. What we wanted was the restoration of the civil and human rights to which we were entitled, and we were perfectly capable of demanding them ourselves. By now, that "we" had expanded beyond women in prison and their children, LSPC's core constituency when I first started working for Ellen. During my first decade at LSPC, I believed that if the public understood the oppression women in prison were facing, it would wake them up entirely and disabuse them of their stereotypes. The reality of who these women were and how the system was abusing them would counteract the dominant narrative of serial killers like Charlie Manson and Jeffrey Dahmer. It would put the lie to the ascendant dehumanization of Black male youth as "superpredators." It was a nice theory, but I was wrong. The floodgates of compassion did not open for women, and public hysteria kept on vilifying men and boys. We had a shot at winning the fight, I now believed, only if we were *all* in: formerly incarcerated people of all genders, all races, all ethnicities, all sexual orientations. Now *that* was an army that would keep on growing.

Not long after Hamdiya joined us, I put my thoughts to words in the paper I called "Save Our Selves," or SOS. It was an expression of our collective need for self-determination, and I sent it around to anyone and everyone doing the work across California and the country. The feedback was so strong we decided to host a convening. Since Linda was affiliated with the Center for Third World Organizing, it was the logical venue. It was housed in a Victorian mansion south of Lake Merritt, a neighborhood that had gone from white and wealthy to Black, brown, and blighted.

Anyone and everyone who had been locked in a cage was welcome. Linda brought her fierce and thoughtful skills to the organizing committee, as we conceptualized what we sought to accomplish, built out the weekend's agenda, and strategized about how to get the word out. We had help on the committee from a younger generation—George Galvis, who I'd gotten tight with during the Critical Resistance conference, and Marlene Sanchez, who left gang life as a teen to help first herself and then others meet their potential through the Center for Young Women's Development. Bringing the OG brothers into the convening was my domain: former Black Panthers, revolutionaries, and political prisoners I'd known from San Quentin, including Elder Freeman, Jitu Sadiki, and Timers Tha and Sundi. We also invited people from outside the Bay Area. Our

217

East Coast representative was a formerly incarcerated sister named Tina Reynolds. Our powerful Southern California contingent included Alex Sanchez, the founder of Homies Unidos, and Susan Burton, who was already becoming my trusted friend and confidante.

Susan was one of tens of thousands of sisters criminalized for their addiction to crack. She turned to self-medication after her young son was struck and killed by a car driven by an LAPD detective. She cycled in and out of prison many times after that, getting no help for her trauma or her addiction. Then she caught a break, got clean, and built a community in South Los Angeles called A New Way of Life for women newly released from jail and prison. Some had served one year, some thirty. Many were experiencing addiction. Just like Free at Last, it stepped into a void and made some magic. I'd met Susan a few years earlier when I was doing some organizing in Los Angeles. The brother I was with knew she had just gotten her first safe home up and running. That lit me up, and we went to visit her at the three-bedroom bungalow she was renting in South LA, near Watts. Susan was operating on a shoestring, sleeping in the living room, holding twelve-step meetings in the garage. As one of the founders of Free at Last, I knew how rare and necessary programs for formerly incarcerated women were, especially women with addiction. As for any run by formerly incarcerated women, they were unheard of. Right off, I knew we were soul siblings in the struggle. I didn't want to make any promises, but I had an idea. I tried to be vague.

"You know what, sistah?" I told her as we were getting ready to leave. "A chicken's gonna fall out the tree."

Not long after that, Karen Shain and I flew Susan up to San Francisco to meet with us. I had just wrapped up a two-year

California Wellness fellowship that I'd landed for my Free at Last antiviolence work. We had an in there, we told Susan, and Karen Shain could write a winning proposal with her hands tied behind her back. How about we applied for one on her behalf? The fifty thousand dollars over two years that Susan wound up getting meant she could finally pay herself a modest thousand dollars a month. Even more important than the money, she got hooked up with a leadership coach who helped her learn how to run a nonprofit.

WHEN WE GATHERED on Friday, March 14, 2003, for our three-day marathon, we looked around and realized we'd pulled it off. Like the Critical Resistance conference, it was intergenerational, multiracial, and multigendered. But this time it was entirely by and for formerly incarcerated people. The Center for Young Women's Development and Young Women United for Oakland even brought clients who'd just gotten out of juvenile detention. Every single person in the room had done time in prisons, jails, juvenile lockup, or immigration detention centers. Some had aligned with warring gangs when they were surviving in cages. They had to check that shit at the door. It was a big ask. But everyone who entered agreed that the oppression we were all facing was a greater uniter than those allegiances were a divider. It wasn't always perfect, and it wasn't always easy, and I can speak for myself when I say egos got in the way down the road. That's how we learned. Still, the vessel for change we committed to building that weekend provided space for our differences. We wrote it into our pledge: *to treat each other with respect and not allow differences to divide us.* Every single one of us in the room that day could call ourselves cofounders. And every new member since can too.

We weren't sure where we were headed yet, but we knew we were moving the needle, and it was electrifying. Suddenly I understood in a most visceral way why those in power didn't want to teach my enslaved ancestors to read and write, didn't want more than three to gather.

George was entrusted with the opening ceremony. He was twenty-five years old and grateful for the honor. Today, every-body's checklist for their social justice conference has an In-digenous invocation and blessing seeking permission from the people of the stolen land and all that. Back then, no one did it. Except for us. Thanks to George, we centered our spirituality. We burned sage. We burned grains from Africa. And we put out a photo board covered with the faces of loved ones who were still in cages and those who had died in cages. We were in a healing mode, a spiritual mode. Just about all of us had been feeling like wallpaper at social justice gatherings organized by the elite. George had compared it to white people driving the freedom bus in the civil rights struggle of the south. That weekend was different. It was as if we'd knocked that other bus driver out of the way, took the fool's seat, and started handing out maps, asking every passenger to play a role in determining where we were headed and how we would get there.

Collectively we identified many areas of focus, but we agreed to start with the discrimination people coming out of prison or jail face every day: the legal, financial, and social barriers impacting our right to employment, housing, food, education, health care, and the vote. We also got clear on the issue of language. We would push back on anyone who called us ex-offenders, ex-felons, ex-cons. We were and are human beings, first and foremost: formerly incarcerated *people*. I'd picked up that line of thinking from Eddie Ellis, a former Black Panther in New York I'd come to both clash with and deeply respect. To this day, if anyone ever calls me or my comrades by a name that doesn't humanize us, I correct them, whether it's a well-meaning ally, the editorial board of a major newspaper, or a bigshot in the White House. It's fundamental. And it's a battle we're still waging.

AT FIRST, IT seemed fitting to me that we name ourselves SOS, for Save Our Selves, after my call to action in the treatise I'd written. It was also a play on the international Morse code signal of distress. But when I suggested that at our gathering, Linda looked at me and rolled her eyes. "I hate it," she said. "This can't be our name." Linda has always been a steadying force. Strategic, fiercely intelligent, generally calm, and honest as hell. SOS, she thought, sounded selfish. It also suggested we were rats on a sinking ship. That *we* were the ones who needed saving. We all agreed it wasn't right. But we were stumped. Until fate smiled on us again about three months later. A small group of us was sitting around a table at the LSPC office when Donna Willmott, who was now on our staff, came bursting in.

"I found our name," she said, breathless.

Donna had just come from the San Francisco County Jail, where she was doing some work with incarcerated women, when she saw the Bertolt Brecht poem titled "All of Us or None." The beauty of it all: the man behind it was Nate Harrington, my childhood friend, my mentor, my teacher. I have no doubt Nate's spirit was sitting with us at the Center for Third World Organizing when we birthed our movement, and by our side as we pulled off the Critical Resistance conference too. He would have become one of our fiercest fighters. The fact that he wasn't alive to join forces with us is a tragedy that still owns a piece

221

of my heart. Nate and I had stayed close. He was a steady visitor to LSPC, and won over lots of party guests up at Margaret and Tricia Littlefield's paradise in Belvedere. His death was a freak accident. In the summer of 1997, during an argument at home with his seventeen-year-old son, he fell down the stairs and crashed through a window of the landing. He died from his injuries. I've done my best to offer love and support to Nate's son over the years as he carried that weight.

When Nate died, he was working for San Francisco's progressive sheriff, Michael Hennessey, helping men and women incarcerated in the county jail with civil legal matters, like divorces and child custody. He'd had a few careers before that, as a criminal defense attorney and an administrative law judge for the Berkeley Rent Stabilization Board. But he wanted to go back to his roots. The year after Nate died, Sheriff Hennessey dedicated the San Francisco County Jail's new law library to him, and honored him by installing a glass case in the lobby filled with his favorite things. The Bertolt Brecht poem "All of Us or None" was there, next to a Snickers bar and a copy of *The Wretched of the Earth,* a 1961 book by the psychiatrist Frantz Fanon that was among the many works of brilliance Nate had shared with me on the yard at DVI. It analyzes the dehumanizing effects of colonization on people and countries, and seeded ideas for the cultural decolonization work the Black Panthers began and that continues today.

"ALL OF US or none" became our core organizing principle. And that helped steer us through some rough water in the six months after that inaugural gathering. We were not the only group of formerly incarcerated people who were starting to come together. On the East Coast, another movement was taking shape. Eddie Ellis, the former Black Panther in New York who led us all in demanding that we be described as human beings, not ex-cons or felons, had launched an organization called NuLeadership Policy Group with another formerly incarcerated brother named Divine Pryor. It was what people refer to as a "think tank"—and both Eddie and Divine had advanced degrees. Their concept was to bust some myths about the formerly incarcerated, in part by demonstrating how capable they and others were of making it in the dominant society. I knew and liked Eddie, and he was in full support of my SOS paper when I shared it with him. I'd wind up speaking at his memorial in 2014. But in between, we had some collisions. As George would say, Eddie and Divine had a theory of liberation that seemed to us to be focused on the "talented tenth." They'd become leaders in their communities, and with that came an assumption that men *like them* should be leaders of the broader movement. Degreed brothers in suits and ties. Our response: We're not Some of Us or None. We're All of Us or None. More than six hundred thousand Americans come out of state and federal prisons every year, and nine million more cycle through local jails. There are more than seventy million people who have a criminal record today. We deserve to be in charge of our own narratives.

223

We'd get into it with Eddie at Critical Resistance South, a New Orleans gathering held in April 2003, just one month after our inaugural Oakland convening. A core group of us All of Us or None cofounders gathered separately to hold our own meeting. Then we joined the larger event – where formerly incarcerated people from sixteen states had come together—to discuss the prospect of taking our concept national. Eddie wanted us to join forces with NuLeadership. We didn't want that.

It got tense in New Orleans. But the older Panthers backed our approach all the way. We didn't want to be coopted. To this day, we say All of Us or None is a grassroots movement, not another nonprofit, though LSPC serves as its fiscal sponsor. Susan Burton was there with us, and she remembers it in a more diplomatic way. That clash came from a feeling of urgency and scarcity. We'd all come to a deep understanding of the prison industrial complex and all the other "isms" that surround it, from capitalism to sexism to classism. We all wanted to seize the moment and run with it. But with that new passion came a fear that there wasn't space for all of us to make it, that there had to be winners and losers. We were new to freedom, new to our profound awareness, scrambling and scuffling to survive. I'd later come to realize, just as Susan had, that there *was* room for all of us. But first, Eddie and I almost came to physical blows. When I look back on my growing pains, this one ranks high.

224

It happened in New York City, the summer after the New Orleans convening. And it was my fault. I'd flown in with Linda Evans and Karen Shain for a conference and decided to call an organizing meeting of All of Us or None. We were here, after all. Why not start building a New York chapter? Eddie was blindsided. It wasn't just that I was operating on his turf without his buy-in, there was a whole East Coast–West Coast tension in the universe of incarcerated and formerly incarcerated people. It was a holdover from the killings of Biggie Smalls and Tupac, and it ran deep. It was ugly, and it was rooted in real violence. I can still remember taking off my jewelry and handing it to Linda. I could feel that switch flipping inside me. Eddie was getting ready too, and everyone who hadn't been in the pen fled the room faster than cockroaches under a flashlight beam.

But our punches never landed. I respected Eddie too much to go through with it. Besides, all those NA meetings, listening to other people work through their anger, were paying off. I stood down. But it was a close call, and it yielded some big lessons: If you are organizing in someone's community, it's nice to come out publicly with them as an overt ally. You need to work on that to make it happen. Number two: If you need to fight it out, don't do that shit in public. That explosion set us back a few years with white supporters and the philanthropic community. After New York, we developed a code of conduct. And years later, when we formed a national collective of organizations working on behalf of the formerly incarcerated, Eddie was right there as a cofounder. By then, I was *almost* as diplomatic as Susan. I recognized that there are many people doing this work who view themselves as large and important due to their accomplishments, because they are. I don't have the right to tell them how to approach this struggle. As the number of formerly incarcerated people keeps on growing, powerful leaders keep emerging across the country. Our collective question has become, how do we build movement together? But on that day in New York, it was me and Eddie both saying, "It's my way." I was green. But I was learning about collaboration and compromise on a number of fronts, some of them painful, and one in particular absolutely joyful.

ON THE MORNING of August 23, 2003, Sheila Hackett, soon to become Sheila Hackett-Nunn, walked out the door of my family home on Hill Avenue in the Menlo Park neighborhood of Belle Haven wearing an ivory dress with matching pearls and carrying a parasol. Then she stepped into a waiting horse-drawn carriage, and that white horse trotted down the street

225

to the park next to the Onetta Harris Community Center, where we committed to our love. I was fifty-two years old. Sheila was forty-seven.

Five months had passed since the collective birth of All of Us or None, and I was taking a leap I doubt I would or could have taken if it hadn't been for Kathy Labriola, my god sister Shirl, Ellen Barry, and all the other women at LSPC who taught me what it meant to be a decent man. It was a process marked by failure. I hadn't always been kind or honest. But I had taken inventory, and I was ready. Sheila made sure of that.

The fourth and final time I asked for her number I was single, with money in my pocket and a burning desire for long-term union with another. Sheila jotted it down on yet another scrap of paper. But before she handed it to me, she told me straight up she was "too old to just be somebody's girlfriend." "And, if we ain't going anywhere in six months," she said, "we ain't gonna be going anywhere at all." Her unapologetic honesty was like clear, cool water. When I asked her what had broken up her first marriage, she didn't blame the brother. She took responsibility. It was her and her addiction. She told me how she used to sleep in her car. I'd been there too. The first gift I gave her was cherries in the middle of winter, because I wanted her to have something rare. She made me reach like that. The horse-drawn carriage was an homage to the beauty of Sheila and the richness she was bringing to my life. But it was also about community. I wanted to show my neighborhood, my family, my people that Black women don't need to settle for something less than what they're worth. That's why I dragged a horse and carriage through the streets of Belle Haven. It picked Sheila up in the very spot where I used to sell dope and took her to the park where I had played Little League baseball. It's not a long way, but it marked a big transition. The streets were no longer calling me. The bony fingers of the old life could no longer reach me.

In my own family, when I thought about wanting women to know they didn't have to settle, I thought most about my little sister, Gloria. The men she chose hurt her, over and over. It was a pattern engraved in some early unreachable place of pain. I wanted love for her then, and I want that now. I also wanted to set an example for the men. The media message back then about Black families seemed to be all about the absence of fathers. I had made my way back to my children, and now there were grandchildren in the picture, with more to come. I'd been plumping the feathers of a marriage bed in my head for a while, preparing myself for a new way of being. I knew that if I was gonna have half of a chance at a monogamous relationship, I would have to be 100 percent clear about my intentions. For so long, I was that person women didn't take home to their families. By the time I met Sheila, their families were coming to me for help. I had gone from being Dorsey to becoming Mr. Nunn, and I wasn't shy about admitting I wanted the whole package. I was prepared to love and support Sheila, to keep improving as a father and grandfather and leading as a brother. David had managed to get on the newer class of antiretroviral drugs, just like I'd predicted when I begged him to go to treatment. He'd been living with me since he got clean, and Sheila knew he would stay right there in the house with us until his soul left this world.

My little brother passed the day after Christmas, in 2004. He was the person who taught me what it meant to die well. His mind was clear, his heart was open, and so was mine. We weren't afraid to talk about death, and we weren't afraid to cry.

My close friend Eric Walker had been a guide in that regard. He was part of the Circle of Recovery, and he taught me a lot about honesty and courage. We watched him die of AIDS before our eyes, without shame. Free at Last's first men's recovery home bears his name. When Sheila and I were planning our wedding, Eric's mother, Mary Walker, was just becoming a minister. It was our honor to ask her to be our officiant. She had no church of her own, which is partly why we chose the park as our venue. Soon after, Free at Last opened our doors to her so she could conduct her services there.

On the day of our ceremony, the sun was strong, and the mood was high. We served fancy-looking apple cider from the dollar store in fancy-looking dollar store glasses. It was an open secret that Sheila was a shopaholic, but she didn't necessarily go for the pricey stuff. She went for all the stuff. So, when Reverend Mary Walker asked her if she'd take me to be her lawful wedded husband "for richer or for poorer," everybody laughed. At the reception, my daughter gave a toast about how relieved she was that she wouldn't have to meet my girlfriends anymore. I'd walked a long road to get to a place where I could love a woman like Sheila. But here we were. Jumping the broom on that August day in 2003 was the most joyful moment in my life.

"Until this day, I was married to the revolution," I said in my own toast to our gathered guests as my tears welled up. "Now the revolution becomes my mistress, and I'm married to a woman of flesh."

Sheila promised to make my life easier, and she fulfilled that promise, carving out a safe haven for us—for me—that was not about work. She gave me a place to recharge, to enjoy, to step back from injustice and struggle. She brought me a peace I had never known.

Still, she knew exactly who she married. There'd be plenty of occasions to come where revolution rode shotgun. Soon, All of Us or None had special baseball caps with gold stitching made up exclusively for sacrificing spouses: Hamdiya's husband, Fred; Linda's partner, Eve; and Sheila, my beloved wife until death do us part.

I OFTEN THINK back to our seminal gathering at the Center for Third World Organizing. Many of us do. We knew we were giving birth to a movement, but I doubt any of us predicted how hospitable the soil we were fertilizing would be to the seeds of our passion, or how united we would remain in our central purpose.

Linda Evans had already brought her Soros Fellowship over to LSPC, where she became a central strategic force as All of Us or None took shape.

Donna Willmott spent years fighting with us to improve prison conditions before moving on from LSPC to other advocacy work. Ida McCray founded Families with a Future, an organization to help children of incarcerated women, and we brought it under the LSPC umbrella as its fiscal sponsor. She went on to get a couple of degrees and work as a rehabilitation specialist for the San Francisco Sheriff's Department.

George Galvis also founded his own organization, CURYJ, or Communities United for Restorative Youth Justice, and stayed deeply connected to LSPC. Today he chairs our board of directors. Marlene Sanchez also devoted her time to us as board president. She's now executive director of the Ella Baker

Center for Human Rights, a storied California nonprofit that works with Black, brown, and low-income people to shift resources away from prisons and punishment and redirect them to building safe and healthy communities.

Tina Reynolds, who represented at our gathering for the East Coast, went on to cofound a New York–based advocacy organization of currently and formerly incarcerated women called Women on the Rise Telling HerStory (WORTH). As for Susan Burton, she became one of my closest confidantes as we both weathered challenges as Black formerly incarcerated people leading nonprofits. Today A New Way of Life provides shelter to women in twelve safe homes across Los Angeles County, where staff with lived experience help connect them with medical and mental health care, education, and job opportunities. Residents can also get pro bono legal help and tap into services to help them reunify with their kids.

Each of us, along with dozens of others who gathered that March weekend in 2003, have touched the lives of hundreds and in some cases thousands of other formerly incarcerated people nationwide, bringing them into the movement's fold. But there was a learning curve.

Chapter 16

BAN THE BOX

BE IT FURTHER RESOLVED, That the Board of Supervisors supports eliminating the requirement that applicants disclose all past convictions on the preliminary application for public employment in the City and County of San Francisco in order to mitigate or eliminate discrimination against people who have been in prison or convicted of criminal activity in the past and to assist with their successful reintegration into the community after prison.

—OCTOBER 11, 2005, *San Francisco Board of Supervisors—ADOPTED*

A few weeks after I married the woman of my dreams, I kissed her good-bye and hopped on a plane to Washington, DC, with a bunch of my homies. As All of Us or None, we were feeling high on our movement and righteous in our cause. Impatient. Possibly a little bit arrogant. We'd managed to get an invitation to speak at the Black Congressional Caucus legislative weekend, and we'd put out the call to formerly incarcerated allies across the country to join us. About two hundred showed up. For many it was their first time on an airplane. What better place to start pushing our agenda, we figured, than in our nation's capital, speaking to Jesse Jackson Jr., Bobby Rush, John Conley, and other famous Black elected leaders we'd only seen on TV? Right? Wrong.

Our trip to Washington, DC, left us covered in the same shit-smelling fertilizer my hazing on *The Merv Griffin Show* had. Unpleasant, yet conducive to growth. We had big plans to talk about felony disenfranchisement in employment, in housing, and in voting. We had a whole platform of changes we believed needed to happen on a national scale—immediately. We never got a chance to share any of it. Our panel was scheduled to start after another one on reentry wrapped up, but the congressional leaders talked well past their ending time. They talked *at* those of us with lived experience, not with us. They told us what they thought we wanted to hear, and they never thought to ask us what we had to say. Their choice of words when describing us pushed my irritability over the top. So I stood up to set those bigshots straight.

"Now I won't call y' all Negroes if you won't continue to call me a felon, convict, or offender," I said. "But if you call me that, I'm gonna be calling all of you Negroes."

The room got so quiet you could have heard ants walking on cotton. I guess my diplomacy needed some brushing up. The situation went downhill from there. Suddenly there was no time left for our panel to convene at all. The Congressional Black Caucus ball was happening that night, and a security sweep was about to go down. At least we had someplace to go. We'd contributed funds to rent a conference room in a nearby church for a gathering about human rights in Haiti that some of our members organized. We hustled to spread the word to Black lawmakers and their staffers to come on over and hear what we had to say. None showed up. Maybe that was for the best, because by the time I walked into that church, I was so mad I thought blood might come out of my eyes.

Some of the people we brought with us didn't feel the sting. They were having an experience of a lifetime just getting this close to famous Black leaders they'd admired. But us All of Us or None cofounders felt disrespected to the core. Linda Evans was crying, something she does when she gets angry. Susan Burton's way was to get quiet. She'd given up her fiftieth birthday and taken precious time away from her safe home and the women who relied on her to come to DC, only to be treated as invisible. She was thoroughly disgusted. I did the yelling and swearing. These Black leaders were willing to call themselves freedom fighters while silencing us. It reminded me of the Democratic Party's betrayal of another grassroots civil rights warrior. "These motherfuckers don't remember Fannie Lou Hamer!" I hollered. That's when Hamdiya sidled over to me.

"Dorsey," she said in a fierce whisper, "you are cussing in a church."

George Galvis was with us, and he was righteously pissed off. But there's a saying in Spanish that he shared with us: *Somos pocos, pero locos*. We may be small in number, but we're crazy and nimble enough to get shit done. When my heart rate finally slowed, we started to break it down. Maybe we were wrong to aim for a national audience when we were just getting started. Maybe we were wrong to come into a space where *they* controlled the microphone. That night, we made a collective commitment to go home and build our base, one *loco* at a time.

233

We would take our message to the streets. Then we'd organize peace and justice community summits—on our own turf and on our own terms. This time we'd do the inviting. Local and state lawmakers who accepted would have no choice but to sit and listen. They wouldn't even be on the agenda. We'd been humbled, and it was a good thing. It redirected us.

RONALD "ELDER" FREEMAN was one of the OGs who'd been with All of Us or None since we convened at the Center for Third World Organizing. He'd helped found the Los Angeles chapter of the Black Panther Party, but I came to know him as a fearless source of wisdom on the San Quentin yard. Elder got out a couple years before I did and was living in West Oakland. He wound up teaching us critical canvassing skills, like how to do mapping and door knocking. Then we spread out in small groups throughout the Bay Area to connect with formerly incarcerated people and invite them to join our cause one house, one street corner at a time.

I'd learned when I was inside San Quentin that to build a grassroots movement, it helps to be close to the ground, to listen to the concerns and grievances of each and every contact. Now I applied some of those lessons. In addition to door knocking and street corner canvassing, we visited drug treatment centers, where we were guaranteed to find people who'd done time. Free at Last, which explicitly and intentionally served formerly incarcerated people, was an obvious stop. So Linda and I headed down together. At six foot five, David Lewis towered over both of us when he told the packed meeting hall we had something to say that made a lot of sense. Then the floor was ours, and I launched into it. "What I'm suggesting to you is that within Narcotics Anonymous, within Alcoholics

Anonymous, the room is also filled with those of us who have committed felonies," I explained. "Some of us right now can get past the piss test. It's the felony we can't get past." Talk about preaching to the choir. I turned to a brother in a red T-shirt and black baseball cap. "How did it impact you, bro?" And his story poured out.

"They had just told me that I was their best trainee," he said, "and when I went to work yesterday, they told me they couldn't use my services. Turns out some other felon had robbed an armored car in the area. I asked them, what did that have to do with me? And they said, 'It's not us, it's the district manager.'" He'd even told his boss upfront about the felony, and the man had thanked him for his truthfulness. When he pointed that out, his supervisor said, "Yeah, but that was before that other felon did the robbery."

With that, the room busted out laughing. This shit was beyond absurd. A sister who spoke next said she'd been on four interviews for a job at IKEA and had even passed the drug test. At the final interview she was told she was a very strong candidate. But then they asked about that box she'd checked. She explained she was an addict in recovery, that she was turning her life around. She never heard another word.

Linda jumped in to broaden the conversation to exclusions and evictions from public housing—whole families kicked to the curb because someone in the household had a drug conviction. By now, the whole room was nodding. They'd lived it. It was time to band together and *do* something about it, Linda said. Vicki Smothers, who'd been serving as vice president of the board of Free at Last since we'd cofounded it more than a decade earlier, was already wearing an All of Us or None hat. "Job, job, job," she said. "I hear everybody talk about how we

235

can't get a job. But All of Us or None is way bigger than just about jobs. So how do we continue this effort? Some of us can't carry this message the way you just carried it."

Vicki had a point. These brothers and sisters needed a vehicle to discuss their collective priorities and practice speaking on their own behalf. "Now that you brought it up, Vicki, I want to organize a chapter of All of Us or None in East Palo Alto and push an agenda, because y'all need an agenda push," I said. "I need to come home and help you to learn how to fight back."

A few months later, we hosted the East Palo Alto Peace and Justice Summit. The city manager was in the room, listening to Vicki and other new chapter members tell their stories. We held other Peace and Justice Community Summits in Oakland and San Francisco, and then took them south to Watts and San Bernardino, building chapters as we went. The consensus: we needed to end *all* forms of discrimination against people with criminal convictions. But we'd pick banning the box on public employment and public housing applications as our first battle. All of Us or None was and still is housed at LSPC, and plenty of our early members were living in San Francisco. So that, we decided, was where we'd start. There was just one problem: none of us knew shit about the workings of government.

THE CITY AND county of San Francisco had a Human Rights Commission, so we figured we'd go there first, since the right to work and the right to housing are human rights issues. We hit the jackpot. A few key staff members made us feel at home and educated us with patience and kindness. They were the ones who suggested we separate the public employment and housing pieces and start with employment first. The issues were handled by separate committees at the board of supervisors, and besides, housing would be a harder win because landlords are an organized lobby and would fight us.

We agreed. Next up, we needed to write a draft resolution and take it to the head of the city's human resources department, Phil Ginsburg. Linda had thought of the phrase "Ban the Box" while puttering in her garden, and over time the work of thousands of us pushed it into the modern lexicon. It all started in San Francisco. Phil Ginsburg thought it sounded too radical. He suggested "Beyond the Box." We refused. I had developed a good sense about compromise. Sometimes incrementalism leads to open doors. Other times, it stops your progress in its tracks. We didn't want to soften our message right out of the gate. Next, city officials suggested our resolution stop short of demanding the box be removed. Why couldn't it just raise concerns about reentry without being so specific? Our answer to that was no again. Phil came on board anyway. We made plenty of compromises as the process unfolded, but we learned to make them selectively and strategically.

What a lot of people do once they've written a draft resolution is shop it around to supervisors to find a lead sponsor. We could have even had LSPC staff do that. But we at All of Us or None wanted this to be all ours, and we wanted it to be so big by the time we took it to a lawmaker that they had to back it. So first, we took it to the streets, spending hours cruising neighborhoods and stopping at transit stops talking to formerly incarcerated people, gathering signatures on a petition, and building our membership. We also went to the media and got interviewed on the radio. That brought in more members. *Then* we shopped it. The first supervisor to say yes was Tom Ammiano, an aging gay white man with a side hustle as a comedian. It didn't take long for us to see the logic in that. When

237

he stood with us, San Francisco was heavy into the fight for the rights of same-sex couples to marry. Ammiano had been a warrior in plenty of earlier battles for the civil and human rights of LGBTQ+ people. We understood each other.

On a Tuesday in late September 2005, we passed through the metal detectors at San Francisco's city hall in a steady stream and made our way up the rotunda's wide marble staircase into the legislative chamber. Two o'clock in the afternoon is one wrongheaded time to hold a public meeting for people with working-class jobs. But we managed to pull together a small army anyway. After all, a lot of our people couldn't get jobs in the first place, which was right on point. We were ready for action, and the handmade signs many of us were clutching made it clear we weren't the constituents who usually filled these seats: *I Am Not My Criminal Record. My Past is Not My Present. End Employment Discrimination: Ban the Box.*

We were there to demand that the city and county of San Francisco stop asking job seekers to list off their conviction history at the very beginning of the application process. We didn't know it when we got started, but the Boston City Council was working on a similar policy change. We'd gotten some advice from allies over there, but beyond that, we were on our own. We were making an ask so radical for the time that even some formerly incarcerated brothers told me I was crazy. One suggested we should be willing to wait ten years before obtaining full record clearance. Obviously he hadn't heard of the presumption of rehabilitation upon the completion of a sentence. He'd been trained to think crumbs were all we deserved. We were about to show him that was a lie. We weren't about to compromise on our overall goal—to end structural discrimination directed against every person with a past conviction.

By the time we packed the supervisors' chamber that Tuesday afternoon, we had not only discovered what a resolution was, we'd written one. A final vote wouldn't come for two more weeks, but today was our chance to make our case. We wore matching T-shirts emblazoned with our logo: the clenched Black Power fist. We were multiracial, multiethnic, but we all knew that fist meant resistance and revolution by the people, for the people. I'd been reminded of its expansive influence more than eight years earlier, as I stood on the guard rail of Mt. Eden prison in New Zealand. There it was, hand drawn on the far wall of the prison yard. The Maori prisoners, it turned out, had formed their own "Black Power Gang" in a nod to our struggle back at home. A global struggle for self-determination. Now, wearing our All of Us or None shirts, we walked up to the microphone one after another to make highly personal arguments to San Francisco's elected leaders—about our struggles to put food on the table when potential employers saw that checked box and tossed our applications straight in the trash. About workplace purges that got us fired from stable jobs we'd managed to snag when suddenly everyone got background checked. One sister who'd worked in the Stanford Medical Center radiology department got axed that way when a patient's ring went missing in another department, despite a decade of stellar work without a single write-up. She'd been paying her taxes, going to church every Sunday, loving and supporting her family. And just like that, she was crushed. She wasn't free. None of us were—not five, ten, or thirty years down the road from our worst mistakes. Our choices were traps. Check the box and get frozen out, or lie and risk getting canned later on.

I had a fancy job title—codirector of Legal Services for Prisoners with Children. But when I got up at that mic to address the board, I spoke not as a nonprofit leader, but as one of more than twenty million Americans still shackled by felony convictions. "I come before the board of supervisors to ask you not to blink," I said, "because for some of us, the city and county of San Francisco represents our lunch counter. And what we came to do is ask you to serve us at this lunch counter. If you blink, you could miss the opportunity to stand on the right side of the civil rights of formerly incarcerated people trying to gain access to employment, trying to gain access to housing, trying to gain access to a reasonable and a humane life."

Two and half years had passed since we gathered at the Third World Organizing Center, and for most of us this campaign marked the first time we were addressing public officials on our own behalf. The discrimination and disenfranchisement we'd experienced was so deep, so constant, that some of us had never talked openly about it to anyone. Throwing off that shame and demanding the civil and human rights to which we firmly believed we were entitled felt revolutionary and cathartic. We wanted that checkbox gone from *all* job applications. But we were starting with the public sector, because elected officials had an obligation to represent us as constituents. Our taxes paid for their employment, and they were denying us ours. Plus, we figured, government couldn't ask the private sector to do something it wasn't willing to do first. Banning the box in public employment—even if we were in the most liberal pocket of California—would set an example. When the board stood with us, we were electrified. Two weeks later, the resolution passed unanimously. That's when the harder work began—helping the city craft its ordinance, the final expression of public policy.

We'd built strong enough alliances inside the human resources department that we didn't have to break down the door.

Ban the Box

They invited us in to sit at that table and work through the hard questions: Which jobs would still require a background check? (Those that involved contact with kids, the elderly, or the disabled.) When, if at all, would people be asked about their past convictions? And how would those convictions be considered? We didn't win every battle. We wanted the city to hold off on asking about conviction history until they made conditional offers of employment. Instead, they agreed to wait until the step before that, once they'd selected finalists. That turned out to be a money saver—a selling point we returned to as we expanded the fight. The deputy director of Human Resources worked with us closely, bringing us into the conversation at every step. At first the city wanted to use language from the US Equal Employment Opportunity Commission, which suggested employers consider the "nature and gravity of the offense." We balked at that. If it wasn't relevant to the job in question, it wasn't relevant period, we explained. He agreed. We were pinching ourselves. He was also solidly on board with the need for human-centered language. We were people, not felons or ex-cons. He understood it so well he made a suggestion of his own: Instead of using the term *criminal record*, how about *conviction history*? We'd borrow that from him and keep it.

241

There was a downside to our warm welcome in San Francisco. We came away with high expectations, which made the slap downs we were about to experience all the more painful. Alameda County and the City of Berkeley came on board fast with Ban the Box ordinances and policies. East Palo Alto was a snap. Oakland took longer than we expected. But our biggest defeat came down south. Susan Burton and other members of the Los Angeles chapter of All of Us or None worked their asses off to get a resolution approved by the Los Angeles

County Board of Supervisors. We packed two public hearings in 2006 with our members. Dozens of allies from local organizations that served the largest concentration of parolees in the state also showed up in support. Supervisor Yvonne Brathwaite Burke, who'd made history as the first Black woman in Congress to represent the West Coast, introduced the resolution. She fought hard for us, calling on her colleagues to be courageous, take a political risk, do the right thing. At the second hearing, we brought in the heavy firepower: Congresswoman Maxine Waters and California State Senator Gloria Romero testified in favor of Ban the Box. The Boston councilman who'd transformed that city's hiring practices even flew out to speak in our favor. When I stepped up to the mic, I pointed out that county bureaucrats had already admitted they didn't run background checks until late in the process. So why make people disclose up front, before they had a chance to show the employer what they're made of? Besides, I said, Los Angeles County had the juice to make an impact far beyond its borders.

242

"In Northern California, we sort of think that y'all are the dog," I told them. "We're just the tail. If you don't do it here, most likely this thing will be a long time coming. You've got a chance to be more than politicians. You get a chance to be leaders. I'm asking you to lead."

They declined, pushing it off for further study. Behind the scenes, the county kept throwing up roadblocks. They wanted FBI checks for everyone. We said no. It went on like that before Supervisor Burke put the resolution in the deep freeze. We had failed. Efforts to work with the LA City Council were unsuccessful too, though city leaders eventually came around.

These defeats were bruising, and Susan and I had long talks about them. The work she did all day and night directly impacted the lives of women coming out of prison. She was picking them up at the Greyhound station in downtown Los Angeles at all hours and bringing them to shelter, fighting with them to get their kids back. Every second of time and ounce of energy she took to try to persuade some politician to do the right thing was time and energy lost making an immediate difference in women's lives. She knew it had to be done, but she was getting skeptical fast. At LSPC, delivering direct services was never our core mandate. We were still litigating when the situation called for it, but our Ban the Box campaign and the grassroots power of our growing AOUON movement was helping me see we could make our own policies. If we were losing, that just meant we needed new strategies.

In the meantime, we'd had enough success to realize we should spread the knowledge. In 2007, we started handing out Ban the Box toolkits at conferences all over the country. Inside were sample resolutions, lists of questions to ask human resources staff, best practices to argue for, sample flyers, petitions, and community organizing suggestions. We also partnered with NELP, the National Employment Law Project, which embraced the cause of Ban the Box like a pit bull gnawing on a bully stick. Ban the Box wins started sweeping through cities and counties in Georgia, Michigan, North Carolina, Florida, and more.

The right to a fair shot at a job is so fundamental that we kept the campaign alive, moving the goal post to secure the rights to be productive contributors to the economy and our own communities. In 2013, we got the state of California to require all cities, counties, and state entities to save that question

243

about conviction history for later in the employment process. The crazy thing is, California wasn't even first. By then similar legislation had been signed into law in New Mexico, Massachusetts, Connecticut, and Colorado, with seven more states coming on board over the next three years. The dominos were dropping. We knew the time had come to push the fight into the private sector. Once again we started with San Francisco, and once again we won when the city's Fair Chance Ordinance passed into law in 2014 with our input. It required all private businesses with twenty or more workers to save that question on conviction history until after a live interview was conducted, or a conditional offer of employment made. Like the public sector ban, it also straight-out prohibited employers from asking about older convictions, juvenile convictions, or arrests that didn't lead to conviction.

244

At the hearing where we each marched up to the mic to share our stories, a quiet woman named Sandra Johnson joined us. Like Susan Burton and so many other Black women, Sandra turned to crack cocaine after suffering deep personal trauma, and got swept up in the punishing drug laws of the 1990s. She'd found out about the hearing from a friend, and it hit close to home. Sandra's record as a paratransit driver for a private company was stellar. She'd even been celebrated as employee of the month. Then, when the company changed hands, the new owners ordered across-the-board background checks and fired her.

At that crowded hearing, one of our people handed Sandra an All of Us or None business card. On the back, it said "formerly incarcerated–run organization." She stared at it in disbelief, then tucked it in her purse. A couple years later, she got in touch—just in time to become LSPC's first Elder Freeman

Policy Fellow. In that paid yearlong position, she learned how to craft state legislation, lobby lawmakers, and bring the house down when she testified. When she first started, she was scared to be in the spotlight, so we sent her to Toastmasters for practice. It was her story that changed the mind of a holdout lawmaker in 2017—and helped us pass the private sector Ban the Box law for the state of California. That's equivalent to banning the box in the fifth-largest economy in the world, and it came down to one woman's truth telling.

We'd been building political muscle year after year. In 2013, we launched our annual Quest for Democracy Day in partnership with All of Us or None, mobilizing two hundred formerly incarcerated people to the state capitol to learn about policy and advocacy work. We also started hosting policy academies across the state, so formerly incarcerated people could get an intimate lesson on how law gets made at the local and state levels and brainstorm their own agendas. By the time Sandra Johnson, who stayed on after her fellowship, helped organize our seventh annual Quest for Democracy Day in 2019, more than six hundred formerly incarcerated people streamed into Sacramento in buses, vans, and cars from All of Us or None chapters all over the state to lobby for a list of bills we backed to improve the lives of people in cages and coming out of cages.

The Elder Freeman Policy Fellowship lives on. We created it in Elder's name after he died of cancer while he was visiting New York in late 2014. His photo is on LSPC's Ancestral Wall. At each All of Us or None meeting, someone knows to put the call out for commitments. That's when people reach into their pockets and throw the ones, fives, and tens down on the table. Some of it goes to pizza and fried chicken. Most of it goes into an emergency fund. We tapped into that fund to help send Elder's brother, Roland, to New York to bring back Elder's body. When Roland unexpectedly died of a heart attack right in the middle of LaGuardia airport, we chipped in to help bring him home too. That's how we showed our gratitude to the man who'd taught us so much. We've kicked in that way for plenty of other families in need too.

Today about 237 million people in the US live in jurisdictions that have banned the box. We even made inroads at the federal level. I almost fell off my chair when President Barack Obama used the term during a 2015 news conference, after issuing an executive order directing the Office of Personnel Management to, you guessed it, hold those questions about conviction history until later in the hiring process. We pushed to extend that ban to all federal contractors—who employ a quarter of the nation's workforce. It took a while. But the federal Fair Chance Act took effect in 2021.

THE BAN THE Box campaigns had me hustling all over the state, and there were other LSPC campaigns keeping me busy, not to mention the time invested in All of Us or None chapter building. My work schedule was so relentless I had to step down from the board of directors at Free at Last. One day, in 2006, as we were getting our asses kicked in Los Angeles County, David Lewis called me and dropped another one of his blunt observations. My brother Ronald had been living in the men's program at Free at Last for a while, working on his sobriety.

"Dorsey, you know, we feeding your brother, we housing your brother, we're doing all this for your brother," David said to me. "What are *you* doing for your brother?"

I walked into the next meeting at Free at Last and looked Ronald in the eye. "I'm not getting short on cars, I'm getting short on brothers," I told him. "If you bring me a year clean, I'll give you my Cadillac." It was a deep green, in mediocre shape, but it meant the world to him. I was in the room with my sister Joyce when Ronald got his one-year chip. She was so happy she stood up and started shouting, "Hallelujah!" She'd been praying for it for so long.

Meanwhile, Sheila kept her promise to turn our home into a sanctuary of love, a respite from the revolution. Even as I worked like a dog, for the first time in my life I made time for vacations. We cruised our asses off, traveling through the Caribbean and Mexico, and we snuck away on short respites to hotel time-shares Sheila owned. Back home, she made holidays feel like holidays. I'd walk into the bedroom on Valentine's Day, and everything would be red. She insisted on a Christmas tree, and I strung lights around the house to make her happy. Sheila also made me think. She had a favorite flower—the calla lily. She loved the soft, clean smell and the way it took its time when it bloomed. Once, she made me sit down at the table with her over the course of three days to watch it slowly open. She kept asking me, "What does it remind you of?" It took me a while, but eventually I figured it out. It reminded me of our first intimacy—gradual, natural, and meaningful. Every Thursday, for years, I brought her flowers. I never missed a day.

247

Chapter 17

THE CONCRETE TOMB

In December 2010, LSPC's board of directors named me executive director. I felt overwhelming fear. I didn't want to be the person who took charge of an organization with such a rich history and wound up failing. I still carried guilt about the way I'd let down the Prison Law Office when addiction came on strong. My daughter's husband, Daniel, helped me find the courage to step into leadership. It was a big responsibility, and my new role made me the first formerly incarcerated nonlawyer we knew of to lead a legal services nonprofit. LSPC was already working in tight partnership with the formerly incarcerated people who were joining All of Us or None and raising their hands to start their own chapters. They were dedicated comrades, and our growing numbers gave us a stronger voice that was helping us build serious policy-making muscle that would just keep on getting bigger. People were waking up to their rights, to the presumption of rehabilitation upon the completion of a sentence. For LSPC's first big fight under my leadership—the push to end indefinite solitary confinement in California—I'd tap into just about every major lesson I'd learned, about how to pair litigation with grassroots activism, how to take our cues from the people caged in the most inhumane conditions, and how to join forces with other legal and prisoner rights organizations. Meanwhile, as LSPC and All of Us or None, we drew on allies we'd been cultivating since our very first Ban the Box victory, who now had some serious juice in state government.

It turned out to be a deeply personal fight. Every human being stuck in isolation and deprived of human touch for years or decades could have been me, especially the Black brothers. More than that, one of them happened to be an old friend.

THE FIGHT TO end indefinite solitary confinement started in Pelican Bay, a "supermax" prison built at the far northern tip of California in 1989. But support would come from every single prison in California's swollen system.

Pelican Bay was built to house the supposed "worst of the worst," in the kinds of conditions the public never heard about until the torture chamber was up and running. It's where the guards and wardens sent every suspected leader or associate of a prison gang they could, and locked them up in solitary confinement *indefinitely*, meaning no end date. The whole supermax concept of extreme isolation was a new phenomenon, and it spread across the country like a dance craze. I'd gotten my taste of solitary. When Kathy Labriola touched me with kindness after a year of deprivation in the Hole, my body shook uncontrollably. But what I endured was a cakewalk compared to the decades of solitude imposed on the men—and a small number of women—held in the state's supermax special housing units, or SHUs. At Pelican Bay, each man was stuck alone

The Concrete Tomb

under fluorescent light in windowless concrete cells for at least twenty-two and a half hours a day, often more, fed through a slot. If they were lucky, on some days, they'd get a shower or a chance to "exercise" alone in another poured concrete box, with fifteen-foot ceilings and just a sliver of sky to look at.

No phone calls or photos were allowed, and visits to the prison were pretty much impossible for family and friends with no money or time to spare. It was too damned remote, and that was by design. Abuse that amounted to torture from guards at Pelican Bay and the state's other big supermax site at Corcoran was rampant, and so was gladiator-style violence between prisoners, orchestrated by guards who then fired their guns into the mess they created. Pelican Bay was especially extreme, and after pleas from men locked up there leaked out in letters, US District Court Judge Thelton Henderson, who'd once been a civil rights advocate, ruled that the use of force and denial of adequate medical care at the prison was unconstitutional. Placing human beings in solitary for years and years on end, he added, also amounted to cruel and unusual punishment—but only for prisoners who were mentally ill, chronically depressed, brain damaged, or developmentally disabled.

251

Henderson's 1995 ruling and the settlement agreement that came out of it was better than nothing, but it didn't acknowledge the full truth—that indefinite isolation in and of itself is a violation of constitutional and human rights for anyone and everyone. That cutting human beings off from kind touch, from the sun, from the sensation of a breeze, and leaving them alone with their thoughts in concrete tombs for years or decades on end was the kind of torture that could *make* a person go crazy.

But *we* knew. Pelican Bay soon fell off the public radar. Not for us though. Ellen and LSPC staff attorney Cassie Pierson had traveled up there for a visit in 2000, hoping to get the local Legal Aid chapter interested in the abuses. That's when letters from prisoners in the SHU started pouring into the office, and Cassie fielded them. Eight years later, after she retired, Carol Strickman joined our legal team and kept those channels of communication open. I was fresh to my role as boss in early 2011 when we at LSPC sent a survey to SHU prisoners in Pelican Bay and Corcoran. What came back was a testament to human suffering and resilience: Four out of five of the men who told us how long they'd been in had spent *at least* a decade in the SHU. A third had been in at least two decades, and a fifth had been sitting in a concrete tomb for a quarter of a motherfucking century. And yet, thanks to the force of their spirits, more than you can imagine were unbroken and undeterred.

By June, men held in sensory deprivation cells at Pelican Bay on what was known as the Short Corridor were organizing, sending out collective statements about their conditions of confinement to prisoner rights organizations and the governor. They were planning a hunger strike, and we at LSPC were at their service. We helped pull together the Prisoner Hunger Strike Solidarity Coalition, joining with Critical Resistance, California Prison Focus, and the Prison Activist Resource Center, abolition and prisoner rights organizations that had formed or expanded since that game-changing Critical Resistance conference in 1998. Then Carol and I got in her car and hit the road for Pelican Bay.

The farthest north I had ever traveled in California was my vacation home in Lake County. I thought that *was* Northern California. But as we headed north on Highway 101 through oak scrub and into the shade of the redwood forests, I realized I had no clue. I fell asleep twice, and when I woke up, we still weren't there. When we got to the prison north of Crescent City we were led into a visiting room, and on the other side of the glass sitting next to a telephone was my friend Paul Jones, who I knew as PJ. PJ was my intellectual ally back at DVI, the one who got shipped out after CO Jerry Sanders was killed by shanking in November 1973. Labeled as BGF forever, he wound up being one of the first men locked up in the Pelican Bay SHU after it opened in 1989. He hadn't seen daylight since. I almost didn't recognize him behind the glass because he'd lost so much color.

I didn't weep that day, though I wanted to. I saved that for the legislative hearing later that summer—the one we at LSPC and AOUON helped set up because Tom Ammiano, the former San Francisco supervisor who had carried our Ban the Box legislation, was now the chair of the Assembly Public Safety Committee. PJ's mental state seemed all right, given the circumstances. Mine was fucked up. I had done time in solitary because guards decided I was a radical threat, maybe a BGF associate. I knew how easily I could have been in PJ's shoes, stuck in a box for decades. The only ways to get out if the system had "validated" you as a gang member was to "debrief"—as in snitch—or die, because with no access to education or a slave job, you couldn't make a case before the parole board. Those who *did* debrief, who chose family over principle, wound up with targets on their backs for life. Worse, many were unable to forgive themselves. That's no kind of choice.

The hunger strikers were inspired by the writings of Bobby Sands, the leader of the Irish Republican Army (IRA) who had staged a hunger strike inside Belfast's Long Kesh Prison. The problem is, he died. So did nine of the other IRA hunger strikers. Imagining that for PJ was breaking my heart.

253

"Hold it, man," I said. "Some of these motherfuckers starved themselves to death. How far are you willing to take this?" His answer was everything I didn't want to hear.

"Dorsey," he answered, "I'm gonna go as long as I need to on this thing."

But what really got me was what PJ said when I asked him who he wanted us to notify in the event that he starved himself to death. It proved challenging to come up with anyone. The brother had been locked away since 1969. So many of his family and friends were dead.

Carol and I interviewed three other men on that visit. One brother started to cry when he saw me. He was so happy just to have the chance to speak with another Black man.

Two prisoners organizing the hunger strike had already filed a lawsuit on their own and were looking for legal representation. When we planned our visit to Pelican Bay, I wasn't sure if I wanted to throw LSPC into the fight. I had some major reservations about suing the prison system. The guards were still the goon squad to me, and their union was a major California power player. I was worried they would find a way to go after LSPC, to undermine us with our funders, to destroy us. Carol talked me out of that tree. I wasn't unjustifiably paranoid. Prison officials pulled my central file during the litigation to investigate me. I learned about that when I tried to get a copy decades later. They told me they lost it.

There was another issue eating at me though. The system had moved these men into the Short Corridor because they were believed to be high-ranking members of the Aryan Brotherhood, Mexican Mafia, Nuestra Familia, and Black Guerilla Family. Shot callers. My personal experience hadn't made me a big fan of white supremacists, and the violence prison gangs engaged in on the inside leaked out to the streets, where youth were killing each other and landing in prison themselves. But as someone whose file had me pegged as a radical because of my intellectual proclivities, I knew not to trust the system's conclusions. A tattoo or a drawing interpreted as suggestive of a prison gang could also seal your fate, as could allegations thrown out into the void of secrecy by confidential informants scrambling to save their own skin.

After our visit, I found myself warming to the idea of litigation. Sitting across from PJ absolutely had something to do with my change of heart. So did Carol's passion. These men, living in conditions that amounted to torture, had found the strength to organize on the inside, though they'd never seen one another's faces. They deserved our help.

Not long after Carol and I took that endless drive to Pelican Bay, Daniel "Nane" Alejandrez called me to talk about the pinch we were in. Nane was a friend and mentor. He had founded Barrios Unidos back in 1977 when I was still doing time in San Quentin. By the mid-1990s it had become a powerful street-based peace movement to bring an end to gang violence.

"Dorsey," he said, "If we gonna put ourselves out there like this, we gotta ask for something that's meaningful."

The ask we settled on for the prisoners planning the hunger strike: "Can you all stop young people from following in your footsteps?" The crazy thing is, they were already on it. That's how oppression can lead to revolution and healing. Those supposed shot callers in the Short Corridor had nobody to talk to but each other. They did it by yelling through the walls, and using the toilets and drains to send messages. And the more they talked, especially about political theory, the more they figured that they were all being similarly afflicted. Not just that, they recognized they were being played, that it was in the interest of the prison system to fuel racial divisions. It was exactly what I'd come to recognize at DVI. One of the Black core organizers, Paul Redd, later told an interviewer that they were all inspired in part by George Jackson, who wrote in *Soledad Brother*, "Settle your quarrels, come together, understand the reality of our situation, understand that fascism is already here, that people are dying who could be saved, that generations more will die or live poor butchered half-lives if you fail to act. Do what must be done, discover your humanity and your love in revolution. Pass on the torch. Join us, give up your life for the people."

Once Nane and I could see where the hunger strikers were coming from, we were all in.

The Prison Hunger Strike Solidarity Coalition that we'd put together on the outside set up a media team, and we all worked our asses off to get the word out, bringing family members of prisoners and students over to the cause and reaching out to our brothers and sisters locked up in other prisons across the state. The coalition even built a portable model of a Pelican Bay SHU cell and took it on the road to rallies and demonstrations.

The first hunger strike went down in July 2011, and more than sixty-six hundred prisoners from thirteen California prisons took part. It lasted nineteen days. By August, thanks to Tom Ammiano, we were testifying before the state assembly. Prison officials were allowing the hunger strikers to phone us—legally, not with contraband cell phones—and the following month, they arranged a legal call with us at LSPC and some other attorneys. Jules Lobel of the New York–based Center for Constitutional Rights was one of them. I'd never even heard of the organization, but one of our former legal interns was working there. That's just one of the ways we seeded the movement. Jules had been following the situation for months and became the lead counsel on the team. Almost all the contact with the prisoners, though, came through Carol, and it was LSPC and AOUON that honored their requests in the fight to publicize the hunger strikes. The legal team stepped in to represent the two prisoners who had already filed their own lawsuit, then later amended it to include a multiracial, multiethnic group of named plaintiffs, Paul Redd among them, and got the case certified as a class action on behalf of *everyone* in the SHU indefinitely in California's prisons.

In the LSPC office we very seldom use the word *clients*. The people putting their lives on the line, living the daily torture, were the people making critical decisions about where to take the struggle. When we say we worked for them, we actually did! We consulted them every step of the way, just like LSPC had done for Charisse Shumate and the other sisters inside when we sued for better medical conditions. When the core group of hunger strikers felt the prison system was stalling in September 2011, they stopped eating again. We helped them hustle support, and this time twelve thousand prisoners across the state refused meals. Soon the litigation team was looping in the UN Special Rapporteur on Torture and consulting mental health experts on the impacts of this kind of endless deprivation on the human body and soul. It was new information, and it sparked international interest in the strike.

The following summer, the Short Corridor hunger strikers put out a statement called "The Agreement to End Hostilities," saying it was time to stop letting CDCR use racial divisions against them. It called for a truce, an end to race-based violence. It was a big moment, even if that peace didn't completely hold.

The third hunger strike was the biggest and longest, starting in July 2013 and lasting fifty-nine days. At its peak, about thirty thousand prisoners turned down meals across the state. The legislature held more hearings, and in 2015, we settled the case. Absent the hunger strike, which created a sense of urgency, I think prison officials would have proceeded with business as usual. We brought so much to the table—grassroots organizing, political education, support from other people fighting for prisoners' rights. It affirmed for me that LSPC was no one-stroke pony. It wasn't an absolute victory. In fact, Jules Lobel of the Center for Constitutional Rights and other cocounsel are *still* litigating the case all these years later to compel CDCR to comply with the settlement. Still, it brought significant change. Within two years, more than fourteen hundred people were released from indefinite solitary to step-down units or into the general population, including PJ. It meant they could get vocational training, go to school, steps that could finally make them eligible for parole. What spoke to me most though was the access they would finally get to human touch that wasn't suspicious or violent.

I OFTEN SAY those closest to the problem are closest to the solution. And I know for a fact my own traumas and human connection to PJ compelled me to get LSPC into the fight. I too had been labeled BGF, just because I had a different political philosophy than my keepers. If the tough-on-crime laws of the eighties and nineties had been in place when I committed my crime, I might be sitting in a box today. But those same deeply felt connections also caused me pain that could have undermined our purpose. Because trauma endures. The same month Carol and I drove up to Pelican Bay, the support coalition we helped create started recruiting members for a mediation team, to serve as the bridge between the hunger strikers and CDCR. I joined. I knew that sitting across the table from the real shot callers, the ones who'd done me and so many people I care about wrong, would not be easy. Still, I reminded myself of the lesson I'd learned when I first served on the Men's Advisory Council in San Quentin: you don't have to like your adversaries to negotiate with them. It still proved to be too much for me. Sitting at the table with leaders of the system I despised for good reasons mired me in anger. Every time I heard these administrators make promises, I was convinced before they closed their mouths that they'd never keep them. Members of the mediation team who hadn't had the misfortune of living in a cage responded politely as my heart rate quickened and thoughts of violence bubbled up: *Man, I'm supposed to do you right now, dawg.*

To me, they were killers in suits. I was back on the tier, so spiritually agitated I knew I had to step down. It was the right thing for the team, and for me. It wasn't healthy—in the same way having to tell that brother on San Quentin's death row that the state was probably gonna start dropping the cyanide soon wasn't healthy. And *that* had led me to a place of darkness where I promised myself I would never return.

259

Chapter 18

"I SPEAK FOR MYSELF. I VOTE."

Sheila was a recovering addict, just like I was. She also had a felony on her record, in her case a direct result of crack cocaine. Still, *felon* wasn't a word I ever associated with Sheila. *Wife* was. *Fierce. Proud. Strong. Beautiful.* She was giving back to her community in a way that would have made Kalima proud, being an asset. And she supported me and my work 100 percent. Early on in our marriage, she collected all her single earrings and had them melted down to make me a solid gold necklace pendant of a clenched fist—the All of Us or None symbol of strength and power. A matching ring came later. The woman lost a lot of earrings. Sheila understood the key to my sobriety wasn't only the big book of Alcoholics Anonymous or the practice of Narcotics Anonymous, it was my political belief system. But *private* was also a word that described Sheila. She hadn't joined All of Us or None or thrown her story into our Ban the Box fight. Outside of her closest circles, she hadn't talked openly about her felony conviction. Until 2008, when she made a very public declaration.

By then LSPC was nearly five years into an ongoing campaign to clarify and expand voting rights of the formerly incarcerated. More than half the people that I did crime with or worked with after I got out of San Quentin knew their Miranda warning by heart: *You have the right to remain silent. Anything you say can and will be used against you in a court of law. You have the right to an attorney. . . .* Beyond that, they mostly had no clue what other rights they had. Nobody had taken the time to tell them. I was in that same boat when Kathy Labriola asked me in early 1975 what my comrades inside and I thought about our voting rights, and my answer was a dumbfounded, "What?" That question—of who has a voice and who doesn't—became central to my life's work.

When we convened at the Center for Third World Organizing to birth the movement that became All of Us or None, voting rights was up there on the wall next to our other priorities. Our goal was to eliminate *all* forms of discrimination against formerly incarcerated people. That included disenfranchisement when we're denied the vote—*and* when the message is so unclear that we sit out the process. Because, even when the law was on our side, we were being disenfranchised by misinformation. So in 2004, while we got to work on our Ban the Box campaign, LSPC and AOUON set off on a parallel mission around voting rights. The national landscape was ugly. Nearly half a dozen states barred people with felonies from voting for *life*. All but two states prohibited voting for people in prison, and in plenty of others, including California, you had to wait until you were off parole. It added up to 5.4 million people across the country being locked out of this democracy. Muzzled. Just like the modern prison system, the silencing of millions of voices was a legacy of slavery. Sure, the Fifteenth

Amendment to the US Constitution granted voting right to former slaves back in 1870. But Jim Crow laws clawed them back, explicitly or through thirty-one flavors of intimidation. It's no accident that felony disenfranchisement hit Black people the hardest. In 2000, we witnessed the consequences in a clear and obvious way when fewer than six hundred Florida votes and one controversial US Supreme Court ruling tipped the nation for President George Bush. Florida was one of those states that banned *all* people with felonies from voting. Those 1.4 million so-called citizens denied a voice in perpetuity included people who'd committed murder, caught a lobster that was too small, or released helium balloons into the air. Just a fraction of those disenfranchised voters could have changed the course of history and made Al Gore our president. Maybe then we wouldn't have gotten into an eternal war in Iraq and Afghanistan that killed the children of other taxpaying citizens. I use that example with people to point out why our vote doesn't just matter to *us*, it matters to *all*.

In 2004, I started driving around with a giant cardboard voter registration form in the trunk of my car. Every chance I got, I used that prop to grab people's attention, remind them of their rights, and sign them up. But getting clear on the law was more complicated than you'd expect. We knew California denied the vote to people confined to prison and to those on parole for felony convictions. That meant people who'd come *off* parole could vote. But what about the seventy-five thousand people cycling through jails who were awaiting trial or doing time for misdemeanors or felony probation (when you're sentenced to jail instead of prison for a felony as a condition of probation)? After plenty of legal research, we at LSPC determined that people in county jail who hadn't yet

263

been convicted or were serving misdemeanors absolutely had the right to vote. On the question of felony probation, we were less clear, so we checked in with California's secretary of state, Kevin Shelley. In a letter to LSPC he affirmed those rights. We were making progress. By this time, All of Us or None had teamed with the ACLU of Northern California to survey counties up and down the state about their take on the issue. What we found was a hot steaming mess. Some election officials had their facts so wrong they told us it was illegal for *anybody* in jail to vote. Close to none were making voter registration forms available.

We had our work cut out for us. Then, in 2005, just as we were gearing up for a public campaign, Shelley flip-flopped on us, directing every county in the state to *deny* voting rights to people doing jail time for felony probation. Next, LSPC, the ACLU, and the League of Women Voters successfully sued the state, and in December 2006, the California Court of Appeal upheld our victory. It was now crystal clear—or so it seemed. Voter disenfranchisement *only* applied to those serving time in prison or on felony parole.

By 2008, we made an all-out effort to spread the word. We were headed for a national election, and Barack Obama was running for president. We needed our voters out in force. In partnership with the ACLU of Northern California, All of Us or None members held news conferences at jailhouses across the state, registering people who were visiting loved ones and passing the word about those loved ones' rights. We carried our voter registration clipboards into city parks and set up our tables on street corners to free the motherfucking vote. All of Us or None members also volunteered to take part in a massive campaign that would plaster their portraits on billboards and bus shelters, in mass mailings, and on postcards. Sheila joined them.

THIRD STREET IS the main artery and gathering place for the Bayview and Hunters Point neighborhoods of San Francisco. Just like my childhood ghetto, the district turned Black and poor after pulling in Southern labor to work the naval shipyard during World War II and then disappearing those jobs. Like Belle Haven and East Palo Alto, Bayview-Hunters Point is full of streets named for root families, especially Black matriarchs who fought like hell to keep their sons safe from police violence, for public housing that wasn't decrepit, for the cleanup of toxic waste sites that were making their families sick. By the time Sheila and I took a drive down there in the fall of 2008 in the two-seat Miata I'd bought for her, Black families were already getting squeezed out by gentrification. But Bayview still represented one of the city's most significant Black communities. That meant there were plenty of passersby whose brothers, daughters, fathers, and sons were cycling through jail or prison. In fact, more than half the people locked up in San Francisco jail at that time were Black, even though less than 10 percent of the city was.

265

Sheila and I parked next to Auntie April's Chicken, Waffles and Soul Food, a block from the historic Bayview Opera House. Then we got out and looked up. There on a giant billboard was Sheila's proud face. There were her smiling eyes, her close-cropped hair that was starting to go gray, and that look: challenging, playful, uncompromising. Next to her image were these remarkable words: *"SHEILA 'I Speak for Myself. I Vote.'"* The small print spelled out the details: Yes, you *can* vote when you're in jail—even if you're there as a condition of felony probation. If you're *out* of jail or prison you can vote too, as long as you aren't on felony parole.

Discrimination targeting people with criminal convictions still ran deep. Victim's rights advocates who didn't understand that holding their thumb on us for eternity wasn't making communities safer were telling lawmakers and the media that none of us deserved the right to vote—ever. To come out as a politically engaged formerly incarcerated person in that climate was an act of courage and strength for every person who did it. For Sheila, a nonmember of All of Us or None who had held her story close, it was an even bigger deal.

Maya Harris, whose sister would later become this nation's vice president, was executive director of the ACLU of Northern California, a friend to me, and a friend to Sheila. She was the one who persuaded her. But a few things happened not long before that put Sheila in a fighting mood. The first involved one of my granddaughters. When both her parents landed in jail, I talked to Sheila about taking her in. But we figured out fast that our felonies permanently disqualified us from being foster parents, regardless of the stability of our home or the quality of our love. The second blow came when Sheila volunteered to work with kids at Belle Haven Elementary School—that school that had hardly done anything for me but teach me how to spell *supercalifragilisticexpialidocious*. Sheila's felony record popped up on a background search, and the school turned her away like a leper. That rejection felt exceptionally humiliating. But the biggest thing that likely motivated her to put herself on blast up on that billboard, the whole reason she had time to volunteer in the first place, was her cancer.

The day we got the diagnosis of Sheila's lung cancer felt almost like a sentencing to me. One of the longest moments I have experienced in this lifetime was sitting there waiting for Sheila to ask her doctor the big question, "How long do I got to live?" If I hadn't worked around all these women at LSPC and done some real growing, I might have jumped in and asked it myself. But it was her question to ask. The answer: "Six months to a year." She'd get more time than that. As we coexisted with the knowledge of our limited time together, we experienced a new level of intimacy. Not long after Sheila started chemotherapy, she asked me to cut off her dreadlocks. Doing that was more sensuous than I could have imagined. It was an act of love. A ritual of commitment. In the months that followed, I learned to hold my wife in a new way. To make love to her in a new way. There's one memory that runs through my mind on repeat. We were flying home from what probably was our last trip together. By then, Sheila was bald. As she walked down the aisle to our seats from the airplane bathroom, I saw her pull off her wig for all to see. I've always thought that marked the moment Sheila got comfortable with the idea of dying. In truth it may have marked the moment when I recognized that I wasn't. I never did cross that bridge, despite many conversations about the inevitable.

267

We stumbled together through Sheila's final months. When she was feeling good enough, we headed up to the modest vacation home I'd bought in Clearlake, where we had planned to retire. There, we hit the casino. We didn't drink or do drugs. Feeding change into those slot machines gave us some respite. As the November 2008 election got closer, I left her side more than I wanted to. I was in a frenzy, running into the nearby park to register homies to vote, flying to Southern California as our Ban the Box campaign wore on. At least I could afford to hire a good friend to sit with Sheila when I was away—resources I didn't have when my moms was dying. Still, guilt and sorrow washed over me.

"Baby, did I squander our time?" I asked her one night as I held her close.

She looked me straight in the eyes and said, "I knew who I married."

Like David's death, Sheila's was a slow-motion exercise in honesty. Together, we planned her final party. We hosted her celebration of life in December 2008 at the Onetta Harris Community Center—where we'd raised those dollar store glasses to our wedding guests a little more than five years earlier. The entire LSPC staff showed up. So did Michael Satris and his wife, Bonnie; Margaret Littlefield and her sister, Tricia. We made up special baseball caps in Sheila's honor. And in front of everyone, we danced our last dance.

Sheila lived long enough to cast her ballot for Barack Obama. That was tremendously meaningful to her. We watched him take the presidency together on election night. Then, on Sunday, January 18, 2009, two days before Obama's inauguration, Sheila Hackett-Nunn died in our home on Hill Avenue, in our bed, and in my arms—right where she wanted to be. The whole time we were married we only had two fights. Before Sheila, I would have said that being the first man in a woman's life carried the most significance. I learned through Sheila that it's equally important to be a good man, and to be the last man.

AT EVERY MAJOR juncture in my fight to ensure all voting rights are respected, I picture Sheila's face on that billboard. Every day I walk into our LSPC offices, I get to see her smiling eyes on the poster from that 2008 campaign hanging on the wall. But warring interpretations of voting rights for people in jail would drive us back to court, especially as the state handed new criminal justice responsibilities to counties in 2011 under so-called realignment. It wasn't until 2015, after another secretary of state had come and gone and a third one more sympathetic to our cause had taken office, that the right of all people in county jail to vote was finally affirmed by California's top election official. Just in case, we made sure it was written into California law through an assembly bill we cosponsored, guaranteeing access to ballots for tens of thousands.

Nearly a dozen years after Sheila died, we scored our biggest voting rights victory. We couldn't have done it without our formerly incarcerated allies across the country. By then, we were united in a forceful coalition, learning from one another's setbacks and victories.

Chapter 19

FROM THE PRISON GATE TO THE WHITE HOUSE GATE

When we All of Us or None cofounders boarded the plane in fall 2003 to attend the legislative weekend of the Black Congressional Congress, we were like babies who'd recently learned to crawl. We knew just enough to get ourselves into trouble. By 2014, we'd navigated painful and joyful lessons, defeats, and victories. We had made Ban the Box a nationwide cause and cultivated alliances in local and California state government. We were ready to take our fight to the next level.

Barack Obama had been in office five years when his people started talking seriously about "reentry." Unfortunately, they were getting it wrong—because there wasn't a soul in the room with them with lived experience. So, in March 2014, I wrote a letter to the country's first Black president, copying Eric Holder, the country's first Black US attorney general. They needed to convene a national strategy session hosted by formerly incarcerated people, I told them. Imagine if in the middle of the historic farmworkers fight for labor rights national leaders had only been talking to lawyers and middle-class students about the needs and rights of farmworkers. The reentry movement was *for* us and *about* us, I wrote. We had to be at the table.

That summer, I walked through those White House gates with a handful of other formerly incarcerated people for a brief sit-down with Valerie Jarrett. The sister was senior advisor to the president of the United States of America and assistant for public engagement and intergovernmental affairs. A high-level mouthful. Crossing the threshold of that house of power and privilege that our slave ancestors helped build felt surreal. It sure wasn't the journey my San Quentin keepers had visualized when they told me they thought I might make a good janitor one day. It wasn't like we just strolled in though. Security was tight, and for a while, we got held up between two gates. That flashed every one of us back to the sally port, waiting to enter a place that was dominated by fear and anger. Just like we did back in those days in the face of pain or humiliation, we started cracking jokes. "I'm not sure I want to go through that second gate. It didn't go so well for me last time," one of my homies said. "Hey," I piped up, "this time I'm not the littlest guy here, so I'm not going in first." Finally that wait ended, and by the time we were sitting down, the sweat on our hands had dried. The echo stayed with me. I'm one of those brothers who's been through the front gates of San Quentin and the front gates of the White House. All day long, I kept pondering the length of that stroll.

The meeting was preliminary, kind of like a first date, or a tasty appetizer before a big meal. That came a few months later, when we returned to the nation's capital to address staff of the Federal Interagency Reentry Council at the US Department of

From the Prison Gate to the White House Gate

Justice. Eric Holder had created the council three years earlier, bringing together staff of twenty federal agencies to address the growing numbers of us who'd been criminalized and written off for life. They invited us in as subject experts on our own lived experience. It sure had been a long time coming.

We entered the building that day as the Formerly Incarcerated, Convicted People and Families Movement, or FICPFM, an umbrella organization that today represents over fifty civil and human rights organizations in three dozen states, all led by people with conviction histories and their family members. With me was Daryl Atkinson, who headed up Forward Justice in North Carolina; Vivian Nixon, who was leading New York's College and Community Fellowship; and Glenn Martin, who earlier that year had founded JustLeadershipUSA in New York. There was also my good friend Susan Burton. Pastor Kenny Glasgow, founder of the Ordinary People Society (TOPS) in Dothan, Alabama, was there, along with Norris Henderson of New Orleans, who led Voice of the Experienced (VOTE), a project he and his caged comrades dreamed up while held at Angola prison. Also with us was Manuel la Fontaine, another proud cofounder of All of Us or None who worked for LSPC and, like George Galvis, is deeply committed to uniting brown and Black voices in the struggle.

That day, we walked into the Department of Justice our full selves, to talk about employment rights, housing rights, voting rights, and more. In hindsight, the gathering didn't lead to as many changes as we'd hoped. But it was symbolic. Looking around we got an aerial view of how much the landscape was changing. Coming together as All of Us or None had been a powerful step, one that inspired others around the country. Now, united as a national collective, we could speak in one voice on behalf of tens of millions similarly situated. That's leverage.

273

Time and maturity had allowed the vision to come to me. It sure as hell wasn't something I'd been capable of when Eddie Ellis and I were taking off our jewelry in New York back in 2003.

OUR MOVEMENT OF aligned organizations from a dozen states was big, loud, and proud from the moment we congregated on Pastor Kenny Glasgow's turf in Dothan, Alabama, in 2011. There were more than fifty of us in the room, including Eddie, each of us representing organizations dedicated to justice for people impacted by conviction history. All of us had already committed to the concept of coming together. I believe Eddie and I had both been humbled by our early arrogance. I know I had come to recognize that our goal was not to build empire. Quite a few organizations led by the formerly incarcerated had sprung up around the country, and we all agreed we had a better shot at securing our full civil and human rights if we coalesced in harmony under one big umbrella. We also knew we could learn from one another—though how much we didn't quite predict. As organizations, we had our differences. Vivien's and Susan's worked exclusively with women. Some had a leadership hierarchy; others, like AOUON, were grass-roots collectives. But every one had a common origin story that led back to a cage. We at All of Us or None also recognized that we needed allies across the country's vast geography. We couldn't be in every corner of every state, though over the next decade we'd sure get closer.

Kenny had come home from an Alabama prison nearly two decades after I left San Quentin, committed to a similar cause. Now he was welcoming us into the community he called the Ordinary People Society, one he built to fight for the rights of formerly incarcerated people to work, vote, be fed and housed.

We modeled the convening after All of Us or None's first gathering at the Center for Third World Organizing, taping large sheets of paper along one wall and using markers to fill in a chronology of the movement stretching back to the early 1980s. I was proud to see my fingerprints on so many of the accomplishments. The goal was to see where the collective movement had been, where we were at, and where we needed to go. The consensus on the latter was to prioritize an end to felony disenfranchisement in voting.

A few years earlier, Kenny and his homies at TOPS had started an annual tradition tied to Bloody Sunday, that day in March of 1965 when twenty-five-year-old John Lewis led six hundred others across the Edmund Pettus Bridge from Selma, Alabama, all the way to Montgomery. Almost everyone knows that history. State troopers beat the shit out of them. That televised brutality marked a turning point in the civil rights movement that led to the passage of the Voting Rights Act. There was a problem though: All these decades later, many of us still couldn't vote. So to draw attention to that unfinished business, a week before the anniversary of Bloody Sunday, Kenny and his people reenacted the march across the bridge backwards— from the Montgomery side back to Selma—to pick up where the movement had left off. It was an act of symbolic genius. When we all convened in Dothan as the Formerly Incarcerated and Convicted People and Families Movement, we traveled the one hundred–plus miles to the Edmund Pettus Bridge and did that backwards march together. It centered our struggle as the latest chapter in an uninterrupted civil rights movement, one we were waging on our own behalf.

Those of us who'd been waging it the longest had been through the Arctic winter. By the time we gathered in Alabama,

275

that was starting to change—and a certain book had something to do with it. *The New Jim Crow: Mass Incarceration in the Age of Colorblindness*, by Michelle Alexander, came out in January 2010. At first, it didn't gain much traction. With Barack Obama in office, too many people seemed to think we were living in a postracial wonderland. Michelle had to hustle to be heard. She spent two years traveling the country in an exhausting journey of book promotion, while Susan Burton and I bought up her brilliance in bulk. In 2012 she finally broke through, landing on the *New York Times* bestseller list. The book would stay there for nearly five years. I'd been framing the prison industrial complex as our era's Jim Crow for a while. I spoke to Michelle Alexander's class about that when she was a visiting professor at Stanford Law School. But the people who listened to Michelle Alexander were different from the people who listened to Dorsey Nunn. The sister is a well-known civil rights lawyer, advocate, and legal scholar who hadn't experienced the misfortune of being called *criminal, offender, inmate, felon, ex-con.* Her book had depth and reach. It transformed the national debate on race and criminal justice, and Michelle's persuasive capacity to change readers' minds put some wind in our sails.

In 2015, four years after our Dothan convening, All of Us or None members drove twenty-four hundred miles back to the Edmund Pettus Bridge for the fiftieth anniversary of Bloody Sunday. President Obama was on the speakers' schedule with a message on voting rights, and more than eighty thousand people turned out to reenact the historic march. Kenny's backward march was usually held one week earlier, but by now our message resonated enough that event organizers included it in the main event. The giant crowd amassed in Selma waited for *us* as we marched toward them from the other side, carrying a banner emblazoned with a slogan Kenny had come up with: "From the Back of the Bus to the Front of the Prison. The Struggle Continues." I take credit for a catchy chant: *"Can you share your civil rights with a brotha like me? I've been convicted of a felony!"* Once we crossed, we turned around, fell back just behind the front lines, and all marched toward Montgomery together. The message was clear: felony disenfranchisement is a denial of democracy and a legacy of slavery.

There were a couple of other chants that rang out on that bridge named for a Ku Klux Klan grand dragon: "Hands Up, Don't Shoot," and "I Can't Breathe." Because the summer before, police had killed Michael Brown and Eric Garner, in Ferguson, Missouri, and New York City. It was a moment of reckoning, and the Black Lives Matter movement was tearing through the country. At last, structural racism against Black and brown people didn't seem so abstract to some Americans. 277 Many were finally waking up to racist oppression disguised as tough-on-crime politics, and we were ready to engage them with concrete ideas to repair the harm.

WHEN WE FIRST gathered in Dothan, I'd been executive director of LSPC for about four months. Being the sole person in charge was an altogether different exercise than being codirector, and I turned to Susan Burton often for advice. I'd already moved LSPC away from a near-exclusive focus on women with the formation of All of Us or None, and our grassroots movement was becoming more central to LSPC's identity with each passing year. Still, for some in the organization, my vision to create yet another entity, this time a nationwide umbrella of organizations led by and for formerly incarcerated people, came out of left field and carried risks. The structure FICPFM had come up with was a revolving fiscal sponsorship. That meant each of the nonprofits represented on the steering committee would take turns, including LSPC. But the steering committee would control the agenda, not the fiscal sponsor. FICPFM would bring LSPC closer to the movement in ways that turned out to be rich and transformational. But I had to navigate some real discomfort, and Susan whispered in my ear along the way. She also offered me guidance when LSPC fell on tough financial times. Our funding wasn't keeping up with our vision. Without my staff knowing, I went without pay for a year. Hamdiya Cooks-Abdullah had become an indispensable member of the staff and was now LSPC's administrative director. She took half pay. We were that committed. Being boss came with the joy of hiring, and I started pulling in so many formerly incarcerated people that at times they've made up 70 percent of my staff. I was carrying forward that gift Michael Satris had given me a quarter of a century earlier, providing breathing room for my staff to learn, make mistakes, grow from them, and dream about what comes next. Some are settling into new identities. For a flash in time I was Ajamu, so I'm sensitive to these changes. I tell people, "You can be whoever you want to be, just tell me a name I can put on the check so you can cash it." They flourish and move on and up, and just about every time they do, I cry. They're part of me.

Being boss also meant I had to fire people who messed up repeatedly despite guidance and patience. It got me thinking about my final months at the Prison Law Office, when crack was colonizing my mind. I'd lie, come in late, or not come in at all. So a little more than two decades after I quit to slink back to my ghetto, I got in my car and drove to the Prison Law Of-

278

fice to see Don Spector. Don, who'd become executive director after Michael Satris left, was still in charge. I walked through his open office door, and before he had a chance to say hello, I apologized.

"What, are you on step nine?" he asked, thinking I was making amends as part of my twelve-step work.

"No, man," I told him. "I'm coming here to say I'm sorry, because what I fundamentally know to be my truth is that I was an asshole as an employee."

Don's a serious guy, but he cracked a smile. Enough said.

THE ORGANIZATIONS BY and for the formerly incarcerated that made up our coalition were having impact at the local and state level across the country. As a group, we were educating one another on tactics and pitfalls, and demonstrating our strength in numbers and geographic reach. But our meeting at the Justice Department with the Federal Interagency Reentry Council in late 2014 led to few tangible changes. The one concrete step forward that came out of it was creation of a position called Second Chance Fellow at the Department of Justice, to bring in the legal perspective of someone who is formerly incarcerated. Our ally Daryl Atkinson landed the one-year gig. We'd been hoping for more, and that left a slightly bitter taste. We'd paid our own way, and Susan complained that our federal hosts didn't so much as offer us a bottle of water. But looking back, our presence likely influenced President Obama's decision to Ban the Box for federal agencies a year later. Susan had predicted he'd do *something*.

"Dorsey," she told me one day, "occasionally I watch football."

"Yeah," I said. "What do that mean?"

279

She grinned. "I ain't never seen a Black man score a touchdown that didn't spike the ball. Barack Obama's gonna show out in his last term."

That day in 2015, when Obama used the term *ban the box* on national television and I almost fell out of my office chair, I had a special guest sitting across from me. Kalima Aswad had just walked off forty-six years in prison. My lifelong mentor was now eighty years old. He'd just learned to take the Bay Area Rapid Transit train that morning in order to come see me. Now, I was finally able to answer his question, "What will you do with your newfound freedom?" I'd used the privilege to fight for him and all others still stuck in cages and coming out of cages. For the remaining four years of Kalima's life, he joined us in that fight.

Michelle Alexander's book, the Black Lives Matter movement, and our own hard work to get our stories out there meant public sentiment toward formerly incarcerated people was thawing. Meanwhile, we—LSPC, All of Us or None, and all the organizations that made up the Formerly Incarcerated, Convicted People and Families Movement—were making sure more of us were politically engaged and voting. That helped cure a major problem we'd encountered back in the 1990s with ballot box legislating when the tough-on-crime free-for-all was at its peak. More formerly incarcerated people going to the polls increased our chances for victory. The first big win for us in California came in 2012 with the Three Strikes Reform Act. It came eighteen long years after that oppressive law first passed, years of continuous and escalating damage to Black and brown communities. The new ballot measure spelled out that the third felony conviction, the one that would strike you out and land you a life sentence, had to be "serious or violent." Most important, it let people who'd been sent away on a nonviolent or nonserious third felony get resentenced. That was huge. Plenty of the people I hired after we helped get that measure passed came out of cages that way. So did a lot of my homies. Two years later, after a lot of hard work and lobbying by LSPC and All of Us or None, California voters passed Proposition 47. That measure busted certain felonies down to misdemeanors and was retroactive, meaning tens of thousands of people could petition to change and expunge their records. It also saved money by locking up fewer people, and directed those savings to drug treatment, mental health treatment, and to keeping kids out of the school-to-prison pipeline.

As our ideas became more palatable to the mainstream, we started getting some love. In April 2016, I flew back to the White House to be honored with a Champions of Change Award for my work around reentry. Hamdiya and Ellen were in the audience. So was Alma, my childhood sweetheart. We were back together yet again. After I acknowledged them, I spoke my truth in other ways—about how freezing formerly incarcerated people out of the workforce doesn't just punish us, it keeps about $65 billion a year out of the economy, hurting our communities. I also took issue with the cherry-picking they seemed to be doing. Everyone in the business of incremental reform was quick to make distinctions between violent and nonviolent, deserving or nondeserving. I believed that to be some serious bullshit. We'd all done our time and paid our debts, I said. Then I posed a question that had half the audience staring at their shoes: "When do you recognize that those of you who work for the government exist off my tax dollars too? You work for me too."

I was honored to be honored. But I'd already learned that talking to federal bureaucrats wasn't the most effective way to bring about change. As FICPFM, we had a new kind of power, and it wasn't dependent on the approval of the chosen few. Our strength stemmed from our diversity of experience, and the sheer force of our numbers. So, in September 2016, we convened the first national gathering since we'd first come together in Dothan. All of Us or None and LSPC hosted in Oakland, and more than five hundred people affiliated with all the rich and varied organizations in our coalition showed up. These gatherings aren't cheap. We fund a lot of scholarships, and house and feed our comrades. But they serve a few key purposes. They allow us to strategize about collective priorities, and to learn from one another's victories and missteps. They also inspire us, which is especially important for those traveling from far-off, conservative places. Coming together confirms for them that they aren't crazy. They can see how others have prevailed and keep on pushing. Gathering in force also makes us visible in all our organizing prowess to policymakers and funders, our special guests.

282

When a tribute to FICPFM founders during the conference opener referred to me as "the godfather of the movement," the crowd started chanting, "Dorsey! Dorsey! Dorsey!" Yes, I cried. Then Kenny Glasgow stood up and vowed to never let my name die. I cried some more. There were decades dating back to my time in cages when I'd felt the loneliness of my struggle, of our collective struggle. Now our community was growing faster than I ever could have imagined, and I felt rich in all this good company. Assistant Attorney General Karol Mason, a sister who'd been in the room with us at the Reentry Council gathering in Washington, DC, two years earlier, came and spoke too. She was honest in acknowledging that the pace of change had been slow, that she'd been pushing her colleagues to take the moral high ground, to be more courageous in the few remaining months of the Obama administration. They'd fallen short.

From the Prison Gate to the White House Gate

The nitty-gritty work involved coming to a consensus on a collective battle. When we took the temperature of the audience using a cell phone voting app, an end to felony disenfranchisement was still high on the list, as it had been back in Dothan. Voting rights. We were uniformly sick of taxation without representation. Desmond Meade, our brother from Florida who sits on the FICPFM steering committee, moderated a panel on civic participation, which posed the question, "Am I a citizen if I don't have the rights?" He would prove to be an important teacher for all of us.

TWO MONTHS AFTER our Oakland conference, Donald Trump got elected, and those channels of communication we'd spent time developing with the federal bureaucracy snapped closed. It was once again time to go local, and Desmond would show us a new way. In September 2018, he hosted our second FICPFM gathering in Orlando, Florida, and this one took all our human power and put it to work on the streets right then and there, to make real change in real time.

We at All of Us or None had learned to write a resolution and turn a resolution into an ordinance, which was the expression of public policy at the local level. We had learned how to craft a bill and find a state legislator to carry it for us, to lobby in numbers, and to change state law. But Susan's frustrations from that early Ban the Box loss in Los Angeles still rang true. Sometimes it took just one backward politician to derail all our efforts. Desmond had found another way: taking a state constitutional amendment straight to the people. If you want to avoid the steep costs of signature gathering, the first step still involves getting a bill past the legislature. That essentially places the issue on the ballot for voters to decide. By the time we got together on Desmond's turf, he had founded the Florida Rights Restoration Coalition, and they'd managed to jump that first hurdle. Amendment 4, to restore voting rights to people with felony convictions, was on the November 2018 ballot. That gave the one thousand of us FICPFM homies who descended on Orlando a mission—to persuade a whole lot of voters to come out in force and push Amendment 4 over the finish line.

Wearing shirts that said, *Your Vote is My Voice*, we took to the streets that weekend, persuading a lot of good people to open the door of democracy to their cousins, neighbors, sisters, friends, and every other person who had served their debt to society. We advocated for that right. We also got people excited about the *exercise* of that right. We gave them a reason to care, to act. And all the while, we were learning. We got familiar with phone banking, campaign text messaging, political issues focus groups, and branding. And we tracked our efforts. Our people knocked on eighteen hundred doors, sent ten thousand emails, and texted seventy thousand people—in a two-and-a-half-hour period. We learned enough to fill a book. Now *that's* the value of a national coalition.

284

November 6, 2018, was a midterm election, and when the polls closed, plenty of liberals across the country were gauging the victory or defeat of Black representation through high-profile races. There were painful defeats. Andrew Gillum, who would have become Florida's first Black governor, lost to Republican Ron DeSantis. In Georgia, Democrat Stacey Abrams conceded her powerful race for governor too. Formerly incarcerated people like me, though, were watching other races that night. And the tears of joy flowed when Amendment 4 cruised to victory. We were also watching the Louisiana polls that night, and we cried some more tears when voters there approved another constitutional amendment. Amendment 2 was the baby of Norris Henderson, another FICPFM steering committee member, and his grassroots crew at Voice of the Experienced delivered. That change to the state constitution requires unanimous jury verdicts to convict people of felonies. Before that, ten out of twelve was all it took to put someone away for life or arrange a state-sanctioned killing. I went to bed with a smile on my face, feeling like we'd kicked the new Jim Crow in the balls, twice.

WE AT ALL of Us or None and LSPC came home to California from Florida with all that new knowledge bursting inside us. We got a bill signed into law by the governor that would let almost all people with felony convictions who weren't on parole sit on juries. Called "the Right to a Jury of Your Peers," the legislation was carried by Berkeley's Senator Nancy Skinner, one of our strongest allies in Sacramento. It passed like a knife through butter. Meanwhile, we were working hard, Desmond-style, to get legislation through Sacramento for our own constitutional amendment that would lift the voting ban for about fifty thousand Californians on parole. For starters, we formed a loose statewide coalition of formerly incarcerated–led organizations. Power in numbers. We knocked on doors asking legislators for their support. We lobbied the ones on the fence, and brought the heat by securing resolutions in favor of the bill, ACA6, from the Oakland and Richmond city councils and from elected supervisors in Alameda and San Francisco counties. We developed a website, ran full-page ads in the *Sacramento Bee*, and got high-profile influencers like Angela Davis and Michelle Alexander to stand with us.

285

It took a minute, but we got ACA6 through the state legislature. That meant we wouldn't have to pay to gather signatures. Our measure was on the November 2020 ballot as Proposition 17—and the work of convincing the public began. I'm old enough and smart enough to know to place my trust in youth, and it was the younger soldiers who helped take the message to Instagram, Twitter, and Facebook. We placed ads through Pandora and Spotify and got ourselves on talk shows all over the state. John Legend, Dolores Huerta, and Danny Glover joined our list of influencers. Our phone banks were on fire. Replicating Desmond's operation, we made more than fifty thousand phone calls and sent out about three hundred thousand text messages. And we did it all at the height of the COVID-19 pandemic. We got creative about that too, distributing more than ten thousand facemasks that said, *Yes on 17—Let All People Vote*. We handed them out in front of stores, at rallies, on buses, on corners, at laundromats, reentry and drug treatment centers, and barber shops, and every place else our staff could gain entry, not just on our Bay Area turf but in Stockton, Bakersfield, San Diego, Riverside, Los Angeles, and East Palo Alto. To ensure our message was touching people incarcerated in the county jails, we delivered hundreds of masks to the public defender's office in San Francisco and Alameda counties and to the San Mateo County private defender. We even created a special-edition newspaper to distribute inside prisons.

Proposition 17 passed with nearly 59 percent of the vote. I couldn't have felt prouder of my community for stepping up. For formerly incarcerated people to engage at this level, at the height of a pandemic, was unprecedented. We had enfranchised fifty thousand new potential voters. Those kinds of numbers can swing local and state elections. Still, I knew that engaging

286

those prospective voters and persuading them that their voices mattered would require a lifetime of ongoing work. I also found myself wondering, would the public figure out that formerly incarcerated people had amended three state constitutions in three years? Would they finally view us as potential assets to our communities instead of liabilities? Because no matter how much I accomplish, it seems, it will never be enough. Part of that is the nature of the struggle. There is so much still to do. Part of it resides inside me.

Chapter 20

THE SHAPE OF THE
HOLE I LEFT BEHIND

Remorse can't be forced by punishment. If you're watching men in cages get shanked, shot, and burned, fighting for your own survival, remorse is meaningless. If you haven't learned about the privilege and sacrifice of love, remorse is futile. If you've been taught to hate yourself, remorse is unattainable.

When I was locked up, my slave masters thought that if I wasn't wailing with snot coming out my nose, I didn't have any kind of feeling about what had taken place in the Newark liquor store that night. False. Because I hadn't snitched, they thought I hadn't accepted responsibility. False again. I took responsibility for my part in what transpired. Snitching wouldn't have made me any less culpable. I gave eleven years of my life when I probably could have done none. And every time I wrapped my arms around my daughter in the San Quentin visiting room, I wondered if there was a child out there who no longer had a father to hug because of the life we wound up taking that night. I absolutely felt sorry. But remorse is something else. Remorse is a seed that requires certain conditions to sprout. When my fight instinct caused me to whip around in the darkness and punch Alma's teenaged niece in the face, that seed was dormant. By the time I sat down across from Denise at Heidi's Pies with a year of sobriety under my belt and committed to being the best father I could be, that seed had sprouted into a sapling. Over the course of decades, as I earned my place as the Nunn family patriarch, it grew into one motherfucking sturdy tree.

People can say they're sorry all they want. It doesn't mean anything. What matters is your practice. Even when I was an addict, what was hardest for me to forgive about myself wasn't that I was using dope, it was the children I walked past on the way to getting high with their parents. What was hardest for me to forgive wasn't my theft of material objects as I was coming up, but deeper, more intangible thefts. I stole a piece of my father's dignity when, instead of accepting his discipline, I attacked him as soon as I got old and big enough. I stole Alma's youth when I got her pregnant at fifteen. I robbed Faydell of her ability to trust when I kept taking up with her former best friend. As for my moms, whether or not she fully realized it, I stripped away a piece of her faith when I asked her to lie for me in court after she swore on the Bible. I think about that continuously. It's why the last place I took my mother before she died was to see the church she cofounded. The damage I did to the people in my closest orbit sank in quick. The damage to that other family came more gradually. Even though I never touched the gun, over time I came to accept that I stole a husband. I stole a father. I left a hole so big that for a long time, I couldn't see its shape. It would reveal itself to me as my love for my own family deepened.

I BECAME A patriarch in stages. At first there was no one else available to step up. Then it became my calling. I cared for my mother as her health failed, hauled my siblings into rehab, buried Pat and then David. I held my wife in my arms until she breathed her last air on this earth and then cried as if a cannon had shattered my soul. I was able to feel those losses, to participate in my grief, because of the depth of the love I had learned to give, and the love I had learned to receive. My remorse was predicated on that exchange.

Denise wound up marrying an engineer with a good heart, a string of college degrees, and a family that hadn't been shredded to pieces by the prison industrial complex. Their daughters, Raven and Sydney, were gifted a life of safety, love, and comfort. I remember the day Denise told me, "Dad, you don't ever have to get them gifts, not for Christmas or anytime. Just give them your presence, so they'll know their grandfather." I've done that with joy. My son, Sockie, didn't know me until I walked holes in my shoes to find him. Not long after, he became a teenaged dad just like I had, bringing Anthony Jr. into the world. But as crack grabbed hold of me, I slunk off in shame, and the distance between us widened. When I really was on step nine of my sobriety program, I visited them to make amends. I was telling Anthony Jr. how much he could trust me now, acting all familiar, when he gut-punched me by asking me who I was.

"I'm your grandfather," I told him. He just looked up at me deadpan.

"Then how come I don't know you?"

291

With that, an eight-year-old boy blew a hole in my heart. I went to therapy for several weeks on that shit. My desire to know him, to have him know *me*, brought me back into Alma's life. So did Sockie's second child, Deajah, who came along later. She was the one who was headed for the child dependency system when both her parents wound up in jail at the same time. Sheila and I couldn't take her. We were both "felons." Besides that, Sheila knew she would likely be losing her fight with cancer. We had to focus on her health and on our love in our final time together. Deajah stayed with Alma for a while, but the two didn't mix, so into the system she went. And guess what? She turned out strong and beautiful, the first in our family to graduate a four-year college. Anthony Jr. turned out just fine too. I'd failed to keep his dad out of jail, though I did make good on my commitment to keep him out of state prison. Saving Anthony Jr. from incarceration became my next priority. When he was a young buck going through his peacock phase and posturing for girls, I was convinced he was getting high. So I marched onto his middle school campus with a jar in my hand, pulled him into the bathroom, and told him to pee in it. The kid turned out to be clean as a whistle. It was the raging hormones talking. I'd been there too. I doubt Anthony Jr. appreciated the gesture at the time, but he sure as shit knew I cared. After that, we got close. There was gang and drug activity all around the boy. When I smelled trouble coming, I stepped in to help him make sound choices. He knew my history, and I reminded him of it whenever I got the chance. It helped him avoid the traps I fell into as a Black teen growing up in a violent community. We could see how hard he was trying to escape his circumstances, so we sent him out of state to a four-year college. He didn't quite finish, but he came home happy, with a beautiful woman and a baby. My grandson is an excellent father, better than me or his own dad were or could be. Saniah, my great-granddaughter, most surely knows every day that she is loved, even if I sometimes think she's spoiled rotten.

For years, my son and my grandson called me by my first name. One of the greatest rewards of my life was when they started calling me Dad and Pops—and saying it in a real way. Lately my grands have all shown up for the movement, which fills my heart with a pride too big to describe. Anthony Jr. started tagging along with me as I lobbied lawmakers in Sacramento back when he was about thirteen. The last time we rode up there together for LSPC's annual Quest 4 Democracy, he was thirty-two. *This* is how time helps a family heal. With each generation I get stronger, and they get stronger too. With each generation I come to a deeper understanding of how I deprived the family of that liquor store owner of a similar luxury.

THE DEPTH OF loss is a measure of love, and for me, the losses kept on coming. In 2014, death ran particularly fast and hard through my life. In the spring, complications from hepatitis C took Ronald, the last of my surviving brothers. In his eight years clean, he worked as a mentor at Free at Last. He managed to buy his own car, and to my delight he became a man who paid me back when he borrowed money.

Denise was next to leave this world. Watching her grow from a child into a powerful woman was one of the great privileges of my life. It's why I advocate so fiercely for prison visits—not solely as a right for prisoners, but as a right for families. Because in-person visits help human beings in cages hold on to their humanity while building relationships that have an opportunity to endure. Visiting makes reuniting possible, giving communities a chance to survive and thrive. Visiting planted the seed for my enduring relationship with Denise. Still, the journey to trust was long. It required work of both of us. And we rolled up our sleeves and did it. In the years before my daughter died, we had a running conversation about class. Denise was more than comfortable being middle class. She'd worked hard to get there, and she tried to convince me that I was solidly middle class too, that poverty is a state of mind I was clinging to. I kept money in my pocket and in the bank, and I saved enough to buy a vacation place up in Clearlake with some good fishing nearby, not to mention a casino. Through sheer stubbornness and the help of friends when I was in need, I still had my family's house, now in the shadow of Facebook and worth a million bucks or more. I had a fondness for luxury cars, so that's what I drove. But the whole idea of being middle class still made me uncomfortable. So did the divergence of my granddaughters' upbringing from my own. Not long before Denise died, I sat in the audience of a Walnut Creek theater watching one of my granddaughters dancing in the Nutcracker ballet and thinking, *This music don't got a beat at all. What am I doing here? How did my daughter get here?* Before that, Raven had auditioned for and come close to getting a role in the movie *Fruitvale Station*, a feature film based on the police killing of twenty-four-year-old Oscar Grant. A transit officer had shot the brother in the back while they had him face down on the platform, and it sparked a deep and justified rage that burned for more than a decade. I'd been in a meeting when Oscar's uncle, Cephus Johnson, walked into the room and said, "Damn, they killed my nephew." Raven was just learning about Oscar Grant. The police killings of Eric Garner and Michael Brown were all over the news. When I saw those images, my first thought was, *These motherfuckers are trying to kill me.* For the girls, it was theoretical: the police are trying to kill *other* Black people. I wrestled with our divergent experiences. Suppose you struggle past all the barriers to get to a place where you can enjoy the best society has to offer, I wondered. When you get there, will you still be as kind?

These questions were gnawing at me enough that I picked up the phone and called Denise. We talked through it all. Before we said good-bye, I told her straight up, "I'm gonna love my grandkids even if I know they're turning out different than me."

One week later, on December 21, 2014, Denise succumbed to sickle cell anemia at age forty-five. She died at a hospital with access to the best medical treatment money could buy. There just wasn't enough available, because sickle cell anemia is a disease nearly exclusive to Black folks. Denise's husband, Daniel, called me as soon as she died, and I came to the room to sit with him as her body went cold. We talked about her beauty and her courage. Then I told Daniel what Denise had told me: If something should happen to her, she wanted Daniel and me to take care of her; if she passed, she wanted Daniel and me to take care of Raven and Sydney. She wanted me to hold those girls tight, to stay in their lives. I wanted that too.

Denise was smart as a whip, fierce, and whole and proud. Sitting at her funeral, listening to her friends tell me who my daughter was to them, was a gift. By now I'd lost a significant part of my immediate family, and when I got up to speak, I explained that I took my comfort from Job. The devil goes to the Lord and says Job may seem like a good servant, but the dude hasn't really been tested. So the Lord takes away all Job's oxen and all his donkeys. He takes away the house, he takes away his family, and even when the man has nothing, he's still got faith. Losing Denise was a blow so large I was feeling lost, and right away I knew I had to find in the situation the place where gratitude rested.

I hear Denise's voice in my head a lot, poking at me about my poverty state of mind. And in a way, she's right. It comes back in part to the commitment I made to Kalima—to be an asset to my community. I need to stay close to my roots so I don't lose sight of who I am, so I never leave my homies behind. Lately, though, I think remorse has something to do with it. I was raised in poverty, and I was in a poverty state of mind the night of my crime. I was enraged at my deprivation and at the racism at its root. And in that state, I felt entitled. Entitled to be served first in that liquor store, before the white man who walked in after us. Entitled to be respected. Entitled to material wealth I'd been denied. When I felt entitled, that's when I became dangerous. That's when I caused harm. In recent years, I remodeled my house, made myself a nice man cave in the garage with a plush lounger and a big screen TV. I've spent some rare money on myself because I can afford to. I don't feel deprived, and I don't feel entitled. Still, I keep thinking there must be some mistake. I can't wrap my head around the fact that I've come to a place of comfort. I find myself marveling at my good fortune and wondering at the same time if I could possibly deserve it. It's in these moments that I almost always think about that man on the floor of the liquor store.

If you asked me what he looked like, I couldn't tell you. I wish I could see his face in my mind. I don't. Instead, it's the meaningful relationships in my own life that crystallize for me what that other family no longer has. I see the shape of his absence. As my love grows, as my loss grows, the lost love of that other family comes into clearer focus. *That* is remorse. And none of it came to me because the state locked me in a cage. That punishment put me in a space where survival was contingent on terrible acts, the opposite of its supposed intent. My remorse came as a result of my own hard work, against all odds, in the face of lingering trauma, with nothing to turn to for relief but the poison of street drugs. My remorse is my victory over punishment. Despite the beatings, physical and spiritual, the degradations that harken back to slavery—*squat, cough, lift up your nuts*—I got myself to a place where I could see the shape of the hole I created.

FOR YEARS, I thought about the family I harmed. But before I could contemplate reaching out to them, there was a hurdle I needed to cross. Anthony Jr. was old enough to know my story. Deajah, the second oldest, knew something of my personal history too. She'd been separated from both parents when they were in jail and was wiser than her years, more savvy than any child should be. Raven, Sydney, and Saniah, meanwhile, were innocence incarnate. We had to have "the talk." Not the sex talk. The other talk. The one every formerly incarcerated person who ever procreated dreads. Whatever the kids might find out about my past, they needed to hear it from me first. Susan Burton and I talked about this in more than a few of our daily calls, and she was gentle but firm with her encouragement. If I wanted honest relationships, if I wanted the kids to love me as wholly as I loved them, I had to let them know the fullness of who I'd been and come to be. After all, prison is built into my DNA. It's the source of my trauma and my passion, the fuel of my daily commitment.

It was Saniah who put "the talk" on the front burner. She was barely old enough to read when she picked up an LSPC

297

newsletter that was sitting on the kitchen table and learned that Dorsey Nunn had done prison time. When she asked me about it in her little girl's voice, my heart nearly skipped a beat. So I took her down to Baskin-Robbins to buy her some ice cream and told her the basics: I did some bad things a long time ago. I had to pay for those mistakes, so I'd gone to prison for a long time. The details of the felony murder charge, I left out—for now. But I knew the time had come to gather the girls together and lay it out. My plan involved a nice chicken dinner. About a year before Denise died, I sat in the car with Saniah, Raven, and Sydney after eating at a fine suburban restaurant. I felt more nervous than I'd ever been before the parole board.

"You're sweating," Sydney pointed out.

She was right. I explained as best I could who I was at nineteen years old. I told them robbing liquor stores was something I'd done more than once, that on this one occasion, it went more wrong than I could have imagined. That it ended with a man dying. Even though I didn't pull the trigger, I told them, I was there. I was part of the chain of events that led to a murder of a man, and I would always regret it. At nine, Sydney was the oldest. "Mom already told us you'd been to prison," she said quietly. It was close to Christmas time, and Raven piped up next.

"That's the saddest Christmas story that's ever been told."

We sat with that for a minute in my Infiniti luxury sedan, the heater quietly humming. Then we headed to the shopping mall. When we got there, the girls wrapped me in a hug. I'd pressed a hundred-dollar bill into each of their small hands— one of those material gifts Denise had told me I never had to give them—and soon they were lined up inside with their Benjamin Franklins to buy some boba tea. That's how innocent they were. So much was swirling in my mind, but protecting these little Black girls rose to the top. I pulled them out of the line. Yes, I got to stealing as a youth growing up in my real estate–created ghetto. But long before I did, I was already a suspect. Presumed guilty. Watching the girls, it was clear to me no boba tea stand was about to break a hundred-dollar bill once, let alone three times. And I didn't want them to be questioned. I didn't want their innocence touched in my presence.

As the next half dozen years passed, the girls didn't ask me hard questions. They accepted me. Thankfully, the lives of Raven, Sydney, and Saniah did not involve prisons or prison visiting rooms. They set my past aside. But Deajah was older and more experienced. By now she was studying at Cal State Hayward. We share the same last name, and other students had asked her about me, bringing up things she didn't know much about. Some had seen me mentioned in Michelle Alexander's book, *The New Jim Crow*. Others had caught a glimpse of me as they sat in the classroom and watched the documentary *13th*, a powerful analysis of the intersection of race, criminal justice, and mass incarceration in this country by sister Ava DuVernay. She took her title from the Thirteenth Amendment to the US Constitution, which did away with slavery and involuntary servitude back in 1865—except when it comes to those of us convicted of crimes, who can still be worked for pennies on the hour. Deajah deserved to know my full truth. So one night in June 2019, just after the family showed up strong for her college graduation, I took her to a Jamaican restaurant in uptown Oakland for some rich-tasting oxtails.

By now, I knew I wanted to reach out to the family I harmed. The wife of the liquor store owner had been in the back room that night. She'd heard the shot and run out to see her husband on the floor. I had reason to believe she might still be around—at ninety years old. I wanted to ask her if she was the same person she'd been at nineteen. Because I wasn't. I wanted her to know I'd dedicated my life to making positive change in my own community. If she was a religious woman, I reasoned, maybe an opportunity for forgiveness would bring her peace on her way out. If she wasn't inclined to forgive, I still wanted to apologize. If she wanted to tell me to go fuck myself, that would be OK too, as long as it didn't cause her harm. I also had reason to believe she had a son who was about my age. I wanted to tell him how sorry I was too. I'd been working it over in my mind. But these kinds of decisions weren't mine alone to make. They could impact my whole family. So I took Deajah into my confidence right there at the dinner table.

"If the person that killed your relative was still alive," I asked her, "how would you feel about meeting them?"

300

Dear Mr. ——,

I hope that this letter finds you and your family in the best of health and happiness always in your immediate reach. My name is Dorsey Nunn, and I am writing to apologize for the tremendous harm that I have caused to you and your family. In 1971, I actively participated in a robbery that resulted in the death of your father. I was subsequently tried and convicted of first-degree murder and received a life sentence in 1972 as punishment for my involvement.

I sweated the writing of the letter. Was I doing it for them? Or was I doing it for me? How could I approach the family in the most respectful way? For help with these questions, I called my friend and colleague Danielle Sered. She pretty much wrote the Bible on how our society needs to stop favoring the nonviolent and unjustly sentenced when it comes to criminal justice reform. *Until We Reckon: Violence, Mass Incarceration and a Road to Repair* makes the strong case that punishment as a core philosophy isn't working. Instead, people who commit violence should be asked to make amends to those they've damaged. That same restorative justice approach the Maori brothers taught me about in New Zealand back in 1997.

I think punishment does nothing to address spiritual and moral debt. I owed an apology not to the state of California but to you and your family. I know it may not mean much after all these years, but I am sorry. I have held on to this apology for much too long, and I will continue to pray that it is not too late for it to be meaningful. If I could change anything in my life, it would be that night. . . . As I grew older, I knew the life that had 301 *been taken also impacted all the people who loved your father and the life trajectory of everyone in his sphere. Each time tragedy has knocked on my door with the loss of a loved one, it made it even more impossible to deny what I had taken. . . .*

With Danielle's help, we mailed the letter to an address where we thought the son was living. I haven't heard back, but I still hope to. At the very least, I hope he read it.

Chapter 21

HOMECOMING

On a mild winter night in December 2021, we brought a catered buffet in to LSPC's new headquarters in Oakland, California, and decked out the generous community room with gold balloons that spelled out W-E-L-C-O-M-E. We'd all weathered the darkness and isolation of the COVID-19 pandemic, going virtual for our monthly All of Us or None meetings. It was time to break bread together. A chance to have a meal without having to code-switch or do a dance. A time to be seen by others who recognize our individual and collective value.

I had thought hard and often about what homecoming meant to me when I finally walked out the gates of San Quentin to so-called freedom. It meant hope, sure, but the reality entailed mostly disappointment, despair, and humiliation. Disappointment that I could see in my own family's eyes that they had no place for me. Despair that women locked their doors when they saw my bulked-up frame walking down the street, and that just about every employer I approached for a job told me no. Humiliation that I had nowhere to go to commune with other formerly incarcerated people but the parole office or a street corner for dope slinging. In those spaces, we were pariahs known only as our worst mistakes. Felons. Ex-cons. Our humanity and dignity had been disappeared. Now there was an alternative, one we'd built ourselves.

We'd gotten notice in 2017 that the San Francisco building on Market Street that housed our office was slated for development. Gentrification was pushing us out. But there was a blessing in that fucked-up truth. We'd had a few landlords since Ellen Barry created the organization back in 1978. As far as I knew, we'd never been late with the rent, so I did the math, calculating that we'd handed over $1,267,000 in rent to those landlords. I'd pulled LSPC through some financially fraught times as executive director, building it up to the point where we had a staff of twenty—nearly three-fourths of them formerly incarcerated, almost entirely people of color. We didn't want others speaking for us anymore, so why would we want to continue to surrender our hard-earned money? It was time to buy. We were living in a post–boom-bust-boom, high-tech economy, so San Francisco was off the table. Oakland was a bit more affordable and had history as a Black town, even if that history was getting erased by the day. The Lionel J. Wilson Terminal at Oakland International Airport is named after that judge whose courtroom I'd trashed back in 1971. The juvenile hall camp is named after Wilmont Sweeney, the brother who defended me in my second case. The federal and state buildings are named after Black men too, not to mention the fact that Oakland was the home of the Black Panther Party. I got with our board of directors, and we plotted out a way to finance it. Then I shopped. One seller stood me up without even hearing what I had to offer. It got under my skin. Was it because we had "prisoner" in the name of our organization? I asked a friend and attorney from my Prison Law Office days. Or did they do me that way because I'm Black?

"Well, Dorsey," she answered with delight in her voice, "it could be both!"

We had a laugh, and I kept on looking. When we found it, we *knew*. In the summer of 2018, we closed escrow on our new home, a single-story building in a mostly residential neighborhood of North Oakland where the Black Panthers used to run. It would become a drop-in, discrimination-free zone for our community while doubling as a headquarters for the brilliance of LSPC, All of Us or None, and the California Coalition for Women Prisoners. Next to the space we planned to build out for our utopia were some paying commercial tenants, including a psychologist who happened to be a sister. That made us landlords, with a steady stream of no-strings-attached income. At $2.5 million, the property was one hell of a down payment on our self-determination. We named it the Freedom and Movement Center. And we dedicated our ample conference room to Carol Strickman, our now-retired former staff attorney who helped litigate the end to indefinite solitary confinement in California prisons.

We hired a formerly incarcerated general contractor, who guaranteed us he'd exclusively employ formerly incarcerated subs. One was Willard "Ali" Birts, who'd recently bailed out of jail with borrowed funds on a bullshit charge that hadn't yet been adjudicated. Ali knew the Nunn name. He knew all my siblings, so I was the one he called at midnight to come pick him up. He had done hard time in prison, come out, and was doing great. But thanks to a love affair gone south, he was now

305

coming to work for me every day wearing a goddamned ankle monitor—at a personal cost to him of $1,030 a month. I'd fight like hell to help him through that chapter of life, starting with stable employment. Ali had a bit of manual labor in his past, but he'd never torn up a building, and he wasn't young. Still, he demolished walls, hung new sheetrock, and learned all kinds of other skills along the way with the rest of the crew.

By the time the remodel was done, we were sitting in a high-ceilinged open space with skylights that was painted with warm-colored accent walls. All the electrical, plumbing, and carpentry was done by the hands of formerly incarcerated men. Formerly incarcerated women had laid the carpet and helped hang photo portraits on our Ancestral Wall. We felt so proud of what we'd accomplished that we knocked on every door in the area to invite our neighbors to a block party as a way of introducing them to our space and our staff. Our goal was to demonstrate what reentry can look like when directly impacted people have legitimate input into all aspects of its development and management. Before COVID drove us online, All of Us or None meetings filled up our community space on the third Thursday of each month. Formerly incarcerated people who needed a place to search for work started stopping by to use a computer.

Now, in the winter of 2021, we were reconvening after a long lull to welcome anyone who'd been released from prison in the previous year to a new kind of center. Our returning honorees were mostly men. Among the few women present was Aminah Rasul, a fiery seventy-two-year-old woman who'd just walked off forty-two years. That's one area Hamdiya and I have committed to improving. LSPC has expanded so much from its roots that we need to double down on outreach to formerly incarcerated women. It was a "come as you are" kind of evening. Some guests wore hoodies, others came styled out in fine suits. I was suffering from fierce sciatica, and the pain down my leg was screaming so loud I could barely hear myself think. So I'd written down my remarks—something I rarely do—to keep it short and remember what I had to say. "Welcome home," I read. "Welcome to the dream that your absence inspired. You are the people we have been waiting for. This place was purchased by formerly incarcerated people because some of us never will forget what we have been through."

The truth is, I never was much for scripted comments. They come out choppy. When I took off my readers and looked up, I realized I had more to say. I got started with an emphatic "Mmm," which generally means the channel from my heart straight to my mouth is about to open wide. No filter. Some of the aged and lined faces looking back at me I'd known in the pen before I started shaving. Others were new to me, with decades of life ahead to practice their brilliance. The best I could do was relate and tell them where I came from.

"Some of y'all in this room, I can look in your eyes and see you all didn't allow them to break y'all," I said. "Well, I never allowed them to break me. And so, when I dreamed, I dreamed big. The two-and-a-half-million-dollar building you sitting in came *after* my life sentence. It came *after* the drive-by shooting that sent me back to jail in 1990. So y'all need to continue to dream. Some of us, when we were oppressed, we could only dream about getting through the gates. But that was the *beginning* of your journey. It wasn't the end of your journey."

I went on to tell them that this place is a place of honesty and truth, with zero backing from the po-po or parole. LSPC has never accepted that kind of funding. This place means safety. It means home. A real home, where they can walk in with their dignity intact and be welcomed for their full potential. "So if you ain't got no place else to go, and you got some burning questions you need help with," I told them, "man, we built this shit for y'all."

Hamdiya spoke next. She'd done twenty hard years in federal prison, and by now she'd dedicated about the same amount of time to our struggle, building movement as one of my most essential collaborators. She stood up to share a little more of herself. Like me and a lot of our guests in the room, she was an elder now too, at sixty-eight.

"Trauma brought me here," she said, "as well as meeting people who didn't judge. Dorsey and Karen Shain were codirectors of LSPC and took a chance on me, and now Dorsey and I can proudly say that together, we built *this*. I couldn't be more proud and blessed to be here today."

Hamdiya and I knew it in our bones: *This* was the culmination of our collective dream. More than litigation, more than policy victories, this community *of us, by us, and for us* was the foundation upon which everything else could rest. And when she and I are sitting in our rocking chairs, it will keep on keepin' on.

"Welcome home, everyone," Hamdiya continued. "You can contact us day or night. And just, be strong. What brought me to the work was knowing people that cared enough to take a chance on me. You'll find that here, and you'll find it with us."

WE NAILED THE meaning of *home* with the Freedom and Movement Center. But home is more than a concept. It's a place to lay your head and lock your door, a place to wash and eat and feel safe. And on that front, I knew our comrades coming out of prison were suffering fiercely. Kathy and Shirl had set me up in an apartment of my own, giving me a place to settle my nerves after more than a decade of degradation and constant danger. But things had changed since those days. Homelessness was on the rise throughout the Bay Area, in part because rents were out of control, and homelessness had a color that for the most part was not white. Gentrification had cleared out most of the aunties and distant cousins and neighbors a brother used to be able to wrangle a place to sleep from. Ali Birts had come knocking on *my* door when he first paroled from prison after two decades because he had no other choice. Our slice of Menlo Park was well on the way to becoming a Facebook town, and most of the other root families were gone. That's how large-scale gentrification ripples outward. Where do you go when you need a couch to sleep on if Miss Maddy's garage that you used to go knock on is no longer available because someone else owns the property? My house on Hill Avenue was one of the few exceptions. If my moms had a flaw, it was taking generosity to a level that impacted all of us in the house. She was a moms to a lot of people who didn't have shit to do with being born from her. That included extended family, her own kids' friends, and some strays we never could place. Once in a while, even today, someone knocks on my door who's been missing for decades. "Do the Nunns still stay here? I hung out with Ronald, Pat, David, and Gloria back in the day. And you must be Dorsey." I was *that* brother to Ali when he needed me.

Still, couch surfing with distant friends is not a housing solution. And after our move to Oakland, it became increasingly apparent just how many people camped near freeway onramps and on underpass sidewalks were formerly incarcerated. A survey of Oakland homeless encampment residents not long after we opened the Freedom and Movement Center found that more than 70 percent had conviction histories.

309

I was deep into puzzling through a solution when I met Lee "Taqwaa" Bonner. A practicing Muslim now clean and sober, Taqwaa had just come home to East Oakland after three decades in a cage—with no place to stay. Like me, when the brother went away, he hadn't turned twenty. Like me, he could barely read. And like me, he had put his time inside to good use. He got an associate's degree, mastered three electrical trades, and finished an electrical apprentice program. Taqwaa also came out with enough money for rent. The problem: landlords kept rejecting his applications because he had a felony and was on parole. No one he knew who he'd done time with was faring any better. His sister and daughter would have gladly taken him in, but they were living in federally subsidized Section 8 housing, and giving him a place to sleep was cause for eviction. So Taqwaa wound up sleeping in his car, just like Ali did while he worked for me. Meanwhile, the state of the East Oakland neighborhood Taqwaa had left behind was causing him distress. His homies used to line East Fourteenth Street in fine Cadillacs. Now they were sleeping in tents. I hired him about a nanosecond after we first spoke, and he became lead housing advocate for All of Us or None, based out of the Freedom and Movement Center. He's also policy and outreach leader for an organization called Just Cities, which supports the Fair Chance Housing campaign. In 2020, that campaign pushed through some of the strongest policies in the country in the cities of Oakland and Berkeley to protect formerly incarcerated people from housing discrimination—Ban the Box for housing. What makes these laws stronger than others around the country is the fact that they apply to just about all kinds of housing—private, Section 8, Federal Housing Authority, and all affordable housing. In almost all situations, landlords or housing

310

providers can't ask you about criminal history, period. They can't mention it in their housing ads or tell you criminal background checks are required. That means formerly incarcerated people can't automatically be frozen out of the private rental market, and families can be united. Just like with Ban the Box for employment, we started it here at home, and we're working with chapters nationally to ripple this change outward.

Those kinds of protections go a long way. But there's still one constituency that needs more help: old-timers coming out after decades in cages. And once we opened our doors at the Freedom and Movement Center, the calls from these old friends just kept on coming.

First there was Catfish, intelligent, principled, and trustworthy. I'd served time with Catfish in Gladiator School, where we'd both been part of the Black Culture Club. We both wound up at San Quentin, where I did eleven years—and he did thirty-nine. I invited him to an All of Us or None meeting, and another brother who had just walked off twenty-seven years happened to show up too. A few weeks later the phone rang, and Don Wilson's voice came on the line. Don and I had served on the Men's Advisory Council together, and it was Don I connected with Michael Satris when he was looking for a lead plaintiff in the class action lawsuit to end double-celling. When I paroled, Don stayed—for nearly four more decades. And on it went, one old homie after another calling me up or strolling in the front door.

We were celebrating their freedom, but the question remained: What is freedom when the system has taken away a person's entire working life? Getting that checkbox off housing applications is a good start. But these elders, these lifers, I realized, they need more. If you've walked off multiple decades, you probably lost your parents and your spouse or partner. You've got no social network. Home isn't home anymore. Some have never held a cell phone. They need trauma counseling. They need skills. They're too old to be doing physical labor. Plus, most of them can't enter the job market in a meaningful way because of the cost of health care. They aren't qualified for Social Security because many of them have only worked as slaves, and their quarterly earnings don't meet the threshold. They need someone to walk with them who can help them take steps to restore relations with their grown children, who can treat them like the adults they are—not infantilize them in a boilerplate program—and let them know with kindness that the dream they had when they went in probably needs to change. Most of all, they need shelter, because street living is a human rights violation for people in their sixties or older.

312 I have been searching for years now for a property that I can convert into supportive housing for these elderly lifers. I even had a deal lined up after a West Oakland pastor offered me the abandoned parsonage on land owned by his church. But bias can be hard to overcome. New leadership came in, and the parishioners got scared at the mere thought of these elders in their midst. So I'll keep looking. My goal is to house five elderly lifers the state might not even release without my promise of a landing place that's more than just a bed. If he still needs a place, one of those beds will have Don Wilson's name on it, because he's still living in a program that restricts his freedom and doesn't quite honor his brilliance. A few times a week, Don puts on a fine suit and matching hat and comes to hang out at the Freedom and Movement Center, where he is always respected. We've taken him to a major gathering in Atlanta and to Sacramento to testify to the state legislature on behalf of All of

Homecoming

Us or None. I plan to hire Ali Birts as our house manager. I also hope to create a vocational center for our elderly tenants, to teach them basic skills that could give them a shot at survival. It's my commitment in action, the one I made when I walked out of San Quentin to be an asset to my community instead of a liability—and to never forget the ones I left behind. My commitment is just graying along with me.

THROUGHOUT THE YEAR in 2021, the pace of prison releases seemed to increase. Some came because of Three Strikes reform, some thanks to an elderly parole program that an appellate court demanded and LSPC and AOUON helped strengthen with legislation that took effect in January. Others still were the result of our direct outreach to district attorneys in our comrades' counties of commitment. It was time to come together, and we at LSPC and All of Us or None spread the word throughout the community that each and every one was welcome at the homecoming dinner.

After Hamdiya and I spoke, and our staff members shared their stories, it was time for open mic. One by one, our returnees stepped up. There was William Charles Gibson, the same William Charles who'd warned me off heroin way back at DVI when I asked him what the deal was with so many men getting out and coming right back. Turns out the brother and I had been in the same kindergarten class in Belle Haven too. His last criminal charge was a nonviolent third strike, and it landed him a fifty-year sentence. He'd wind up serving twenty-seven of them. William Charles was a natural with a mic in his hand. He seemed relaxed. "I've been home a few days ago, five months," he shared in the smooth, singsong voice I remember from decades back. "In those five months, I'm surprising myself in some of the things that I accomplished already. I go to work every day now. I just got out of a transitional house two days ago. I'm living life on life's terms."

William Charles had followed my work and kept in touch. He'd called me for advice from inside and again when he got out. I'd taken him shopping along with a brother named Lonnie Morris, who'd walked off forty-four years when he was released in late May 2021. We did the rounds: Target for clothes shopping and iPhone boosters. And lunch at a restaurant where Lonnie, a Muslim, could get halal food. Now Lonnie took the mic, telling us he wouldn't have made it if hadn't been for Allah or the creator. Each of us has a belief system we hold on to in order to survive. That's the one that gave Lonnie the strength to persevere, despite all the grief he got from the board of parole hearings, who didn't want to let him out because he wouldn't name his crime partner. Nearly a half century had passed, and his position hadn't changed. To get out, Lonnie had to take his case to a judge, who sided with him, saying the fact that Lonnie wouldn't snitch had nothing to do with whether he was safe for release. I could relate. But even with a judge's order to CDCR to cut him loose, the tug of war continued. It took a hearing with forty people lined up on Zoom—including some former prison staff—to testify on Lonnie's behalf for him to finally win his freedom.

At our homecoming dinner, we got through the speakers and a group photo too, and then, as the evening was wrapping up, we were told there was one more brother on the agenda. Minister King X, known to me from his time inside as PyeFace, did eighteen years in the concrete tombs of Pelican Bay, where he became codirector of California Prison Focus, one of the organizations in our Prisoner Hunger Strike Solidarity Coalition.

Homecoming

Minister King X had been a key ally in the battle for an end to indefinite solitary confinement. He was also a principal peacemaker in that historic 2012 agreement to end hostilities. When he paroled, I provided him with office space at our new building. Every year, the brother gives out an award that's modeled on the Oscar statue, crafted by a formerly incarcerated artist. Now, as our gathering was wrapping up, Minister King X took the mic and, flashing a big smile and fancy grill, announced that this year's award was for me. When I walked up to accept it, he stopped me in my tracks. "Wait, there's more," he said with a grin. "Somebody wants to say something to you right here."

At first, I didn't recognize the baritone voice coming out of the cell phone. *Congratulations, Dorsey. I saw it coming a long time ago* . . . Then it hit me. It was PJ. My PJ, *the* pivotal person who persuaded me to get LSPC involved in the litigation. By the time PJ got out of solitary confinement and into the general prison population, he'd been in a box alone for twenty-seven years.

I thought about PJ a lot during the pandemic. He was elderly, white haired. He walked with a cane. It was time to come home. His committing offense occurred in San Francisco. So I called up then San Francisco District Attorney Chesa Boudin, who was fully on board when it came to respecting the humanity of people we've thrown into cages. He'd wind up getting recalled for that. "Some of the stuff that you're working on," I told Chesa, "here's a guy who fits all of it."

Four months later, in August 2021, PJ walked free. He'd served fifty-two years in prison.

PJ kept talking through King X's phone, but I was too emotional to hear his exact words—I just heard his voice, deep and steady. Making a difference for these brothers had been at the heart of my commitment from the start. To play a part in PJ's release was more rewarding than anything I could presently imagine. To hear his voice pushed me over the top. I clutched that award in my hands like it was made of diamonds.

"I could take you to my office over there, and I got presidential awards I could show you," I said as the tears came. "But if it ain't coming from one of us, it don't mean that much to me. I done had my BMWs. I done had my Cadillacs, and I'm driving a Benz. But with all of y'all missing, it don't mean nothing. It don't mean nothing."

Before we opened the doors that night, I'd asked Hamdiya to keep track of how many years each person in attendance had lost to the system, so we could tally it at the end. Now, one of our staff members came up and whispered the total in my ear: Six hundred and forty-six years. That almost did me in. "That's what they stole." I was preaching now, yelling, really. "That's how much was up in this room today."

Each of those newly released brothers and the one seventy-two-year-old sister went home that night with a goodie bag. Tucked inside, with snacks and socks, was $250 in cold hard cash—and it didn't smell like Hai Karate. It was my way of saying, *I'll see the $200 in gate money you motherfuckers haven't increased since 1973 and I'll raise you by $50.*

Chapter 22

"SLAVE, WHO IS IT THAT SHALL FREE YOU?"

My career is winding down, because the time has come. I'm an elder, and even if I will never know how to relax, I understand the importance of passing the torch. I am proud of so much, but I think I can say I am most proud of all the young warriors I've helped cultivate who are advancing the work. They do it in baby steps and in leaps so vast they could span the Grand Canyon. They make me rub my eyes in a double take and say, "Goddamn! Look at what *we* built." It's why I love to bring us together for national convenings, so we can sit with one another's brilliance, learn new tactics, fine-tune our mission, and fuel up for the ongoing fight.

We started the Formerly Incarcerated, Convicted People and Families Movement back in Dothan, Alabama, in 2011 in part because All of Us or None couldn't be in every corner of every state. But I got up one day and took a count, and we were growing beyond my expectations. So in March 2022, I decided to host a national convening of all our AOUON chapters. We gathered in Oakland and started off by taking a ferry to Alcatraz Island, the home of what was once this country's most oppressive prison. Because there was something up inside that stone and steel building that I wanted to share.

If you'd been standing at the island ferry port that morning, you would have seen the fog start to clear while the gulls wheeled and called to each other in a wind that wasn't too fierce and wasn't too cold. Then, as the ferry boat that carries tourists over from San Francisco got closer, you would have noticed all the Black and brown faces. Those were my people. There were nearly two hundred of us, and as we came walking off that ferry, you would have made out the shape of that fist of power and struggle on a whole bunch of brightly colored All of Us or None T-shirts. They had come from New Jersey, Florida, Wisconsin, Pennsylvania, Georgia, South Carolina, Kentucky, Illinois, and too many other states for me to even remember, not to mention All of Us or None chapters across California.

The story behind what we were about to see together stretched back five years, when Michelle Gee, who worked for the National Park Service, invited me to the island prison to attend a charette—a fancy name for a brainstorming session. Alcatraz draws more than a million tourists a year, and they mostly come to experience a Disney-style take on one of the most inhospitable prisons in our nation's brutal history. They laugh about Al Capone and the Bird Man and hear stories of other famous men stripped of their liberty and dignity up on this rock. They listen to the audio tour and hear a G-rated version of the pain and violence that compelled men to break out of that wind-battered fortress and plunge into frigid waters in a last bid for freedom. For me, one look at the Alcatraz cells took

318

me right back to San Quentin. Those cages were the same size, same layout, as the ones where my keepers had me under lock and key for years. I could hear the slam and echo of the steel gates. There was that smell of fear and sweat that reminded me of the bottom of a slave ship. The hairs on the back of my neck uncurled. So I made Michelle an offer: "How about Legal Services for Prisoners with Children pays out of our own pocket to bring a bunch of formerly incarcerated people right into your office for another charette, where you could hear from people who've lived it?" I asked. "Because what you all are laying out in this exhibit is *our* lives." Michele said yes. And when we all piled into her office, I felt a whole lot more comfortable. We brainstormed about how to put something in place that didn't just explain the history of the prison industrial complex, but also showcased our humanity. We persuaded her to broaden the scope of the exhibit, because when *we* go to prison, it's not us alone who are impacted. Our families and communities suffer.

The permanent exhibit opened in 2021, aiming to teach those millions of tourists—most of them not Black or brown—about our country's approach to punishment. *The Big Lockup: Mass Incarceration in the United States* didn't include everything we asked for. But we'd gone from being on the fringe of the conversation to being at its center, and that alone was a significant victory. The exhibit reflected the movement that we had built, and I had no doubt it would challenge the narrative around mass incarceration for many Alcatraz visitors. The Park Service expects it to stay in place for the next three decades. That's how much we at All of Us or None have changed the conversation.

The part of the exhibit that I feel most proud of addresses the prison industry as a direct legacy of slavery. One wall details the Thirteenth Amendment's exception clause, which allowed involuntary servitude, slavery by another name, to survive and thrive inside prison walls. On display are slave shackles right next to a pair of modern handcuffs. The connection is clear as day. On the other side of the room, there's an interactive display that asks, "What Are Your Thoughts? Mass Incarceration Relates Back to Slavery." Some big red poker chips are stacked next to see-through plexiglass bins marked *yes, no,* or *maybe.* On that day when our AOUON chapters convened to see it, Bobbi Butts, our sister from the Riverside chapter, was hogging those chips, feeding them one by one into the *yes* slot like a gambling fiend and preaching about it as she went.

"How many times can I vote? Until there's no more, until there's no more," she shouted, feeding those chips in one after the next. "This is for our ancestors. This is for our families."

320

If I'd had my way, I wouldn't have given people a chance to say no or maybe, because there's no doubt the exception clause got stuck into the Constitution to preserve the institution of slave labor. And there's no question involuntary servitude is, was, and always has been the fuel in the tank of the prison industrial complex. We know it because many of us in the room have been forced to donate our labor for pennies on the hour, at times in dangerous conditions, always to make other people rich. Removing this last vestige of slavery from the California Constitution had become our biggest fight at LSPC and AOUON. Because the California Constitution, like more than half the states in the nation, has its own exception clause, Article 1, Section 6: "Slavery is prohibited. Involuntary servitude is prohibited except to punish crime." We're still deep into the battle to raise awareness and gain public and political support. Seven other states are already ahead of us.

"Slave, who is it that shall free you?"

Colorado voters changed their constitution in 2018 to ban involuntary servitude in that state's prisons and jails. Utah and Nebraska did the same in 2020. In November 2022, Alabama, Oregon, Tennessee, and Vermont voters made those changes to their state constitutions at the ballot box.

We are working to make sure California is next. Meanwhile, our All of Us or None chapters across the country are backing campaigns in other states too, including Pennsylvania, Wisconsin, Missouri, and Georgia. We're also supporting efforts to remove the exception clause from the Thirteenth Amendment of the US Constitution. Because we envision a United States where all people, without exception, are free from slavery and involuntary servitude, and where all people are protected by their state and federal constitutions.

The shit jobs that most of us worked for pennies on the hour inform our conviction. As I undertake the final major campaign of my career, I also hear the voice of Geronimo from nearly half a century ago, prodding me to look the San Quentin warden in the eye and demand minimum wage for our labor. It's well past time to act.

WHEN I CONVENED the 2022 national conference of All of Us or None, I gave it a name that felt right and real: "Building the Movement from the Inside Out." We'd been doing that, and it was time for us to back up far enough to take in the bigger picture of our collective efforts. So many of our chapters started with a single person who gathered up a small flock and got to work, and from that boots-on-the-ground place, we were winning big victories. Our own registration numbers had us smiling: About three dozen chapters from more than two dozen states were represented in that hotel conference room near the

Oakland airport. Across the country, we'd been knocking out voting rights victories and Ban the Box victories in employment and housing. We were working on participatory defense to help our people get out of jail and avoid prison time. We were also using our powers to change state laws, get people elected, and kick others who weren't serving us out of office on their asses. The John Lewis Voting Rights Act may have stalled, but we hadn't. "What I want you to see," I hollered into the mic when I got up to welcome the crowd, "is that we are already national."

I also had news to share that would have made Denise smile, though the people closest to me won't believe it till it happens. "I think I got two more years and I'm fittin' to sit down," I announced. "But I don't want to sit down until I'm absolutely sure, at least with All of Us or None and LSPC, that the next generation has somebody that's as committed to what this cause is as I've been." My goal, I told the crowd, was to find an LSPC managing director who could shadow me until I felt comfortable enough to retire, because that's what seventy-three-year-old men are supposed to do. This would likely be my last national conference. And looking out at our collective power was just the medicine I needed. I especially wanted to bring these younger soldiers into the room with us older homies and the wisdom we had to offer. I was gifting them a roadmap, the same favor Kalima had done for me.

"You need to see who *we* are," I told them, "so you can see who *you* are."

Desmond Meade had come from Florida, Norris Henderson from Louisiana, and the three of us kicked off the conference. We all knew they'd had major ballot box victories in 2018, around voting rights and unanimous jury verdicts. But what had us on the edge of our seats were their other victories, where formerly incarcerated people didn't just have the right to vote, they got out and *exercised* that right, bringing about big change. We were building an empowered new electorate.

In Florida, Desmond's people had helped an underdog candidate for state attorney crush her establishment opponent. In Louisiana, Norris's efforts had done in a seventeen-year incumbent sheriff who had called our proud voting constituency of formerly incarcerated people criminals and crackheads. Well, we whupped his ass. We were no longer waiting to gain our power. We were using our power. Because the fight is never for 51 percent of the vote. The fight is for the margin, and in local elections that can come down to a thousand votes. On the state level, in many contests it's probably less than thirty thousand votes. That's how you get your homies motivated to register to vote and to exercise that right.

Half a century after I walked into DVI as a young man who hadn't started shaving, I sat there basking in the presence of love. It provided one of many opportunities to learn a lesson that comes to me in stages—to favor gratitude over discontentment. It got me thinking about something Assata Shakur told me when I flew to Havana back in the late nineties to interview her about women in prison. The sister had fought the good fight with the Black Liberation Army and never stopped struggling for justice. Still, she said, she thought the revolution had done far more for her than she had for the revolution. Taking in the crowd in front of me, that's exactly how I felt.

These democratic gatherings meant to shake the foundations of the criminal injustice system had been at the heart of my sustenance and my strategy for decades. And now I could see all that history laid out before me. There was Ellen Barry, who passed the baton to me to run LSPC. Aminah Rasul was there—one of the first incarcerated women LSPC had worked with back in the 1970s, now free at seventy-two years old. There was Hamdiya, my right hand, and sometimes my left one too. Nane, who founded Barrios Unidos, and George Galvis, who created Communities United for Restorative Youth Justice, were also in the audience. They'd been key to building bridges to our Latinx brothers and sisters.

Throughout the day, we caught up on our victories. My favorite part came when members of each chapter got up to share what they were up to. The depth and power of the work confirmed to me that our movement was more alive than ever. It seemed like every corner of our nation was represented before me, and all these ambassadors shared the same vision we'd arrived at on butcher paper with Day-Glo sticky dots back in 2003 at the Center for Third World Organizing. Cincinnati, Ohio, was in the house. So was St. Louis, Missouri; Kenosha, Wisconsin; Chicago; North and South Carolina; Philadelphia; and chapters from a whole bunch of other states. California chapters covered Los Angeles/Long Beach, Sacramento, Bakersfield, Oakland, Santa Cruz, and more.

As the conference wound down, I took back the mic. There was one more person in the room I needed to acknowledge. She was sitting in the front row at my table, and her name was Alma. Alma, my childhood sweetheart, now my sweetheart again in the winter of my life. Back when I was young, I probably needed Alma more than I loved her. Now, I believe I love her more than I need her. The two of us have been engaged in this dance for more than fifty-five years. We became great-grandparents together. We still fight like cats and dogs, but we've had more good years than bad. We still keep our own places. But more and more, we share a deeper place together.

"Slave, who is it that shall free you?"

Alma never complained that the broom Sheila and I jumped together on our wedding day hung above the bed until I was finally ready to take it down—in 2021. She gave me the space to grieve. In fact, it's Alma who sometimes reminds me of Sheila's birthday and the anniversary of her death, telling me, "I think it's time for you to go put some flowers on her grave." Alma taught me the difference between dormant and dead. Sometimes, love never dies.

As the conference program wrapped up, Lonnie Morris, the brother who'd walked off forty-four years, worked the crowd with a petition to get a measure on the ballot that would repeal California's Three Strikes law once and for all. PJ, my friend and ally who'd walked off fifty-two years and spent more than a quarter century in the Hole, had accepted my invitation to the conference. But I hadn't seen him around, so as we were winding down, laughing and talking, I gave him a ring. Turns out he was sitting in his room. No one had told him it was OK to come down. That's what more than half a century in a cage will do to a man. PJ made it for the banquet, and the brother sat at my table.

Eating that rubber chicken with him made me think about Denise again, and why I can't bring myself to feel middle class. I will never risk leaving the PJs, Lonnies, and Aminahs behind. I fought for their freedom, and they *still* aren't free. None of us are. Not yet. If somebody were to ask me, "What does freedom look like?" I'm not sure I'd be able to describe it. I do know it doesn't necessarily mean what I thought it did during all my years inside. I've seen broken men out here in the "free" world, where we struggle to hold on to Malcolm. We struggle to hold on to Martin. We struggle to hold on to Fannie Lou Hamer. We struggle to hold on to Frederick Douglass. Meanwhile, I've met men inside with the fortitude of thousands, with minds as free as eagles. Prison tried to break me. No doubt. It beat me and bruised me. But I came out unbroken and undeterred, committed to chasing that cause of freedom for each and every one of us.

AS THE YEAR came to a close, I was able to check one important task off my list: I hired a brilliant sister to step into that newly created role of LSPC managing director, a position that will help me work up the courage to step away. Then I got right into planning one of my favorite annual rituals. Way back in 2000, a couple of us from Free at Last worked out a deal with a sympathetic San Quentin guard to give us children's bicycles that the men inside had refurbished. Then we located all the neighborhood kids we could find who had a parent or guardian in prison. Those bikes would become gifts to those kids from their incarcerated parent. Because if anyone knows how good it feels when your daddy gets you a bike for Christmas, it's Dorsey Emmett Nunn. And that bike doesn't have to be purple, and it doesn't have to be stolen.

At first, we called our event the Big Bike Giveaway, but as our concept expanded, we changed it up to the Annual Community Giveback. Because everybody, our thinking went, is entitled to participate in philanthropy. It can't just be something rich people do. The act of giving back is an act of being in community. For years now, every formerly incarcerated volunteer who helps us haul those bikes around, assemble them, and adjust them has a chance to give some away to children on behalf of their parents in prison—and get a contact high from the joy on those faces. Most of these newly minted philanthropists are getting to do something they couldn't when they were living in cages. These days, All of Us or None runs the Community Give-back out of the Freedom and Movement Center in Oakland. We stopped getting bikes from San Quentin years ago. I was done transacting with that system. These days, we raise the funds to buy those bicycles ourselves. At just about every event, I fess up to my teenaged habit and throw out a question: "How many of y'all have stolen a bike?" Every year, the hands of a whole bunch of formerly incarcerated volunteers shoot up. "Well," I tell them, "now's your chance to give one back."

December 10, 2022, turned out to be one stormy Saturday, but the pelting rain that came in waves after a long drought didn't spoil our fun at the Twenty-Third Annual Community Giveback. I had recently learned I was the recipient of an es-teemed James Irvine Foundation Leadership Award, an honor expected to bring a quarter-million-dollar infusion into LSPC to shore up our work. A camera crew was there to document the festivities. There was face painting for kids, and some good-tasting barbecue under a massive tent that kept us dry. Don Wilson was there, holding court inside in a fine suit. And then there were the bicycles—about 240 of them, each spoken for by mothers and fathers in prison who'd registered. One woman was clutching the hand of her nine-year-old grand-daughter, whose daddy was locked up in California State Prison in Sacramento on a fifteen-year sentence. Before I knew it, she was passing me her cell phone so I could talk to the brother himself, so he could thank me. I could hear the emotion in his voice. And I let him in on what we were up to.

"I'm doing the work out here, giving away these bicycles on behalf of y'all inside," I said. "I'm fittin' to step down here soon, and I'm making sure the work will still be going when you get out. So tell everyone on the inside that here at the Freedom

327

and Movement Center, we're looking forward to welcoming you home."

That brother's mama was standing next to me, and now she was crying. She just kept shaking her head, and saying, "It's beautiful. It's beautiful. So many of them are out here now, giving back." But the peak of my day came when that nine-year-old girl got on the phone to thank her daddy for her new pink bike. That's when I knew: I may be retiring, but I'll never stop giving back.

NOT LONG AGO, I went to the funeral of Mrs. Gertrude Wilks, that root family matriarch who founded the Nairobi Day and High School in East Palo Alto when she recognized the public school system had failed us all. She'd been a community matriarch for six decades, serving on East Palo Alto's first city council and harnessing the community's power of prayer when the crack epidemic was tearing us apart. When I walked into her memorial service, it marked the first time someone looked at me and said, "Dorsey, go sit with the elders." Mrs. Wilks had planned her own send-off, and the traditional gospel song she chose said it all: "May the Work I've Done Speak for Me."

Nobody needed to speak for Mrs. Wilks at her funeral. We didn't have to stand up and say, "Job well done." The shit spoke for itself. I decided right then and there what song will be playing when my time here ends.

I know in my head that I've accomplished a lot, but I don't always feel it in my heart. Trauma casts a long shadow, and healing is a process. I still wrestle with anger. But I've learned how to stand down, how to breathe, how to recognize that I'm capable of being fucking wrong. Since I've held my job as executive director, there've been times where I've called Hamdiya and told her flat out, "This is not a good day for me to come to work." Enough said. I know when I need to cool off. And she knows that I know. It's clear as day that trauma is at the root of it, and when I retire, I might just take some time to attend to those old harms in a compassionate way.

I've also recognized that I am a source of deep and abiding love. I brought Joyce, my oldest sister and second moms, to live with me in 2019 at the Hill Avenue house—the same house she and I had sunk our sweat labor into fixing when it was a concession stand for the open-air crack market out front. The same house where David and Sheila had died under my loving care. For nearly three years, I cooked for Joyce, cared for Joyce, laughed with Joyce, and bought her cartons of menthol cigarettes she wasn't supposed to smoke. In the end, kidney disease, heart disease, and breast cancer ganged up inside her. Just days before I hosted my people at Alcatraz, Joyce died, surrounded by family who loved her. Joyce's God was joyful and loving. She went out without fear, and at her memorial we celebrated her life.

As I find myself in the winter of my own life, I've been thinking about my legacy. I've spent my life working to create a narrative that's more potent than the notion that punishment works. It doesn't. And we can't get to the healing as long as our criminal justice system is leaning on that crutch. We got to kick that shit out from under our prison industrial complex. Because it's punishment that keeps that system from stating the obvious: That they're practicing white supremacy. That they're practicing slavery under another name. We are not slaves.

I am proud to have played a key role in bringing these plain facts into the national conversation, without apology. These

329

days, as formerly incarcerated people, we aren't just demanding the full power of our citizenship, we're exercising that power. I have always been comfortable doing the work. It is my life's purpose. And until death takes me, I will remain unbroken and undeterred.

ACKNOWLEDGMENTS

When and while I was thinking of writing this book, I would hear the voice of Manuel LaFontaine in my head, telling me I needed to tell my own story before someone else did. I was comfortable with that latter notion because I always thought someone else would be writing about me. If it wasn't a book, I thought it might be an obituary that would make me sit up in my coffin. Still, I took Manuel's advice. Moving forward with a book would require some concrete financial support, so I pitched my idea to Lateefah Simon of the Akonadi Foundation, and then to Helena Huang and David Rogers of the Art for Justice Fund and the Ford Foundation. Lateefah, Helena, and David, thanks for not discouraging me because I thought we needed another book inspired by movement. I have pitched a lot of different things over the course of the last fifty years, but never anything this personal. Y'all made this book happen. And Bonnie Jones, thank you for pitching in with an early donation before we secured foundation support. Your belief in me dates back decades and is forever appreciated.

I know that acknowledging everyone who has partially accompanied me on a remarkable journey is impossible. I entered a world where racism, classism, prejudice, and discrimination were much more prevalent than our current practices, which still leave much to be desired. Many of the people I was raised with suffered as a result, and many of us who were influenced by this reality carried the trauma into bad decision-making. So I want to acknowledge all the friends and family who walked with me through those times. The ones who loved me when I wasn't easy to love and fed me when I was incapable of feeding myself, and those who housed me so I wouldn't have to suffer in inclement weather in extremely trying times. To my moms, pop, brothers, sister, wife, and daughter who all preceded me in death, I hope they will allow you to read my book in the after-life, even with cuss words.

I want to acknowledge my homies who I ran the streets with, who didn't forecast that many of us would wind up in prison but nevertheless prepared me to survive being arrested as a teenager for murder, and who helped me stay strong enough not to snitch. Compromised values are hard if not impossible to regain, and being unwilling to snitch didn't make me any more or less guilty. Thank you for preparing me to walk through the prison gates at a point in history where prison violence was much more pronounced, in fact, historic. Thank you for the loy-alty, even when many of our steps were missteps and we hadn't yet had the time to figure things out.

To all the brothers who coordinated the political education classes on the yard at Deuel Vocational Institution (DVI): thank you for feeding me the books to read even when I stumbled through them slowly, because reading was particularly chal-lenging at first. Thank you for trusting me with books that had been censored but had been copied in long hand; it seemed at that time the forbidden fruit tasted better. Nate Harrington, if you can hear me in the afterlife, thank you for asking the many questions to see if I had read what had been assigned and to see if I understood what I had read. The reading was so inspirational that many years later, I traveled to Cuba and met Assata Shakur. I also went to South Africa in hopes of meeting Nelson Mandela. You helped make the world bigger than the small cells I occupied and the community that I came from. Jalil Muntaqim and Geronimo Ji-Jaga Pratt, you made it easier for me to travel by sight when faith was weak and questionable. Thanks for being examples that resistance was possible and absolutely required, even when immediate victory was not guaranteed. There are so many people on my list I want to acknowledge, but our past is too sensitive for me to name them.

Outside of my mother and father, I want to thank the two young women (Alma and Faydell) who had children (Anthony and Denise) with me when we were still children. Y'all gave me the greatest gifts of all: some way of thinking of myself other than as prisoner B-39669, and other than as a person in extreme and constant pain. My children held my hopes when I couldn't hold on to anything or anyone. You were the new life I thought about more often than my elders, the human beings I thought would still possibly be living if I had to endure an extremely long and tedious prison sentence. You gave me an additional reason to develop better reading and writing skills.

Kathy Labriola and Shirl Miles, it was absolutely refreshing when you started to visit me. Your entrance on the scene gave me a yardstick to measure my sanity since prison could sometimes feel like an insane asylum. The conversations during the course of your visits helped me hold on to my sanity and figure out what parts of me I should keep and what parts of me I should leave behind when paroling. It was during these visits

333

that I worked on healing. Your visits also affirmed that at least a few people in the outside world thought I was worthy of their investment of time, and that I had a greater value than just as a slave of the state. You also provided a very different perspective than the men I was locked up with, most of who were not in stable relationships. You were instrumental in my growth and inspired me to consider the political circumstances of women and feminism. You saved me much pain and in turn assisted plenty of other women I met later in life.

I also want to acknowledge all the people I worked with at the Prison Law Office the first six years after I got out of San Quentin. Thanks for not asking me why I would choose to work less than two hundred yards from the front gate I walked through upon being released. You made me feel I was part of a community with a cause I had embraced long before I exited prison. I will always be grateful for the patience you showed and shared with me. To Michael Satris, lost to an unexpected heart attack in 2020, your easygoing love and enduring support were critical to my survival. As for other Prison Law Office comrades, you proved to be much more than just coworkers when I slid into the darkness of addiction. Karen Schryver, Margaret and Tricia Littlefield, Sean McCloskey: without your intervention, I doubt if I would be writing this acknowledgment with better than thirty-two years clean, having cofounded one of the largest and oldest recovery centers in San Mateo County. It was your love and kindness that challenged me to look at myself and pointed out that I was in the fight of my life if I was going to maintain my freedom. Millard Murphy, thank you for the letter you wrote requesting the justice system give me another chance. Margaret Littlefield, you are the only person who has ever bailed me out of jail. Thank you for being there for me, and for sharing your home and family.

Someone once told me that ignorance is bliss, but no one ever told me consciousness requires something greater than idleness or indifference. I want to thank all the recovering addicts who showed me this and demonstrated there was a way out of madness, particularly those people at Project Ninety who hung out with me in my early recovery.

Ellen Barry, thank you for giving me my first job interview after I decided to leave the treatment center. You paid me more than I thought I was worth at that time. But more important, I want to thank you for the opportunity to advance a political agenda through organizing. I knew I was called upon to fight for the full restoration of the civil and human rights of incarcerated and formerly incarcerated people. The first right we sought was a matter of collective courage: the right to speak in our own voice and the demand to be called a person instead of a criminal offense. I am also grateful to all the comrades and friends I got a chance to meet on this journey.

The people I ultimately got a chance to organize with—Karen Shain, Donna Willmott, Heidi Strupp, Linda Evans, and Manuel LaFontaine among them—we worked so seamlessly at times it was hard to recognize we were in the struggle for civil and human rights. When I look back, I know it was my honor and privilege to have had you in my life at just the right time. Hamdiya Cooks-Abdullah and Susan Burton, thanks for meeting the challenge of longevity and allowing me to process whatever came up for me, especially all the times I needed to vent. People seem to move better when they are not carrying the burden of anger. You saved so many others from enduring harsh words and bad tone, especially when I became the executive director and some people could not see me as their comrade but only as their boss. And to Heidi Strupp, our longtime bookkeeper at LSPC, you taught me to pay attention to the money and that was an important blessing.

I would be completely remiss if I did not acknowledge all you who were in the Timers group and welcomed me as one of you: Arthur "Tha" League, Sundi Tate, Emory Douglas, David Johnson, Luis Talamantez, Fred Abdullah, and Ida McCray. During our period in Timers, y'all once again rooted my movement dreams and hopes. It should not have surprised any of you when All of Us or None appeared on the horizon.

I also want to acknowledge all people who were a part of developing the Formerly Incarcerated, Convicted People and Families Movement, especially Daryl Atkinson, Norris Henderson, George Galvis, Bruce Reilly, Desmond Meade, Vivian Nixon, Deanna Hoskins, David Ayala, and Hamdiya Cooks-Abdullah. We stood as a united front before the White House and the US Department of Justice, and I do not believe they would have been able to see us if any of us had walked in alone. It is our collective work that gains traction nationally. I have learned so much from current and former steering committee members. Finally, I want to thank my coauthor Lee Romney, our editor Marthine Satris and copy editor Anitra Budd, and the rest of the team at Heyday who made the book possible: Emmerich Anklam, Gayle Wattawa, Kalie Caetano, Chris Carosi, Marlon Rigel, Archie Ferguson, Diahann Sturge-Campbell, former development director Emily Grossman, and Heyday's publisher Steve Wasserman.

—Dorsey Nunn

Acknowledgments

* * *

Over my more than three decades in journalism, a few subjects have stood out as particularly inspiring. Dorsey Nunn, you are one of them. It has been a privilege, an honor, and a beautifully complex challenge to help you bring your story and the story of the movement you helped pioneer to these pages. Thank you for the opportunity to channel my journalistic skills into a new type of storytelling, and for allowing me to contribute to a movement that, due to the force of your collective work, is ever bending toward justice. Above all, thank you for your trust. To Marthine Satris, acquisitions editor at Heyday Books, thank you for your gracious and thoughtful touch. You helped me stay tethered to the big picture and to Dorsey's voice. A great big thank you to the following people who took the time to sit down for interviews between 2019 and 2022, supplementing personal memory and adding context: Kathy Labriola, Linda Evans, Hamdiya Cooks-Abdullah, George Galvis, Joyce Lee, Michael Satris, Ellen Barry, Margaret Littlefield, Tricia Littlefield, Susan Burton, Norris Henderson, Al Haysbert, and Vincent Schiraldi. Lastly, to my husband, Russell Baldon, thank you for your love and patience throughout this process. I could not have made this creative stretch without your support.

—*Lee Romney*

REFERENCES

These references contain the key published resources—newspaper articles, reports, books, documentaries, et cetera—that informed each chapter of this personal history.

CHAPTER 1   INNOCENCE UNAVAILABLE, GUILT NOT REQUIRED

Arizona Daily Star. "Town Is 'Nairobi' to Militant Calif. Negroes." December 29, 1968. newspapers.com.

Arizona Republic. "Militants Want Name of Nairobi." March 11, 1969. newspapers.com.

Daily Palo Alto Times. "It's Expensive to Indulge Prejudice." August 10, 1955. newspapers.com.

Hearings Before the US Commission on Civil Rights, 86th Cong. 636–656 (1960) (statements of Elsa Alsberg, executive director, Palo Alto Fair Play Council; and Lee B. Spivack, real estate salesman).

Oakland Tribune. "Ex-Leader Rips Realtors on Bias Ban," November 20, 1963. newspapers.com.

San Francisco Examiner. "Cultural Center with Soul," June 29, 1969. newspapers.com.

San Francisco Examiner. "Negroes Firebomb Peninsula Market." September 30, 1966. newspapers.com.

San Francisco Examiner. "Police Still Guard Scene of Menlo Park Riot." April 21, 1969. newspapers.com.

Times (San Mateo, CA). "Battle Plan Filed for S.M. County's War on Poverty." August 28, 1964. newspapers.com.

Times (San Mateo, CA). "Circular Accuses Police in M.P. Row." April 22, 1969. newspapers.com.

Times (San Mateo, CA). "Club President Out in Segregation Row." December 8, 1954. newspapers.com.

Times (San Mateo, CA). "New Nairobi Center Opens on Sunday." June 24, 1969. newspapers.com.

Times (San Mateo, CA). "Police Call for Race Seminar." June 28, 1963. newspapers.com.

Times (San Mateo, CA). "Quick Work Averts Near Riot in E.P.A." September 30, 1966. newspapers.com.

Times (San Mateo, CA). "Race Violence in E.P.A. Tract." December 7, 1954. newspapers.com.

Times (San Mateo, CA). "Ravenswood Shares in State Grant." September 13, 1963. newspapers.com.

Times (San Mateo, CA). "Seven More Fires Set in So. County." August 19, 1965. newspapers.com.

Times (San Mateo, CA). "Sheriff Sees No Trouble in County." August 16, 1965. newspapers.com.

Times (San Mateo, CA). "'Wrong Hands, Wrong People.'" August 26, 1966. newspapers.com.

CHAPTER 2 GLADIATOR SCHOOL

Argus (Fremont, CA). "Execution Not Sought for Nunn." September 28, 1971. newspapers.com.

Argus (Fremont, CA). "New Trial Granted in Newark Murder." October 21, 1971. newspapers.com.

Los Angeles Times. "2nd Inmate Dies of Stab Wounds." July 4, 1972. newspapers.com.

Los Angeles Times. "Man Hurls Tables at Judge and Jury." September 10, 1971. newspapers.com.

Oakland Tribune. "Jury Convicts Newark Killer, 20." January 15, 1972. newspapers.com.

Oakland Tribune. "Life Term for Murder and Robbery." February 4, 1972. newspapers.com.

Peninsula Times Tribune (Palo Alto, CA). "Heavy Surf Capsizes Boat; Two Menlo Park Men Drown." September 21, 1970. newspapers.com.

CHAPTER 3 COMMITMENT TO KILL

Californian (Salinas, CA). "Deuel Inmate Found Stabbed." October 17, 1972. newspapers.com.

Californian (Salinas, CA). "Deuel Inmate Fatally Stabbed." June 5, 1974. newspapers.com.

Santa Cruz Sentinel. "Prison Officials Suspect Plot." December 2, 1973. newspapers.com.

CHAPTER 4 MAO'S LITTLE RED BOOK

Cummins, Eric. *The Rise and Fall of California's Radical Prison Movement.* Stanford, CA: Stanford University Press, 1994.

Jackson, George. *Soledad Brother: The Prison Letters of George Jackson*, New York: Coward-McCann, 1970.

CHAPTER 5 LIFELINES

Nunn, Dorsey. Letters to Kathy Labriola, 1974–1981. **341**

CHAPTER 6 THE LEGAL AVENUE—A DIFFERENT WAY TO FIGHT

Berger, Dan. "Prison Nation." In *Captive Nation: Black Prison Organizing in the Civil Rights Era*, 223–224. Charlotte: University of North Carolina Press, 2014.

Berger, Dan. "We Are the Revolutionaries: Visibility, Protest, and Racial Formation in 1970s Prison Radicalism." Ph.D. diss., University of Pennsylvania, 2010.

CHAPTER 7 STEPPING UP MY GAME

Crawford, Mary. "Light Goes on at Tunnel's End for State's Lifers." *San Francisco Examiner*, July 3, 1978. newspapers.com.

Hager, Philip. "State Prisons almost Filled to Capacity." *Los Angeles Times*, March 30, 1979. newspapers.com.

Napa Valley Register. "'Cruel and Unusual' Lawsuit at Quentin." June 16, 1981. newspapers.com.

Reiterman, Tim. "San Quentin: Stuffed to Overflowing with Hard, Hard Men." *San Francisco Examiner*, August 18, 1981. newspapers.com.

Reiterman, Tim. "Quentin Today: Tranquil or 'Ready to Blow'?" *San Francisco Examiner*. August 20, 1981. newspapers.com.

Ryan, Marie Vida, Dona Good, and Gale Chan, *California Prisoners 1977 and 1978 Summary Statistics of Felon Prisoners and Parolees*. Sacramento: State of California Health and Welfare Agency, Department of Corrections Policy and Planning Division, Management Information Section, n.d., ca. 1979, www.ojp.gov/ncjrs/virtual-library/abstracts/california-prisoners-1977-and-1978-summary-statistics-felon.

Sacramento Bee. "San Quentin's Black, White Inmates Parted." July 14, 1977. newspapers.com.

Santa Cruz Sentinel. "Everyone Has Cellmate in State Prisons," June 13, 1979. newspapers.com.

CHAPTER 9   WHAT KIND OF BIRD CAN'T FLY?

Kelso, J. Clark, and Brigitte A. Bass, 1992. "The Victims' Bill of Rights: Where Did It Come From and How Much Did It Do?" *Pacific Law Journal* 23, no. 3 (1992): 843–879. scholarlycommons.pacific.edu/cgi/viewcontent.cgi?article=1059&context=facultyarticles.

Méndez, Miguel A. "The Victims' Bill of Rights—Thirty Years Under Proposition 8." *Stanford Law & Policy Review* 25, no. 2 (March 2014): 379–434. law.stanford.edu/wp-content/uploads/2018/03/mendez.pdf.

Reiterman, Tim. "One Arrested, Two More Sought in Black Guerilla Family Slaying." *San Francisco Examiner*, May 6, 1982. newspapers.com.

Uelmen, Gerald F. "Victims' Rights in California." *St. John's Journal of Legal Commentary* 8, no. 1 (Fall 1992): 197–204. digitalcommons.law.scu.edu/facpubs/359.

CHAPTER 10   BREATHING ROOM

Cooper, Claire. "Measure to OK Double-Celling Rejected by Senate Committee." *Sacramento Bee*, March 28, 1984. newspapers.com.

Navarro, Mireya. "Legal Group's Battle against San Quentin Crowding." *San Francisco Examiner*, August 31, 1983. newspapers.com.

Press Democrat (Santa Rosa, CA). "Murder Parole Bill Dies after Fain Lawyer Testifies." May 24, 1984. newspapers.com.

San Francisco Examiner. "Court Denies Parolee Visit with Prisoners." August 26, 1983. newspapers.com.

References

Smith, Joan. "Criticism at Quentin by Blacks." *San Francisco Examiner*, August 23, 1985. newspapers.com.

Smith, Joan. "He's Looked at Life from Both Sides." *San Francisco Examiner*, October 2, 1985. newspapers.com.

Wilson, Bill. "Work, Training Plan for Prisoners Debated." *Sacramento Bee*, October 24, 1982. newspapers.com.

CHAPTER 11 CLASS ANALYSIS

Green, Stephen. "State Can't Build Prisons Fast Enough, Study Says." *San Bernardino County Sun*, December 21, 1989. newspapers.com.

Kell, Gretchen. "'Disturbing' Finding on Number of Blacks in Jail." *Sacramento Bee*, November 2, 1990. newspapers.com.

Pogatchnik, Shawn. "California Leads U.S. in Inmate Increase: Prisons: State's Growth Rate in 1980s More than Doubles National Average. Rise in Drug-Related Crimes and Tougher Enforcement Are Factors." *Los Angeles Times*, May 21, 1990. www.latimes.com/archives/la-xpm-199–1-mn-168-story.html.

San Francisco Examiner. "Cloudy Future facing East Palo Alto." November 23, 1977. newspapers.com.

Schiraldi, Vincent. "Life behind Bars Is No Way to Build Character." *Los Angeles Times*, February 12, 1990. newspapers.com.

Schiraldi, Vincent. "Props. 114, 115, 120: What Sponsors Didn't Tell Voters," *Sacramento Bee*, June 22, 1990. newspapers.com.

Schiraldi, Vincent. "Smart, Not Just Tough, about Crime." *Sacramento Bee*, February 20, 1990. newspapers.com.

CHAPTER 12 RUNNING SHOES

An Act to Amend Section 2601 of the Penal Code, Calif. Rev. Code Ann. § 2601 (FindLaw, 2019) (approved July 7, 1996).

Breithaupt, Brad. "Women Inmates Sue to Be with Kids." *San Bernardino County Sun*, June 6, 1985. newspapers.com.

Californian (Temecula, CA). "Don't Punish Families." July 14, 1996. newspapers.com.

de Lollis, Barbara. "Health Care in Prisons Called 'Worse,' Demonstrators Rally at Chowchilla Prison after an Inmate Dies." *Fresno Bee*, October 5, 1997. newspapers.com.

Greene, Judith. 2002. "Getting Tough on Crime: The History and Political Context of Sentencing Reform Developments Leading to the Passage of the 1994 Crime Act." In *Sentencing and Society: International Perspectives*, edited by Cyrus Tata and Neil Hutton, 1–32. Hampshire, UK: Ashgate Publishing Limited, 2002. www.justicestrategies.org/sites/default/files/Judy/GettingToughOnCrime.pdf.

Jones, Jack. "Suit Forces Better Care of Pregnant Prisoners." *Los Angeles Times*, April 21, 1987. newspapers.com.

Los Angeles Times. "Prop. 120: Yes on Prison Bonds." May 18, 1990. newspapers.com.

Marks, Claude and Eve Goldberg. "Charisse Shumate: Fighting for Our Lives." Produced by Freedom Archives and the California Coalition of Women Prisoners, 2004. Video, 40:09. vimeo.com/19050308.

Morain, Dan. "Era of Higher Tension Seen at State Prisons; Inmates: Officials Are Revoking Privileges as 'Three Strikes' Adds to Crowding. Some Fear More Unrest." *Los Angeles Times*, February 20, 1995. newspapers.com.

Morain, Dan. "State Politicians Take Aim at Inmates' Bill of Rights: Corrections: Anti-Crime Fervor May Doom the Statute Signed by Reagan. It Allows Conjugal Visits and Lets Prisoners Wear Their Hair at Any Length." *Los Angeles Times*, May 1, 1994, www.latimes.com/archives/la-xpm-199–5-01-me-52831-story.html.

Rosenfeld, Seth. "Women Inmates Sue over Medical Care." *San Francisco Examiner*, September 15, 1985. newspapers.com.

Weintraub, Daniel M. "'3 Strikes' Law Goes into Effect." *Los Angeles Times*, March 8, 1994, www.latimes.com/archives/la-xpm-1994-03-08-la-me-threestrikes-wilson-samuel-timeline-story.html.

CHAPTER 13 FREE AT LAST

Breton, Marcos. "'Murder Capital' an Island of Decay amid Wealth." *Sacramento Bee*, January 11, 1993. newspapers.com.

Burnett, Sandy. "Counselor Can Talk the Talk of Men and Women with HIV." *San Francisco Examiner*, September 25, 1998. newspapers.com.

Californian (Salinas, CA). "East Palo Alto Becomes Nation's Murder Capital." June 5, 1993. newspapers.com.

Flinn, John. "E. Palo Alto: 'Bodies Piling Up.'" *San Francisco Examiner*, January 3, 1993. newspapers.com.

Nelson, Valerie J. "Ex-Con Helped Men Turn Lives Around." *Los Angeles Times*, June 16, 2010. newspapers.com.

CHAPTER 14 PREACHING TO THE CHOIR

Critical Resistance: Beyond the Prison Industrial Complex. Conference held at the University of California, Berkeley, CA, September 25–27, 1998. criticalresistance.org/wp-content/uploads/2018/09/Critical-Resistance-1998-Conference-Program.pdf.

Davis, Angela Y. *Are Prisons Obsolete?* New York: Seven Stories Press, 2003.

Morrison, Neal and Luana Plunkett. "Critical Resistance: Beyond the Prison Industrial Complex, Part 1: Visions of Freedom." Produced by the Critical Resistance Production Collective. Filmed September 1998 in Berkeley, California. Video, 57:01. archive.org/details/ddtv_183_critical_resistance.

Zane, Maitland. "East Bay Organizers Believe the Punishment Is the Crime." *SFGATE*, September 18, 1998. www.sfgate.com/bayarea/article/East-Bay-Organizers-Believe-the-Punishment-Is-the-2990512.php.

CHAPTER 15 ALL OF US OR NONE

Brand, William. "Ex-Convicts Fighting for Their Rights." *Oakland Tribune*, August 1, 2004. newspapers.com.

Cooks, Yvonne, Linda Evans, and Dorsey Nunn. "Prison Should End when Term Is Up," *Oakland Tribune*, July 30, 2004. newspapers.com.

Goldberg, Eve, dir. "Enough is Enough." Filmed in 2003. Video, 18:54. www.youtube.com/watch?v=_ka_nokbvHs.

Goldberg, Eve, dir. "Locked Up, Locked Out." Filmed in 2007. Video, 23:02. www.youtube.com/watch?v=uwloxbndVHs.

CHAPTER 16 BAN THE BOX

America's Invisible Felon Population: A Blind Spot in US National Statistics: Statement before the Joint Economic Comm. on the Economic Impacts of the 2020 Census and Business Uses of Federal Data, 116th Cong. (2019) (statement of Dr. Nicholas Eberstadt, Henry Wendt Chair in Political Economy, American Enterprise Institute). www.jec.senate.gov/public/_cache/files/b23fea23-8e98-4bcd-aeed-edcc061a4bc0/testimony-eberstadt-final.pdf.

Avery, Beth, and Han Lu. *Ban the Box: U.S. Cities, Counties, and States Adopt Fair-Chance Policies to Advance Employment Opportunities for People with Past Convictions.* New York: National Employment Law Project, October 2021. s27147.pcdn.co/wp-content/uploads/Ban-the-Box-Fair-Chance-State-and-Local-Guide-Oct-2021.pdf.

Employment Policies and Procedures Regarding Criminal History, Res. 764–05, San Francisco Board of Supervisors (2005). www.sfbos.org/ftp/uploadedfiles/bdsupvrs/resolutions05/r0764-05.pdf.

Evans, Linda. *Ban the Box in Employment: A Grassroots History.* Oakland, CA: All of Us or None, A Project of Legal Services for Prisoners with Children, 2016. www.prisonerswithchildren.org/wp-content/uploads/2016/10/BTB-Employment-History-Report-2016.pdf.

Evans, Linda. *Ban the Box in Housing, Education, and Voting: A Grassroots History.* Oakland, CA: All of Us or None, A Project of Legal Services for Prisoners with Children, 2016. criticalresistance.org/wp-content/uploads/2014/04/B2B2_Final.pdf.

Nunn, Dorsey. "Formerly Incarcerated People's Policy Academy Launches in Los Angeles." *San Francisco BayView*, February 4, 2014. sfbayview.com/2014/02/formerly incarcerated-peoples-policy-academy-launches-in-los-angeles/.

Romney, Lee. "Ex-Inmates Win New Law Requiring California Employers to 'Ban the Box.'" *CalMatters*, October 14, 2017. calmatters.org/justice/2017/10/ex-inmates-behind-push-expand-ban-box-california-employers/.

Romney, Lee. "Group Pushes to Loosen Limits on Ex-Inmates." *Los Angeles Times*, March 3, 2006. newspapers.com.

Shannon, Sarah K. S., Christopher Uggen, Jason Schnittker, Melissa Thompson, Sara Wakefield, and Michael Massoglia. "The Growth, Scope, and Spatial Distribution of People with Felony Records in the United States, 1948–2010." *Demography* 54, no. 5 (October 2017): 1795–1818. sarah.shannons.us/uploads/4/9/3/4/4934545/shannon_etal_2017_demography.pdf.

CHAPTER 17   THE CONCRETE TOMB

Amnesty International. *USA: The Edge of Endurance, Prison Conditions in California's Security Housing Units.* London: Amnesty International Ltd, 2012. www.amnesty.org/en/documents/amr51/060/2012/en/.

Center for Constitutional Rights. "Ashker v. Governor of California Case Timeline." Last modified June 9, 2023. ccrjustice.org/home/what-we-do/our-cases/ashker-v-brown.

Legal Services for Prisoners with Children. "LSPC Hunger Striker Support Timeline." Published August 2015. www.prisonerswithchildren.org/wp-content/uploads/2015/08/LSPC-Timeline-w-Letterhead.pdf.

Prison Legal News. "Permanent Injunction Issued in Madrid." April 15, 1996. www.prisonlegalnews.org/news/1996/apr/15/permanent-injunction-issued-in-madrid/.

Rederford, Robin, Lauren Liu, and Stephen Butts. *A Cage within a Cage: A Report on Indeterminate Security Housing Unit (SHU) Confinement and Conditions.* San Francisco: Legal Services for Prisoners with Children, 2012. www.prisonerswithchildren.org/wp-content/uploads/2013/01/Cage-Within-A-Cage.pdf.

Reiter, Keramet. "The Origins of and Need to Control Supermax Prisons," *California Journal of Politics and Policy* 5, no. 2 (2013): 146–167. escholarship.org/content/qt4wv4t689/qt4wv4t689_noSplash_1c413c66c9d6bc8d92bc4f9fbc4b1409.pdf?t=nhww9y.

Rodriguez, Sal. "Historic California Assembly Hearing on Solitary Confinement." Solitary Watch, August 24, 2011. solitarywatch.org/2011/08/24/historic-california-assembly-hearing-on-solitary-confinement/.

CHAPTER 18 "I SPEAK FOR MYSELF. I VOTE."

Harris, Maya. *Making Every Vote Count: Reforming Felony Disenfranchisement Policies and Practices in California.* San Francisco: ACLU of Northern California, 2008. www.aclunc.org/sites/default/files/asset_upload_file228_7648.pdf.

Rojas, Aurelio. "A Vote of Confidence for Felons." *Sacramento Bee,* September 12, 2004. newspapers.com.

CHAPTER 19 FROM THE PRISON GATE TO THE WHITE HOUSE GATE

Formerly Incarcerated and Convicted People and Families Movement. "2016 Conference Program" (FICPFM First National Conference, Oakland, CA, September 9–10, 2016). ficpmovement.wordpress.com/2016-ficpfm-national-conference/2016-conference-schedule/.

Nunn, Dorsey. "A Note from AOUON Founding Member Dorsey Nunn." *All of Us or None Newsletter* 2, no. 9 (December 2020): 2. prisonerswithchildren.org/wp-content/uploads/2020/12/NEWS-Dec2020-final.pdf.

Romney, Lee. "Formerly Incarcerated Activist Fights to Give People a Chance to Change." *Los Angeles Times*, March 13, 2015. www.latimes.com/local/california/la-me-dorsey-nunn-20150313-story.html.

US Department of Justice. *The Federal Interagency Reentry Council, A Record of Progress and a Roadmap for the Future*, 2016. nicic.gov/federal-interagency-reentry-council-record-progress-and-roadmap-future-0.

CHAPTER 20   THE SHAPE OF THE HOLE I LEFT BEHIND

Sered, Danielle. *Until We Reckon: Violence, Mass Incarceration, and a Road to Repair*. New York: The New Press, 2019.

CHAPTER 21   HOMECOMING

Glover, Julian. "Alameda Co. Becomes First in US to Restrict Landlords' Use of Background Checks." *abc7 Bay Area*, December 22, 2022. abc7news.com/housing-bill-alameda-county-fair-chance-landlord-background-checks/12599501/.

Nunn, Dorsey, and Ali Birts. "Electronic Monitoring and Prison Industrial Complex: We Speak with Dorsey Nunn and Ali Birts about Electronic Monitoring and How It Economically Cripples Communities." By Anita Johnson and Davey D. *Hard Knock Radio*, KPFA-FM 94.1, July 15, 2019.

Bas, Nikki Fortunato, and John Jones III. "Oakland Passes CA's Strongest Fair Chance Housing Law to Support Returning Community Members." *News* (blog). City of Oakland website, February 21, 2020. Last updated January 7, 2021. www.oaklandca.gov/news/2020/oakland-now-has-the-states-strongest-fair-chance-housing-law.

City of Berkeley. "Rental Housing Providers Cannot Ask about Applicants' Criminal History." Fair Access to Housing. Accessed July 10, 2023. berkeleyca.gov/doing-business/operating-berkeley/landlords/fair-access-housing.

Tsai, Tim. "Standing Together: A Prevention-Oriented Approach to Ending Homelessness in Oakland." Research project, Master of

Public Policy Program, UC Berkeley Goldman School of Public Policy, Berkeley, CA, October 2019. bit.ly/HomelessPrevention2019.

CHAPTER 22 "SLAVE, WHO IS IT THAT SHALL FREE YOU?"

National Park Service. "The Big Lockup: Mass Incarceration in the U.S." Golden Gate National Recreation Area. Last updated November 2, 2021. www.nps.gov/goga/thebiglockup.htm.

Rios, Edwin. "Movement Grows to Abolish US Prison Labor System that Treats Workers as 'Less than Human.'" *Guardian*, December 24, 2022. www.theguardian.com/us-news/2022/dec/24/us-prison-labor-workers-slavery-13th-amendment-constitution.

Taaffe, Linda. "East Palo Alto Educational Pioneer Dies at 91: Gertrude Dyer Wilks Aimed to Give Black Students Equal Opportunity in the Classroom." *Palo Alto Online*, January 23, 2019. www.paloaltoonline.com/news/2019/01/23/east-palo-alto-educational-pioneer-dies-at-91.

Uggen, Christopher, Ryan Larson, Sarah Shannon, and Robert Stewart. *Locked Out 2022: Estimates of People Denied Voting Rights due to a Felony Conviction*. Washington, DC: Sentencing Project, 2022. www.sentencingproject.org/app/uploads/2022/10/Locked-Out-2022-Estimates-of-People-Denied-Voting.pdf.

ABOUT THE AUTHORS

Dorsey Nunn began advocating for the rights of California prisoners and their families while incarcerated. He knows punishment is not the answer to crime, and completing a sentence does not end restrictions to freedom. In the decades since his release, he hasn't held a job that wasn't centered on fighting for the rights of those living in cages or coming out of cages. As codirector of Legal Services for Prisoners with Children (LSPC), in 2003 he cofounded All of Us or None (AOUON), a grassroots movement of formerly incarcerated people working on their own behalf to secure their civil and human rights. AOUON is now the powerful policy and advocacy arm of LSPC, which Nunn has led as executive director since 2011. Collective victories include ending indefinite solitary confinement in California, expanding access to housing and employment for formerly incarcerated people, and restoring the vote to those on parole and probation.

Lee Romney spent twenty-three years at the *Los Angeles Times*, where she developed an expertise in the mental health and criminal legal systems. She left the paper in 2015 to pursue in-depth projects close to her heart and learn the craft of audio storytelling. Her journalism has aired on *Radiolab*, *Reveal* from the Center for Investigative Reporting, KQED-FM's *California Report Magazine*, KALW-FM's *Crosscurrents*, NPR's *Here & Now*, and *Making Contact*, and has been published by *CalMatters* and the *Guardian*. She has been a National Fellow for the USC Annenberg Center for Health Journalism and is the recipient of many honors, among them a Regional Edward R. Murrow Award. Lee is now working with a former public defender on *November in My Soul*, a deeply reported podcast that explores mental illness, confinement, and liberty through an intersectional and historical lens.